Lapshinova-Koltunski, Ekaterina. 2013. VARTRA: A comparable corpus for the analysis of translation variation. In *Proceedings of the 6th Workshop on Building and Using Comparable Corpora*, 77–86. Sofia, Bulgaria.

Levshina, Natalia. 2017. A multivariate study of t/v forms in European languages based on a parallel corpus of film subtitles. *Research in Language* 15(2). 153–172.

Neumann, Stella & Silvia Hansen-Schirra. 2013. Exploiting the incomparability of comparable corpora for Contrastive Linguistics and Translation Studies. In Serge Sharoff, Reinhard Rapp, Pierre Zweigenbaum & Pascale Fung (eds.), *Building and Using Comparable Corpora*, 321–335. Berlin: Springer.

Rozmyslowicz, Tomasz. 2014. Machine Translation: A Problem for Translation Theory. *New voices in translation studies* 10(11). 145–163.

Chapter 1

Introduction

Oliver Czulo

Silvia Hansen-Schirra
University of Mainz, Germersheim

Contrastive Linguistics (CL), Translation Studies (TS) and Machine Translation (MT) have common grounds: They all work at the crossroad where two or more languages meet. Recently, all three have shown a strong affinity towards using multilingual (parallel and comparable) corpora. In MT, for instance, parallel data collections serve as training material for translation models, as well as for related issues from computational linguistics like multilingual grammar induction, automatic lexicography, etc. Translation scholars use corpora and strive for empirical models of the translation process (including translation strategies or specific properties of translated text). For professional translators, multilingual corpora serve as reference works that enable quick interactive access and information processing. Contrastive linguistics uses corpora both to ground its findings empirically and to uncover differences in linguistic features that have not been studied before. Furthermore, multilingual corpora have found their way into lexicography and grammar writing.

Despite their inherent relatedness, methodological exchange between the three disciplines is rare. For instance, when parallel corpora are used in CL or MT, factors like translation direction or translation properties and strategies are largely ignored. Also, MT in particular is agnostic about dimensions like text type or register. At the same time, the use of multilingual annotation and query techniques is often restricted to the most basic techniques in CL and TS - if applied at all.

This special issue touches upon areas where the three fields converge. It results directly from a workshop at the 2011 German Association for Language Technology and Computational Linguistics (GSCL) conference in Hamburg where

Oliver Czulo & Silvia Hansen-Schirra. Introduction. In Oliver Czulo & Silvia Hansen-Schirra (eds.), *Crossroads between Contrastive Linguistics, Translation Studies and Machine Translation: TC3 II*, 1–3. Berlin: Language Science Press.
DOI:10.5281/zenodo.1019679

researchers from the three fields presented and discussed their interdisciplinary work.

The volume begins with a contribution by Steiner who takes a broad perspective on the topic of cross-fertilisation between CL and TS on the one hand and what he refers to as "relevant sub-fields of Computational Linguistics", extending to MT, on the other. He discusses three methodological approaches to inherently multilingual tasks and how they could serve as valuable blueprints for other disciplines, including operationalization of hypothesis testing on lexicogrammatical data from parallel corpora, study of textual cohesion in originals and translations, and integration of product- and process-based data. Steiner concludes with suggestions about how the above-mentioned disciplines could profit from each other.

Korzen and Gylling present a study on the structure of Italian and Danish texts both from a contrastive and a translational perspective. Using samples from Europarl, Korzen and Gylling reveal differences in information density and clause linkage between the two languages in a contrastive fashion. They then go on to formulate some simple translation rules based on their findings.

The progression from contrastive investigations to translation-oriented observations is also characteristic of the contribution by Zinsmeister, Dipper and Seiss. Taking examples from German-English bitexts from the Europarl corpus, the authors contrast the realisation of abstract anaphors in the two languages. They then examine translation-specific differences in the realisations and how the findings from the contrastive analysis may help improve translation procedures.

Thunes aims at linking perspectives from TS and MT explicitly. Based on the crucial to TS theory notion of text type, she develops a classification of translation complexity for two text types. Thunes then applies her classification to MT by proposing to use it as a diagnostic for the feasibility of MT for text types in general.

Kremer, Hartung, Padó and Riezler present a study on how human translation could benefit from MT-generated data. In their experiment, translators were asked to translate adjective-noun pairs. Based on a phrase table created by an SMT system, possible adjective translations were suggested to the translators. The results of the study show significant improvement in translation quality.

The concluding contribution of this volume by Carl and Dragsted reports on a process-oriented study, a field of research from which both TS and MT can benefit. The authors investigate the "monitor model", a hypothesis by which a monitor disrupts the default mode of literal translation in case a problem occurs. In their experiment, subjects either copied or translated a source text. In the contribution, the results from the reading and writing process of copyists and translators are contrasted, and insights into the role of the decoding task are presented.

While the studies contained in this volume draw from a wide variety of objectives and methods, and various areas of overlaps between CL, TS and MT are addressed, the volume is by no means exhaustive with regard to this topic. Further cross-fertilisation is not only desirable, but almost mandatory in order to tackle future tasks and endeavours, and TC3 remains committed to bringing these three fields even closer together.

Germersheim, June 2012
Oliver Czulo, Silvia Hansen-Schirra

Chapter 2

Inside the monitor model: processes of default and challenged translation production

Michael Carl

Barbara Dragsted
Copenhagen Business School

It has been the subject of debate in the translation process literature whether human translation is a sequential and iterative process of comprehension-transfer-production or whether and to what extent comprehension and production activities may occur in parallel. Tirkkonen-Condit (2005) suggests a "monitor model" according to which translators start in a literal default rendering mode, and a monitor interrupts the default procedure when a problem occurs. This paper proposes an extension of the monitor model in which comprehension and production are processed in parallel by the default procedure. The monitor supervises text production processes, and triggers disintegration of the translation activity into chunks of sequential reading and writing behavior. To investigate this hypothesis, we compare text copying with translation activities under the assumption that text copying represents a typical literal default rendering procedure. Both, translation and text copying, require decoding, retrieval and encoding of textual segments, but translation requires in addition a transfer step into the target language. Comparing reading and writing behaviour obtained in the copying and translation experiments, we observe surprisingly many similarities, which also suggests similarities in the underlying processes. Copyists deviate from the default literal text reproduction into more effortful text understanding, and much of the translators' behaviour looks like simple text copying. During translation as well as during text copying we observe that translators and copyists resort to sequential reading and writing patterns which seem to be triggered through target text production problems.

Michael Carl & Barbara Dragsted. Inside the monitor model: processes of default and challenged translation production. In Oliver Czulo & Silvia Hansen-Schirra (eds.), *Crossroads between Contrastive Linguistics, Translation Studies and Machine Translation: TC3 II*, 5–30. Berlin: Language Science Press. DOI:10.5281/zenodo.1019685

1 Introduction

In his seminal book, Gile (1995) suggests a stratificational translation process model, in which a translator iteratively reads a piece of the ST and then produces its translation. First the translator creates a "Meaning Hypothesis" for a ST chunk (i.e. a Translation Unit) which is consistent with the "context and the linguistic and extra linguistic knowledge of the translator" (p. 107) before the translation is produced. Similarly, Craciunescu et al. (2004) claim that "the first stage in human translation is complete comprehension of the source language text". Only after this complete (i.e. *deep*) comprehension is achieved can the translation be produced. Also Angelone (2010) supports that translators process in cycles of comprehension-transfer-production and that "uncertainties" of translators can be attributed to any of the comprehension, transfer, or production phases.

Some scholars challenge this view, stating that translation processes can also be based on a *shallow* understanding and that ST understanding and TT production can occur in *parallel*. According to Ruiz et al. (2008) "the translator engages in partial reformulation while reading for the purpose of translating the source text". They assume that in parallel processing "code-to-code links between the SL and TL [are involved] at least the lexical and syntactic level of processing". Similarly, Mossop (2003) claims the existence of "direct linkages in the mind between SL and TL lexicogrammatical material, independent of 'meaning' ", and that a translator "automatically produces TL lexical and syntactic material based on the incoming SL forms".

In a study comparing reading behaviour for different purposes, Jakobsen & Jensen (2008: 16) investigate (among other things) the difference between test persons reading a text for comprehension and reading a similar text in preparation for translating. Their study showed that reading purpose has a "clear effect on eye movements and gaze behaviour" and they suggest "that a fair amount of pre-translation probably enters into the reading of a text as soon as it is taken to be the source text for translation".

Although it is unclear what is exactly meant by "pre-translation", such findings are obviously in contrast with the eye-mind[1] hypothesis when assuming a stratificational model of translation. Reading with "a fair amount of pre-translation" implies certainly different mental activities than reading for understanding. Since in both cases the eyes remain on the ST it may be difficult (if not impossible) to disentangle which fixations in the logged gaze data are to be linked to text

---

[1]There is no appreciable lag between what is fixated and what is processed (Just & Carpenter 1984).

understanding and which ones are due to pre-translation, and hence either the eye-mind hypothesis has to be weakened or the stratificational model of translation has to be reconsidered.

We assume, with Tirkkonen-Condit, that "literal translation is a default rendering procedure, which goes on until it is interrupted by a monitor that alerts about a problem in the outcome. The monitor's function is to trigger off conscious decision-making to solve the problem" (Tirkkonen-Condit 2005: 407-408). In our interpretation, the literal default rendering procedure implies parallel, tightly interconnected text production and comprehension processes: while the mind is engaged in the production of a piece of text, the eyes search for relevant textual places to gather the required information needed to continue the text production flow. When this default procedure is interrupted by the monitor, we can observe gaze patterns on the ST or on the TT which indicate comprehension- or production-related translation problems. Similarly, Ruiz et al. (2008) suggest that "lexical and syntactic properties may follow different time courses", so that different levels of understanding are obtained at different stages in the concurrent reading/production processes.

In this paper, we will show examples of unchallenged, parallel processing in text copying and translation production. We will also point to passages of conscious, effortful text production which suggest a more disentangled relation between comprehension and production. Similar to Ruiz et al. (2008), who distinguish between shallow/parallel and deep/sequential[2] processes in translation,[3] we find that translators switch between the two modes, but more frequently engage in shallow/parallel processing. In addition, we find that deeper understanding in the decision-making processes is triggered through translation production problems, rather than difficulties in ST understanding. This finding coincides with Gile (1995: 110) who reports that deeper understanding of the ST may emerge through problems in TT production, rather than when first reading a ST passage. He points out that the translation practice indicates processing from a production-based perspective:

> Oftentimes, the translator does not test Meaning Hypothesis until after verbalizing it in the target language (...) Frequently, he or she only realizes there is a problem when trying to read the first target-language version (...) in other words, when already in the reformulation phase.

---

[2] Shallow-deep refer to the level of the translator's (conceptual) representation during the translation process, while parallel-sequential refer to the observable coordination of comprehension (eye gaze movements) and production processes (keystroke presses) in time.

[3] Respectively horizontal/parallel vertical/serial in in their terminology.

A clear-cut allocation of "uncertainties" to one of the stratificational processes becomes difficult, since such processes do not normally exist independently in the translator's mind. Not only is it infeasible (or impossible) to distinguish between comprehension and pre-translation activities during reading for translation, but also the borders between ST understanding and TT production problems become blurred.

In order to investigate the basic literal default rendering procedure, we first look at text copying. We take it that copying (i.e. re-typing) a text is much more a shallow/parallel process than translation: 1) apart from a lexical encoding and decoding (John 1996), text copying does not, in theory, require any deep ST (or TT) understanding, 2) copying can proceed in parallel to a maximal degree, since no revision[4] and no lexical or structural transfer is required. Typing patterns and speed would thus essentially depend on the typing skills of the copyist. Comparing copying behaviour and translation behaviour would reveal the additional effort of translation.

Our investigation is based on empirical data obtained in 10 copying sessions and 15 translation sessions. The experiments were recorded using the Translog 2006 software, which logs keystroke and gaze movements during a reading, translation or text production task. §2 gives an overview over the text type and the translators' activity data. In §3, we first describe a cognitive model of text copying, which predicts word comprehension and typing time. We then illustrate the model with two copying examples. The first example shows an instance of unchallenged copying, the second example shows how text understanding plays a role, also when copying a text. §4 discusses four passages from a translation experiment and compares it to the copying data. We look at instances of unchallenged parallel and sequential translation processes and at two instances of challenged translation which requires re-reading of the source and the target texts. The examples show that much of the translation process resembles text copying, and that deeper understanding processes are triggered through text production problems. While these examples show individual patterns, the last §5 provides evidence that distribution of pauses in translation is similar for different translators translating the same text.

---

[4]Some revision may be going on, for instance correction of typos, but these activities are of a different kind than most of those in translation revisions.

2 Experimental data for copying and translation

We investigate and compare user activity data of two experiments, a copying experiment and a translation experiment. In §2 and §4, we re-use and analyze a subset of the translation data that was collected by KTH. Jensen for his PhD thesis (Jensen 2011). The copying data which is discussed in §2 and §3 was taken from an experiment which Sjørup (2011) conducted for her PhD thesis. Some statistics about these translation/copying processes are shown in Table 1. In §5 we re-use translation data which was collected in the context of the Eye-to-IT project (http://cogs.nbu.bg/eye-to-it/). All process data was collected with different goals and for different purposes over several years in the CRITT/CBS under controlled conditions; all process data is based on processing short English texts between 110 and 170 words long.

2.1 A copying experiment

In the first experiment, an English financial text about bank loans was copied by 10 English L2 speakers. The text consisted of 9 sentences, totalling 169 words (punctuation marks are counted as one word), and 945 characters, which makes an average of 5.59 characters/word. For data acquisition, Translog 2006 was used (Jakobsen 2010), which divides the screen into two windows. The upper window plots the source text, or in this case the text that had to be copied. The translator typed a copy of this text into the lower window. While most of the reproduced texts had the same number of words, none of them were identical to the source text. Besides a number of typos, there were also productions of semantically (or phonetically) similar words. In several instances, "votes" was reproduced as "voted"; "issuers ability" as "issuers' ability" (which was actually incorrect in the source text, and corrected in the reproduction), in one case "any" was retyped as "the", in another case "choke" as "chose" and "card" was reproduced as "credit card". This indicates to us, that a decoding and "understanding" of the texts has clearly taken place during copying where even instances of explication can be observed.

Table 1 plots some of the process data for the 10 copying sessions. It shows that the text was reproduced in less than 3 minutes by one translator (4), and in more than 7 minutes by another translator (7), which is a factor of approx. 2.5 between the fastest and the slowest copyist. The figure also shows that the number of deletions varies between 27 (for the fastest copyist) and 94 (for one of the slowest copyist). The median typing speed of all 10 copyists is 282.81ms per character (average 266.27).

Table 1: Process data for copying sessions

	Translation task				Copying task			
	time	keys	del	ms/key	time	keys	del	ms/key
1	265762	916	49	290.13	255342	1100	80	232.23
2	396390	999	49	396.79	388155	1113	94	348.75
3	654681	1053	107	621.73	193344	982	28	196.89
4	259094	918	40	282.24	169039	980	27	172.49
5	260644	848	22	307.36	260530	1021	48	255.17
6	350854	973	67	360.59	278291	1044	59	266.56
7	411156	959	49	428.73	430353	1009	40	426.51
8	349750	965	47	362.44	228016	994	33	229.39
9	379272	967	58	392.22	288249	1035	54	278.50
10	209142	937	57	223.20	273975	1069	69	256.29
11	322110	979	41	329.02				
12	380643	971	33	392.01				
13	316730	1083	81	292.46				
14	352497	969	76	363.77				

2.2 A translation experiment

In the second experiment, 15 translators translated an English (L2) text into Danish (L1), using a similar Translog setting. This text was a news text about the Olympic Games in Beijing, which consisted of 5 sentences and 160 words (845 character length) with an average word length of 5.32 characters/word. Table 1 (left) shows the translation process data of the 15 translation sessions. The median inter-keystroke delay in this translation task was 362.44 ms/character (average 360.19), which is about 1.4 times more than in the copying task. The time spent by the slowest translator (654 seconds) is more than 3 times higher than that of the fastest translator (209 seconds), but looking at the difference of inter-keystroke delay, this difference reduces to 2.79, since many more keystrokes (particularly deletions) are produced by the slow translators than by the fast translators. There are slightly more corrections (deletions) during translation than during copying: approx. 5.14% and 5.68% of all keystrokes are deletions in the copying and translation tasks respectively.

The analysis suggests that differences between copying and translation are not as large as one might expect: ST reading and TT production activities occur in both the copying and the translation tasks, whereas transfer from source language to target language only takes place in the translation task. If we assume a stratificational translation process model, which proposes that only one activity – ST understanding, TT production, or transfer – can take place at any one time, we are left with less than 100ms per ST character for transfer from the source to target language. While this might be an appealing model for some, we give evidence below that reading (ST understanding) and typing (TT production) can occur in parallel, which leads us to a different set of conclusions.

2.3 Gaze behaviour during reading, copying and translation

As mentioned earlier, it has been found that different reading purposes imply different gazing patterns (Jakobsen & Jensen 2008): e.g. the gaze behaviour in reading for understanding is different from reading for translation, which is different from reading for text copying. Dragsted (2010), for instance, observes on average 3.2 and 5.7 fixations per word by expert and student translators respectively in a translation task, while less than one fixation per word was measured during reading for comprehension for normal college students.[5] That is, there are approximately 3.5 times more fixations on the ST in a translation task than in a text comprehension task. Dragsted assumes that the additional ST fixations are likely to result from the planning of TT production and the effort of transforming ST expressions into meaningful TT[6]. Thus, more than 2/3 of the ST reading effort during translation seems to be linked to translation-related activity and the planning/validation of TT production.

The number of ST fixations during copying in our data was, on average, 1.8 fixations/word, and varied between 207 and 538 fixations for the 169 word text. Text copying thus requires approximately twice as many fixations on the ST than reading for comprehension. During translation drafting we measured between 309 and 595 fixations on the ST. For a text of 160 words, the average was 2.4 fixations per ST word. These figures are much lower than those reported by Dragsted (2010). One explanation might be that we only count fixations during translation drafting; there are additional ST fixations during initial orientation and in the revision phases.

---

[5]http://www.learninginfo.org/eye-movements-reading.htm
[6]But we maintain that it might be impossible in detail to figure out which fixations belongs to which of the processes.

3 Text copying

In this section we will first introduce a cognitive model of text copying, i.e. reading and re-typing. We will then empirically evaluate the model in two copying examples. Whereas the first example in §3.1 confirms the model for unchallenged, smooth copying, the second example, §3.3 shows that comprehension difficulties may play a role in the copying process.

3.1 A cognitive model of typing

John (1996) suggests a three step model for text copying. First a perceptual operator perceives a written word. Then a cognitive operation retrieves the spelling of the word from long-term memory, and finally a motor operator finds a key on the keyboard and hits it. John makes a distinction between copying of single (sequences of) characters and more complex symbols. For the more complex symbols, like words and syllables, a cognitive operator is required to retrieve the spelling of the word from memory long-term memory and to initiate the typing of each character. Hence, the perception of a word and its typing requires the encoding (perception) and decoding (memory retrieval) of the symbol. With the assumption that a skilled typist produces about 30 gross words per minute (gwpm), John arrives at the following model:

1. A perceptual operator reads a word of about six letters and encodes it in 340 ms

2. The cognitive operator has a cycle time of 50 ms to retrieve the spelling and to activate the typing of the characters from the spelling list

3. A motor operator needs 230 ms on an alphanumeric keyboard at a rate of about 30 gwpm

In addition, John assumes that each of the operators works serially in themselves (only one keystroke can be processed at any one time) but that they can work in parallel with each other, with the serialization restrictions that:

- perception has to be complete before getting the spelling or initiation of a character can begin.

- once a character has been initiated with a cognitive operator, the motor operator cannot be stopped.

- the perceptual processor (eyes) stays three words (chunks) ahead of the cognitive processor.

John uses this model to analyze which of the three operations is the limiting factor in text copying. She finds that the overall typing speed depends primarily on the time needed for motor activity, rather than for perception or cognitive control. In line with other researchers, John assumes that the 50ms for cognitive cycle time are constant, and hence typing skills are often the limiting factors.

Comparing this model with the figures in the previous section, we note that some of the typists type much quicker than the time predicted for 30gwpm and are able to copy a text in 75% of the time predicted by John. The average measured typing time is, however, about 115% of the predicted 230ms, which suggests that some of our copyists need more time for the motor actions, and/or they engage in additional (reading) activities during which the copyist performs no typing. The next two sections will look at some examples in more depth.

3.2 Copying an easy text

The first example illustrates the typing process of the 3rd sentence of the copied text:

(1)   *The rise in unemployment has spattered a once-profitable business with red ink.*

The sentence consists of 13 words (including sentence final full stop) with 80 characters (including inter-word blank spaces). One of the copyists copied the sentence in 21 seconds with 5 typos. Figure 1 shows the progression graph: the vertical Y-axis plots the original sentence which was to be copied; the horizontal X-axis represents a time line in ms in which the reading and typing activities take place. Single fixations on the source text are marked by a blue circle. Typing activities consist of text insertions (in black) and deletions (in red) shown on the time line.

The figure shows a time segment of 21 seconds between ms 58,000 to around 81,000 in which the sentence is being copied. At the beginning, the typist first gazed at the two words "The" and "rise" before starting to type. Two typos occurred in the first word when reproducing "The". These typos were immediately corrected. Perrin (2003) suggests a short-hand form to represent writing activities, where corrections are represented in square brackets. In this notation, the typing pattern would be represented as: "Th[i-][r-]e", which is read as follows:

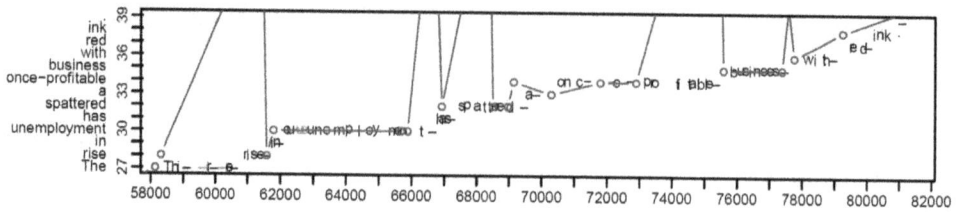

Figure 1: A progression graph for unchallenged text copying

First the typist writes "Thi-".[7] Then "i-", the blank space (i.e. "-") and the "i" are deleted, then "r-" is typed and deleted, until finally the correct "e" is typed. There are thus 4 correcting keystrokes in the production of "The". The typist goes then on immediately with the typing of "rise", without looking back into the source text. There are two fixations just before ms 62,000, one on "rise" and one on "unemployment", the latter while already typing "in". From the progression graph it appears that the word 'in' was actually not looked at; however, it is likely that this word was in the parafoveal scope of the fixation on "rise".

The copying process then goes on smoothly. There are two more typos and deletions, but the typist seems to copy the text without much hesitation, looking in general only one word ahead in the source text. In some cases the typist verifies the spelling of a word that is being typed (e.g. "spattered" around time stamp 69,000), and in other instances she scans the next word already while still typing the previous word (e.g. also "spattered" around 67000 ms).

According to John's model, a skilled typist would minimally need 80 * 230ms for keying the 80 characters, plus an initial 390ms for reading the first word, 340ms for perception of the first word, and 50ms for retrieval of the spelling list. Counting the 7 typos as 2 keystrokes each, the predicted typing time, according to John's model, amounts to approximately 22 seconds. Compared with the observed typing time of 23 seconds, the prediction is pretty good with an error rate of less than 5%. While the model thus seems to be quite exact for predicting the overall time needed when typing activities go smoothly, it does not seem to be so precise for predicting the gaze activities and the structure of the gaze/keystroke coordination: John's model predicts a three words look-ahead; however, in many cases only one word is looked ahead from the word that is currently being copied, and longer (or more difficult) words, e.g. "unemployment" and "once-profitable", may trigger re-fixations, whereas some short words are not fixated at all.

---

[7]The blank space is represented as a dash "-" in the graph and in figures below.

3.3 Copying difficult texts passages

The following (2) illustrates the impact of reproducing unusual idioms on the coordination of gaze and typing activities. More difficult/unusual or surprising source text passages trigger extended reading behaviour and reduce the copying speed. (2) shows the 6th sentence taken from the same text as (1):

(2)   *The industry's claim that the **bill will choke off** access to credit is a bit rich given its own rush to reduce its unsecured lending.*

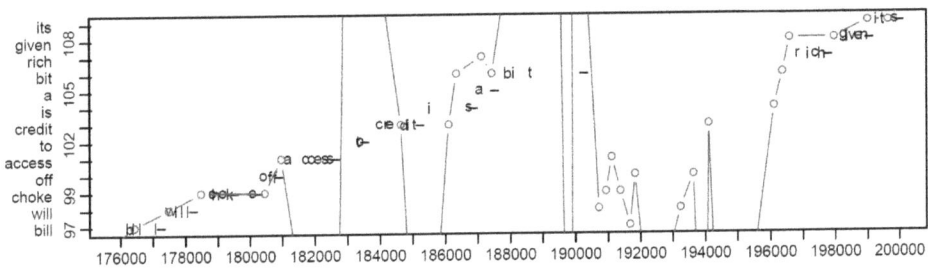

Figure 2: A writing progression graph for challenged text copying

Figure 2 shows the progression graph of the fragment in bold, which contains the expression "to be (a bit) rich".[8] The fragment has 13 words, which are copied in 24 seconds. It consists of 61 characters which, according to John's model, should be typed in approx. 14.5 secs. However, the typist needs 24 secs, with a pause of approx. 8 seconds between seconds between seconds 189 and 197, just before copying the word "rich". Note that "rich" is the head word of the idiom "to be a bit rich", and the idiom might not be known to the typist, English being her/his L2.

We observed twice as many fixations in the more difficult copying in (2), as in the unchallenged copying activity of the 13 word sentence in (1) (see Figure 1). Copying of the fragment in (1) was achieved with 21 fixations, which amounts to 1.6 fixations per word. In contrast to this, there were 39 fixations on the ST when typing the more difficult 13 words fragment in Figure 2, which amounts to an average of 3 fixations per word.

Since we can safely assume that there is no problem in decoding, encoding or typing the word "rich", we believe that the extended reading activities of the

---

[8] According to the free dictionary (http://idioms.thefreedictionary.com/rich): "to be (a bit) rich" is something that you say when someone criticizes you to show that you do not think they are being fair because they are as bad as you.

ST segment indicate a verification or clarification of the idiom meaning, which seems to be unnecessary in a copying task.

It is also interesting to note that the additional reading activity occurs immediately before "rich" is being typed, despite the fact that "rich" was already previously gazed at around ms 187,000. During its first reading "rich" was obviously not recognized as problematic – at least there was no extended reading of the context. The monitor seems to run in the background and triggers conscious re-reading when passages are unclear, even during text copying. This indicates that 1) text understanding also takes place during text copying and 2) the understanding of more challenging expressions takes place when keying in the words, rather than (or in addition to) when initially reading the source text. This is in line with the citation of Gile (above) who states that production processes seem to trigger additional testing of "Meaning Hypotheses" which does not occur when initially reading the text. In the next section we will look at reading behaviour during translation and observe a similar pattern, where reading activities are triggered by TT production problems.

4 Translation

In this section we look at translation activities. We distinguish between sequential and parallel activities. The term "sequential" is used when a translator either reads (the ST) or writes (the TT) at any one time. During "parallel" activities, the translator reads and writes at the same time.

4.1 Parallel reading and writing

Figure 3 shows an example were parallel translation activities occur. It represents a translation progression graph for the translation of an English source sentence into Danish in example (3):

(3)   a. English source sentence:
        Police officer Chris Gregg said that Norris had been acting strangely around the hospital

      b. Danish translation:
          P[i]olitiins[ep]pekt[rør]ør Chris Gregg sagte at Norris havde opført sig sært på h[i]o[p[si]s]sp[o]italet

As in the previous progression graphs, the vertical axis plots the ST words while the horizontal axis represents a time interval of 28 seconds (seconds 149-177) during which the translation is being produced.

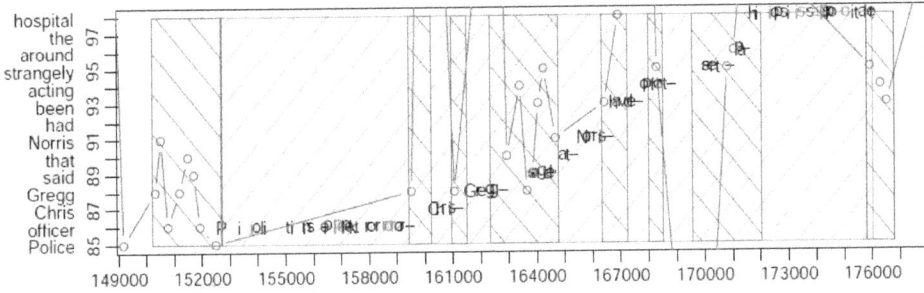

Figure 3: The translation progression graph shows parallel reading and text production.

In a copying task the produced text is identical to the ST which has been copied,[9] and therefore each ST word can be trivially aligned with its identical word in the produced copy. This is different in a translation task, where a single word in the produced translation can represent several words in the ST and vice versa, and discontinuous strings further complicate the translations process. For instance, Danish "Politiinspektør" is the translation of two English words. Thus,it is a 2-to-1 alignment, the translation of which appears in Figure 3 on the line of "officer" whereas the "Police" line is empty.

Typing activities are clustered into production units (PUs), marked in (red) upwards hatched boxes. A PU consists of successive typing activities, where no pause of more than 1000ms occurs between successive keystrokes. A PU is intended to represent coherent writing activities of a segment of text. The value of one second was chosen in line with a previous study (Carl & Kay 2011) which report that a production pause of more than 1000ms in text production is likely to represent a shift of attention towards another segment. A PU thus subsumes all subsequent keystrokes which are part of the same chunk. According to this criterion, the entire sentence in Figure 3 was typed as one coherent production unit.

---

[9]This should be in principle the case. However, we also found cases where copyists inserted or deleted additional punctuation marks, typos and even words.

The (blue) circles are ST fixations and the downwards hatched boxes represent "fixation units". A fixation unit (FU) consists of a sequence of coherent ST[10] fixations, where no pause of more than 400ms occurs between the end and the beginning of two successive fixations. A FU thus represents a ST reading chunk. There are two large FUs in the progression graph in Figure 3. The first occurs during the time between seconds 149 and 152, at the beginning of a new sentence. The translator's eyes moved back and forth in the chunk "Police officer Chris Gregg said that Norris". After this the translation "Politiinspektør" was typed, including a number of typos which were immediately corrected (deleted characters are in red), but the following typing of the proper noun goes smoothly.

Obviously reading is not steady. The eyes jump over two, sometimes three words, back and forth, until a segment of text is understood well enough to start typing a translation. Note that the measured reading time in the sentence onset (circa 3 seconds) approximately corresponds to the perception and decoding time predicted in John's model: the 7 words would require 2380ms to perceive (at a rate of 340ms per word) plus the retrieval operation brings us to 2.5 seconds.

A second FU occurs between seconds 162 and 165. Here the fragment "Gregg said that Norris had been acting strangely" is read by jumping back and forth in the chunk. In contrast to the first FU, this reading activity occurs while typing the translation of "Gregg said that". Such parallel translation activities characterize experienced translators (Carl & Kay 2011), capable of typing a translation while already reading ahead in the ST, whereas translation students resort frequently to an sequential mode, as will be discussed in §4.2.

The Danish translation in 3 consists of 12 words with 79 characters and 12 typos. According to the copying model above, a typist would need 24 seconds to key in the sentence. If we subtract the 3 initial seconds between time stamp 149,000–152,000 where the beginning of the sentence was scanned, and which is supposedly due to the translation activity, we measure 25 seconds production time vs. 24 seconds predicted by Johns model, an error of less than 5%. The translation was thus produced approximately at an expert copyists' speed, plus an initial orientation which amounts to 10% of the typing time. The second FU shows that reading, translating and writing can take place in parallel, and transfer does not necessarily require additional (measurable) time, as compared to the copying task. However, there is more gaze activity on the ST than in the case of unchallenged copying in (1).

---

[10]We only show here fixations on the ST. TT fixations are currently not processed with the software.

We may call this translation activity TRANSCODING, i.e. substituting words or phrases in one language system by corresponding expressions in the target language system. It is an instance of the literal default rendering procedure, as discussed earlier.

4.2 Sequential reading and writing

Figure 4 shows an example of mainly sequential translation activity. The translator is either reading a ST segment or writing a piece of TT, and the average translation time per character increases dramatically. The figure plots the translation progression of a sentence-final segment and the first words of the next sentence. The produced translation is shown in (4):

(4)   English source text:
      ...strangely around the hospital. **Only the awareness of other hospital staff** ...
      Danish translation:
      ...underligt på hospitalet, **kun [andre]andre hospitalansattes opmærksamhed** ...

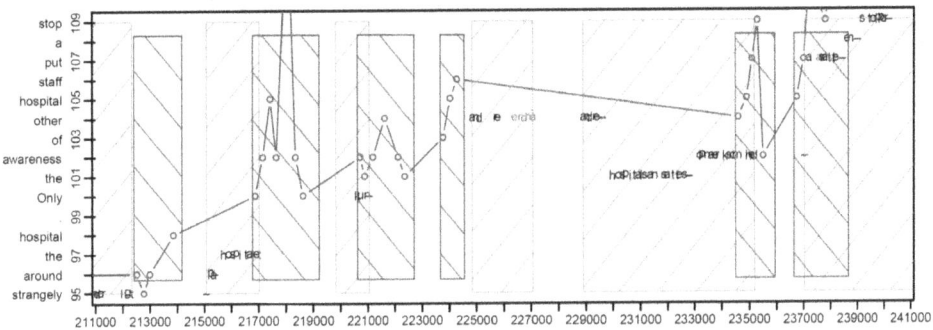

Figure 4: The translation progression graph shows sequential reading and text production.

Presumably, due to a syntactic reordering in the translation of "the awareness of other hospital staff" (see Figure 5), there is some reading activity before the translator starts translating the second sentence and between seconds 221 and 225 just after typing "kun" (translation of "only"). As noted above, a translation progression graph visualises the temporal development of translation equivalents. Units of translation equivalences (i.e. alignment units) were manually aligned in the final translation product, and the allocation of each keystrokes to one of those alignment unit are computed based on an algorithm described in Carl & Jakobsen (2009). The alignment units may be more complex than merely a 1-to-1 relation. Figure 5 shows the more complex translation where an insight-out alignment is intermingled with a discontinuous English phrase. Four English words (a101, a103, a105, a106), the compound noun "hospital staff" together with the definite article "the" and the preposition "of" are translated as b99: "hospi-talsansattes". The keystrokes in time which produce this translation appear in the translation progression graph of Figure 5 on line 101. The words "awareness" and "other" change the order in the Danish translation and appear respectively on line 102 and 105, but are typed in the reversed order. Figure 5 shows the label "s", a semantic equivalence between the English function words and their Danish translation, while the compound noun component has no label. Kromann (2003) gives more background on this alignment schema, but we do not make use of the labels in this investigation. Obviously, the translator had to read 6 words ahead to produce this translation. However, s/he did not read further ahead than that, and thus took into account just enough, but not more context than was required to produce the translation.

The bold part in the translation 4 consisted of 7 words with 42 characters, and was produced in approximately 19 seconds (timestamps 217000–236000). Including the 5 typos (*andre* 'other') was first typed then deleted and then typed again) the copy model predicts 12.3 seconds for typing.

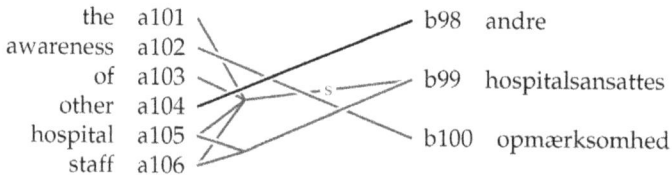

Figure 5: Translation fragment from Figure 6

There are two pauses of 3 secs and 3.8 secs, in each of which the translator reads more or less the same seven words ahead of the ST word that is currently being translated. The first reading activity fits approximately with Johns' reading model, which predicts 2380 ms for perception of seven ST words, the additional reading time (approx. 0.5 second) may be allocated to transfer activities. We assume that the second pause, after typing "kun", is triggered by the "monitor" leading to a non-literal translation and a token reordering in the target text. The translation challenge is relative small syntactic re-phrasing of the English "of" construction into a Danish genitive. We are thus in a position to deconstruct the 19 seconds measured translation time of the 7-word segment into 1) ST reading time, approx 2.5 seconds 2) transfer and monitor time, approx. 4.3 seconds and 3) typing time, 12.2 seconds. Note that the 4.3 seconds correspond approximately to the transfer time of 42 characters, as predicted in §2.2, and 12.2 seconds measured typing time are, again, pretty close to John's 12.3 seconds prediction.

In contrast to (3), where we looked at parallel reading and writing, we observe a sequential reading/typing behaviour, in which only one of the activities is carried out at the same time. While there might be approximately the same amount of ST reading in a parallel and in a sequential translation mode, the overall translation time doubles in the latter one, since activities occur sequentially. Even though there seems to be some sort of "alerting" from the translator's cognitive monitor, it is perhaps not appropriate to assume a "deep" understanding of the text when reading 3 to 6 words ahead. In the next section we will look at more challenging instances of translation.

4.3 Instances of challenged translation

While the examples in Figures 3 and 4 show instances of unchallenged translation, where translation production proceeds smoothly in a parallel (3) or in an sequential mode (4), with only some words look-ahead, we will now look at more challenging translation problems which are more time consuming. This translation activity is characterised by delayed text production and associated with extended reading activities into the ST or TT context, beyond 5 or 6 words from the current translation position, or a production pause exceeding by far the expected decoding time predicted by John.

In this and the next section we look at two examples illustrating translation problems which trigger extensive re-reading of the TT 5 and Figure 6) and re-reading of the ST ((6) and Figure 7). The fragments in 5 consist of 30 English words which are translated into 38 Danish words. From this sentence, we investigate more closely a ST segment of 13 words, which is reproduced in bold in (5):

(5) English source sentence:
  *Although developing countries are understandably reluctant to compromise their chances of achieving better standards of living **for the poor, action on climate change need not threaten economic development**.*
  Danish translation:
  *Selv om udviklingslandene forståeligt nok tøver med at risikere at ødelægge deres muligheder for at opnå en bedre levestandard **for de fattige, behøver tiltag over for klimaforandringer ikke at udgøre en trussel mod deres økonomiske udvikling**.*

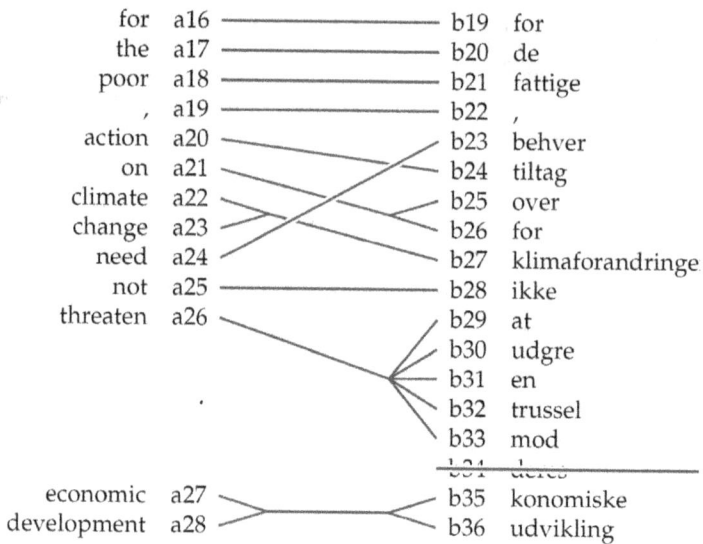

Figure 6: The alignment of the fragment in Figure 5

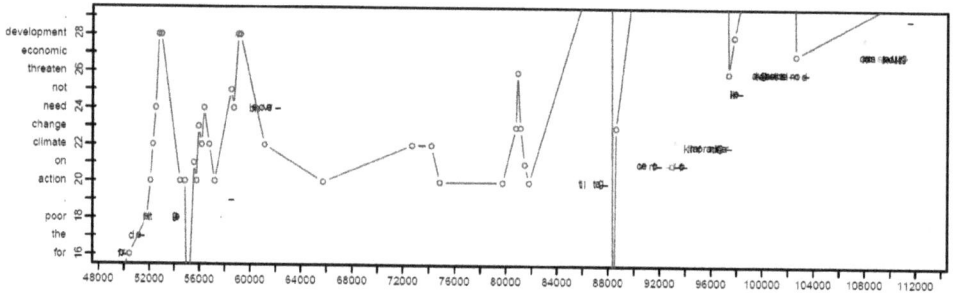

Figure 7: Translation progression graph of a translation problem

The translation progression graph in Figure 6 plots the unfolding of the translation of the fragment in bold in (5). The first three words "for the poor" did not pose any problems: the translator produced a monotonous, literal word-for-word translation into Danish, with only very little look-ahead into the ST. This unchallenged translation production was followed by a scanning of the entire main clause between time stamps 52,000 and 60,000. With the main clause at the second position, the finite verb needs to be clause initial in the Danish translation while the structure is SVO in the English source. The translator thus typed the translation of the finite verb ("need"), obviously without having a clear idea of how to render the remaining parts of that sentence. There is hence a second phase of more than 20 seconds between time stamps 62,000 and 86,000, in which the translator mostly re-reads the target text. The progression graph shows few fixation points, particularly between timestamps 62,000 and 80,000. The figure only shows the gaze movements on the ST window, but from studying the log file we know that the translator was concerned with re-reading the produced target text, obviously trying to find an appropriate translation solution for the current ST segment. Between 80,000 and approx. 82,000 the translator re-read the problematic ST chunk, maybe to verify or confirm a translation solution, before starting typing the translation from time 86,000.

Figure 7 shows the alignment of the translation which corresponds to the time segment in Figure 6 and the bold part in 6. While Figure 6 illustrates *how* the translation was produced, Figure 7 shows *what* was produced in the target text. It shows several cases of re-ordering: i) a syntactic re-ordering of the finite verb *need* ('behøver'[11]) moves into the first position in the Danish clause. Note that only after this was done, the long pause described above occurs. ii) The progression graph in Figure 6 suggests that the main problem here was the rendering of "action on" which does not have a suited literal translation into Danish and requires a lexical choice. The alignment in Figure 7 also shows that iii) "threaten" is translated into an entire phrase, and and extra words ("deres") is inserted which do not have an English equivalent.

Despite the large number of modifications, here too, the translator only reads the minimum amount of text that is required to continue text production. Note that, as in the previous example, the translation of the finite verb is already typed before the translator knows how to render the remaining part of the clause. We assume, here too, that there is no problem in understanding the English source text, rather re-reading of the texts is triggered through production problems, for each of the syntactic and lexical re-organization problems. Parts of the translation are successively typed out as soon as enough context has been read, even if the continuation of the translation is still unclear. This anticipation may sometimes be misguiding and require a re-reading of the ST as the next example will show.

4.4 Erroneous translation anticipation

Another example of a challenged translation is shown in Figure 8. This progression graph plots an instance of a translation problem, where the translator re-reads the (already translated) context of the source sentence. Similar to the example in Figure 1, the translator scans past context in the ST to retrieve information that is necessary to continue production.

---

[11]Diacritical characters (åøœ, etc.) as in 'behøver', 'udgøre', 'økonomiske' etc. are lost in Figure 7.

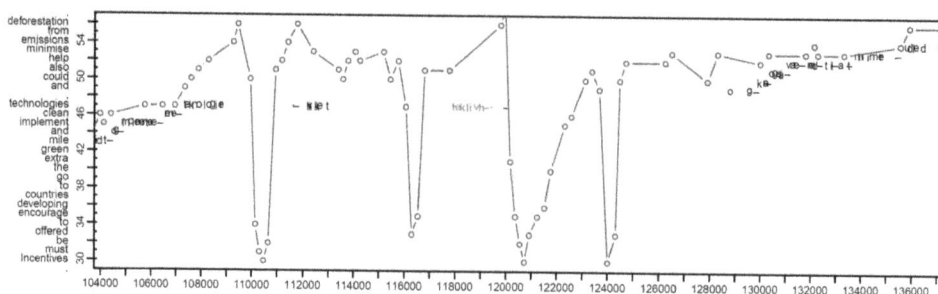

Figure 8: Translation progression graph with backward looking activities

The translation progression graph in Figure 8 plots the production of the bold part in 6, in which the English sentence consists of 28 words, and its translation into Danish consists of 31 words:

(6) English source sentence:
*Incentives must be offered to encourage developing countries to go the extra green mile **and implement clean technologies, and could also help minimise** emissions from deforestation.*
Danish translation:
*Der skal tilbydes incitamenter til at opfordre udviklingslandene til at tage det ekstra grønne skridt **og implementere rene teknologier, [hvilket] og kan også være med til at minimere** udledninger fra skovrydning.*

Similar to the previous example, here too, the beginning of the plotted part shows unchallenged translation. Already while typing the translation for "technologies" around time stamp 108,000, the translator reads ahead until the end of the sentence. She then looks at the beginning ("Incentives must be offered"), and reads the end of the sentence again. Then the translator writes the relative pronoun "hvilket" (around time stamp 112,000) which is deleted 6 seconds later (between timestamps 118,000 and 120,000). After repeatedly re-scanning the entire source sentence, the translator continues with fluent typing at time stamp 129,000 and produces an almost literal, word-for-word translation of the English original.

In this process, which lasted about 30 seconds, it is interesting to note how reading and text production interact. Presumably, the lack of a subject in the English clause "and could also help minimise emissions from deforestation" and its sentence final position has made the translator think that this might be a relative clause of "technologies", despite the fact that English "and" does not translate into a Danish relative pronoun. It is only after writing the relative pronoun ("hvilket") and after re-scanning the source sentence several times that the translator realises that the English clause is a main clause conjunction (with an omitted subject "Incentives"), and not a relative clause of "technologies".

The typing of the relative pronoun suggests a misguided expectation on the part of the translator which had to be sorted out and which required extra reading effort in the ST context. The example shows that there may be only a partial understanding of the text when a translator starts typing its translation, and that more advanced meaning representations are generated "on the fly" when needed, and only to the extent that they are necessary to proceed with text production. As shown in the previous examples, this extended need for understanding is triggered by problems associated with text production rather than a lack of ST comprehension. In reading research it is well known that the reader constructs an analysis of the syntactic structure of a sentence in a highly incremental manner, usually on a word-by-word basis (Staub & Rayner 2007). Our data show that this might be similar in translation production, going back to the source text when this procedure does not work out.

5 Distribution of ST fixation

As discussed in the previous examples, the fixations and fixation units on the ST are not equally distributed over the ST. At some points we observe long fixations and re-fixations on the texts, while other parts are translated smoothly without much problems. We have also seen that – in our examples – the extended gazing duration on the ST is triggered by production rather than comprehension problems.

While extended gaze activities on the ST or TT reflect, thus, text production problems, the question remains whether different translators translating the same text face similar problems at the same text positions. We therefore looked at the amount of ST gaze activity between the typing of every two successive alignment units n and $n+1$, and compared the relative amount of ST gaze duration of five translators before typing the translation of a word n. The result for the five translators is plotted in Figure 9.

That is, for each of the 5 translators T=1...5 we calculate the gaze duration GT on the ST window and the gaze duration GTn just before and during the production of the translation unit n. We then compute for every translator T

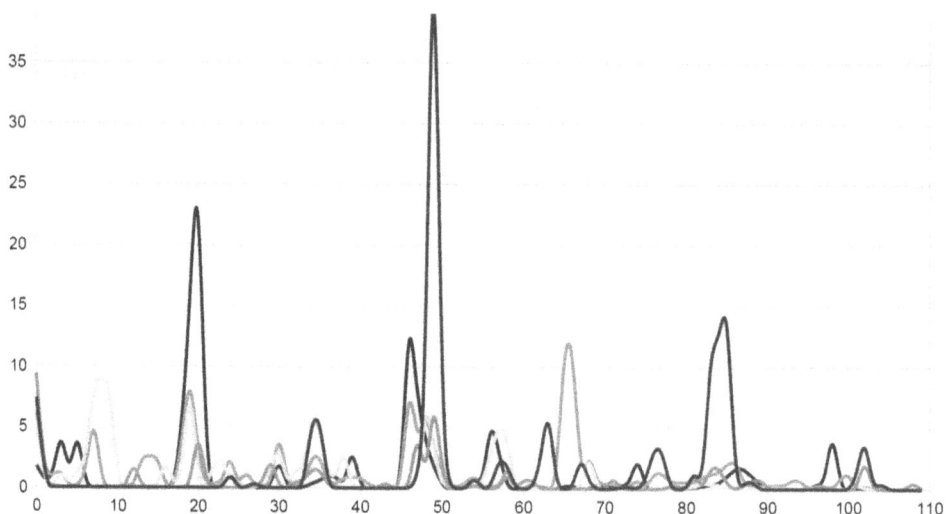

Figure 9: Relative amount of fixation duration (in ‰) before/during of the translation of the n-th ST word

the portion (in ‰) of gaze time for each unit n by the ratio $GTn*1000/GT$[12]. For instance, the ST gazing time during the 8.5 sec pause in Figure 8 before and during the translation of word #49 "and" will be allocated to the GT49, and appear as a peak in Figure 9.

The graph in Figure 9 overlays the proportion of the gaze time that each translator spends on the ST before typing the translation of a word. The horizontal X-axis enumerates all the words of a 110 word ST. The vertical Y-axis shows the relative amount of ST gaze time spent before typing the translation of the ST words. The Y-axis overlays the proportion of ST fixation duration (in ‰) before/during translation production for the five translators. For instance, around ST word #48, one translator spends almost 40‰ of her observed ST gazing time before she produces a translation of the word, while the other translators spent between 5‰ and 14‰ of their gaze time at the same location. The source sentence between ST word number 30 to 56 is represented in Figure 8, while the graph plots the translation progression between words 43 to 52. In Figure 8 we see that much gaze time is spent before "og", the translation of ST word 49 ("and"), is typed. Figure 9 shows that all translators spent substantial time at this position, indicating that they all had presumably similar problems identifying the reference of the verb in the clause starting with "and". Note that while the sentence

---

[12] The amount of gaze time for each unit i also normalised (divided) by the number of ST words that this unit contains.

starts at word position 30, it is only when the conjunction must be translated at word position 49 that all translators have extended reading activities in the ST.

Another example of more than average ST gazing time is around word #19 in Figure 9: all but one translator showed increased reading activity before typing "og", i.e. the translation of ST word #19 "need". Figure 6 shows a translation progression graph of the fragment between ST word #16 and #28. It shows that in some cases all translators spend increased gaze time on the same ST sequences, for other sequences none seems to invest much reading effort and there are still other sequences at which some translators spend much and others no reading time.

6 Conclusion

We have compared two experimental settings, a copying task and a translation task. In the copying task, a copyist read an English text and typed the same text on a keyboard, while in the translation task the translators produced a Danish translation of an English source text without making use of additional aids like dictionaries or collocation tools. Keystrokes and gaze movements were recorded using the Translog 2006 software. While translators mostly copied and translated the text smoothly, looking only a few words ahead in the ST, we also observed at some instances that the text production triggered extended reading activities, e.g. when the meaning of an idiom was unclear. This behaviour can be observed during translation and when copying a text. Interestingly, the extended reading activity did not occur until the idiom was to be reproduced (typed), and not when it was first read.

We discuss instances of unchallenged text production, which are similar in text copying and in translation (1 and 3). We also provide examples that show difficulties when formulating (render and address) the translation rather than a ST comprehension problem. 2 showed that word meaning is processed also during text copying. A production pause occurred when typing an expression that was difficult to understand, rather than when reading it the first time. Similarly, also during translation a "monitor" triggers extended reading when faced with production problems. That is, translations of a phrase are already typed before the translator exactly knows how to render the remaining part of that phrase. Whereas in most cases the initial translation "guess" is appropriate and the translation could go on, Figure 8 shows that this is not always the case. We take this as an indicator that translation production (and text copying) may start with a partial (literal) understanding, and that (ST) meaning emerges and consolidates as the translation develops. Two types of behaviour can be distinguished:

- much of the translation drafting is unproblematic and approximately within the time limits predicted for text copying by Johns' TYPIST model[13]. Translators look only a few words ahead into the ST from the position which they are currently translating. Literal translations are produced in such a parallel reading/writing mode decoding and encoding are processed simultaneously. We suspect that the degree of parallel activity depends on experience and typing skills of the translator. A touch typist would more likely exhibit parallel processing behaviour, similar to the one in Figure 2, while a translator with less developed typing skills would show more sequential translation patterns.

- at some points in the translation extensive reading behaviour could be observed, signalling more serious translation problems. Depending on the type of problem, it may be necessary for the translator to re-scan the ST or the TT. In both cases, the increased reading activity seems to be triggered by a TT production problem rather than by a ST comprehension problem. That is, in the examples discussed above, we observed that the ST was understood, and meaning hypotheses were generated only to the extent required to keep on producing target text. If, for whatever reason, TT production cannot go on smoothly, and the typing flow is interrupted, the missing information needs to be retrieved. This may lead to the re-reading of a ST passage with a view to verification or reinterpretation, and/or the revision of the produced TT.

We do not exclude that a translator may re-read a difficult ST fragment several times before starting to translate it, but we did not encounter examples of such behaviour in our data. All behavioural patterns that point to translation problems (i.e. re-reading of ST or TT passages) were triggered by *production problems*. There are more pauses during translation than during copying, indicating more sequential reading/writing processes in translation, while the absence of such pauses indicates more parallel reading and writing activities during copying. This confirms the hypothesis that there are more interventions of the monitor during translation than during copying. Looking at gaze activities we found that the number of ST fixations during parallel unchallenged translation activities is approximately identical to those of unchallenged copying while there were more ST fixations during sequential translation activity.

---

[13]This conclusion is based on our translation material from English into Danish, two relatively close languages with similar word order.

In a stratificational comprehension-transfer-production theory of translation this behaviour is difficult to explain. If the ST would first have to be completely understood before a translator starts translating it, why would the translation activity have an impact on the ST reading behaviour? Instead, we assume that "Meaning Hypotheses" are constructed to the extent and at the moment they are needed to continue the task at hand. Different meaning hypotheses are required for different kinds of activities, e.g. a technician reading a car repair manual needs a different kind of understanding than a translator translating the text into another language. The reading purpose, thus, determines what kind and depth of meaning representation is required. During translation and text copying, the ST meaning is often only elaborated and tested in the writing process – which leads to the surprising conclusion that comprehension does not precede, but follows text production.

References

Angelone, Erik. 2010. Uncertainty, uncertainty management and metacognitive problem solving in the translation task. In Gregory M. Shreve & Erik Angelone (eds.), *Translation and cognition*, 17–40. Amsterdam: Benjamins.

Carl, Michael & Arnt Lykke Jakobsen. 2009. Towards statistical modelling of translators' activity data. *International Journal of Speech Technology* 12(4). 124–146.

Carl, Michael & Martin Kay. 2011. Gazing and typing activities during translation: A comparative study of translation units of professional and student translators. *META* 56(4). 952–975.

Craciunescu, Olivia, Constanza Gerding-Salas & Susan Stringer-O'Keeffe. 2004. Machine translation and computer-assisted translation: A new way of translating? *Translation Journal* 8(3). http://www.translationjournal.net/journal/29computers.htm.

Dragsted, Barbara. 2010. Coordination of reading and writing processes in translation: an eye on uncharted territory. In Gregory M. Shreve & Erik Angelone (eds.), *Translation and cognition*, 41–62. Amsterdam: Benjamins.

Gile, Daniel. 1995. *La traduction. la comprendre, l'apprendre*. Paris: Presses Universitaires de France.

Jakobsen, Arnt Lykke. 2010. Logging target text production with Translog. In Gyde Hansen (ed.), *Probing the process in translation: Methods and results* (Copenhagen Studies in Language 24), 9–20. Kopenhagen: Samfundslitteratur.

Jakobsen, Arnt Lykke & Kristian Tangsgaard Hvelplund Jensen. 2008. Eye movement behaviour across four different types of reading task. In Susanne Göpferich, Arnt Lykke Rasmussen & Inger M. Mees (eds.), *Looking at eyes. Eye tracking studies of reading and translation processing* (CSL 36), 103–124. Kopenhagen: Samfundslitteratur.

Jensen, Kristian Tangsgaard Hvelplund. 2011. *Allocation of cognitive resources in translation: An eye-tracking and key-logging study*. Copenhagen: Copenhagen Business School dissertation.

John, Bonnie E. 1996. Typist: A theory of performance in skilled typing. *Human-Computer Interaction* 11(4). 321–355.

Just, Marcel Adam & Patricia A. Carpenter. 1984. Using eye fixations to study reading comprehension. In David E. Kieras & Marcel Adam Just (eds.), *New methods in reading comprehension research*, 151–182. Hillsdale: Erlbaum.

Kromann, Matthias Trautner. 2003. The Danish Dependency Treebank and the DTAG treebank tool. In *Proceedings of the Second Workshop on Treebanks and Linguistic Theories (TLT 2003)*, 217–220. Växjö.

Mossop, Brian. 2003. *An Alternative to 'Deverbalization'*. Tech. rep. Toronto: York University. http://www.yorku.ca/brmossop/Deverbalization.htm.

Perrin, Daniel. 2003. Progression analysis (PA): Investigating writing strategies at the workplace. *Pragmatics* 35(6). 907–921.

Ruiz, Carmen, Natalia Paredes, Pedro Macizo & Maria Teresa Bajo. 2008. Activation of lexical and syntactic target language properties in translation. *Acta Psychologica* 128. 490–500.

Sjørup, Annette C. 2011. Cognitive effort in metaphor translation: An eye-tracking study 1. In Sharon O'Brien (ed.), *Cognitive explorations of translation* (Continuum Studies in Translation), 197–214. London: Continuum International Publishing Group Ltd.

Staub, Adrian & Keith Rayner. 2007. Eye movements and on-line comprehension processes. In Gareth Gaskell (ed.), *The Oxford handbook of psycholinguistics*, 327–342. Oxford: Oxford University Press.

Tirkkonen-Condit, Sonja. 2005. The monitor model revisited: Evidence from process research. *META* 50(2). 405–414.

Chapter 3

Text structure in a contrastive and translational perspective: On information density and clause linkage in Italian and Danish

Iørn Korzen

Morten Gylling
Copenhagen Business School

This paper argues that both human translators and machine translation systems can greatly benefit from contrastive studies of text structure. Due to the great terminological and definitional confusion regarding structures in texts, the paper first discusses the main viewpoints on these issues and then outlines the two most significant differences between Italian and Danish text structure. One regards the notion of information density: Italian tends to accumulate the same information in shorter text spans and to include a larger number of Elementary Discourse Units in each sentence than Danish. The other regards clause linkage: A higher percentage of Italian clauses is morpho-syntactically and rhetorically subordinated by means of non-finite and nominalised verb forms. Danish text structure, on the other hand, is more informationally linear and characterised by a higher number of finite verbs and topic shifts. These typological differences are transferred into some simple translation rules concerning the number of Elementary Discourse Units per sentence and their textualisation. Each rule is illustrated by a number of examples taken from the parallel part of the Europarl Corpus.

1 Introduction

It has been pointed out that in some aspects Translation Studies (TS) and Contrastive Linguistics (CL) overlap each other. Some scholars talk about "common

Iørn Korzen & Morten Gylling. Text structure in a contrastive and translational perspective: On information density and clause linkage in Italian and Danish. In Oliver Czulo & Silvia Hansen-Schirra (eds.), *Crossroads between Contrastive Linguistics, Translation Studies and Machine Translation: TC3 II*, 31–64. Berlin: Language Science Press. DOI:10.5281/zenodo.1019687

grounds" between the two, for instance, that they are both "interested in see-ing how 'the same thing' can be said in other ways, although each field uses this information for different ends" (Chesterman 1998: 39). Another more recent and methodological common ground is the emergence of corpora that serve as empirical bases for TS and CL research (Granger 2003).

However, in spite of such "common grounds", the fact remains that only a limited number of TS scholars have applied CL to their research in order to obtain an awareness of systematic differences between two or more language systems. Vice versa, only a few CL scholars take advantage of TS knowledge of translation norms and strategies. This paper aims to illustrate how TS can benefit from CL findings, as a sort of response to Chesterman's appeal (1998: 6):

> Although these [TS and CL] are neighbouring disciplines, it nevertheless often appears that theoretical developments in one field are overlooked in the other, and that both would benefit from each other's insights.

Our point of departure is CL, but where both CL and TS typically confine their investigations to lexical and syntactic levels, we will focus on the textualisation and structure of larger text segments, i.e. segments beyond the boundaries of clauses and sentences.

Structures in texts have been massively investigated from different angles and under different terms: discourse structure, text structure, rhetorical structure, in-formation structure, temporal structure, etc.,[1] and particularly between the three first mentioned terms, discourse, text and rhetorical structure, there is great ter-minological and definitional confusion and overlap. In §2, we shall therefore briefly examine a few of the most important viewpoints regarding these issues and outline the definitions chosen in our own research. In §3, we shall describe Italian and Danish text structure on the basis of a relatively large comparable text corpus, the Europarl Corpus, whereas §4 will be dedicated to the perspec-tives of our research results for translation, supported by a number of "felicitous" Italian-Danish translations from the parallel Europarl texts.

2 Structures in texts

2.1 Discourse, text and rhetorical structures

Especially discourse (structure) and text (structure) have been subject to different definitions in the literature. For instance, in the *International Encyclopedia of Linguistics*, Chafe notes:

---

[1]See Hoey (1991) for a discussion of structure vs. organisation of texts.

The term *discourse* is used in somewhat different ways by different scholars, but underlying the differences is a common concern for language beyond the boundaries of isolated sentences. The term *text* is used in similar ways. Both terms may refer to a unit of language larger than the sentence: one may speak of a "discourse" or a "text". (Chafe 2003: 440)

Irmer (2011) is a recent example of a scholar who similarly uses the terms interchangeably: "Generally, a *text* or a *discourse* is a sequence of natural language utterances." The same viewpoint is found earlier in Stubbs, who adds:

Sometimes this terminological variation [between text and discourse] signals important conceptual distinctions, but often it does not, and terminological debates are usually of little interest. (Stubbs 1996: 4)

Halliday and Hasan use both terms in their definition of a "text":

A *text* has texture and this is what distinguishes it from something that is not a *text*. ...The texture is provided by the cohesive RELATION which is set up where the INTERPRETATION of some element in the *discourse* is dependent on that of another (Hasan & Halliday 1976: 2-4, our italics).

Similarly, we find in Rijkhoff 2008: 90 both terms, discourse and (co-)text, used for linguistic material, as the scholar affirms: "[D]iscourse in the sense of co-text is a linguistic entity."

On the other hand, there are scholars according to whom "text" refers to written language and "discourse" to spoken language. For instance, Stubbs (1983: 9) notes that "One often talks of 'written text' versus 'spoken discourse'", and similarly Riazi states:

The first [approach] is 'discourse analysis', which mainly focuses on the structure of naturally occurring spoken language, as found in such 'discourses' as conversations, commentaries, and speeches. The second approach is 'text analysis', which focuses on the structure of written language, as found in such 'texts' as essays and articles, notices, book chapters, and so on. (Riazi 2002: 4)

However, this distinction is rejected by other scholars:

Discourse ...refers to both text and talk, and these not as two separate genres to be compared and contrasted, but rather as overlapping aspects of a single entity. As the object of study, spoken discourse is 'text', much as words spoken in a speech are commonly referred to as the text of the speech. In this sense, 'discourse' and 'text' are synonymous. (Tannen 1982: ix),

In non-linguistic and non-semiotic circles, *text* is sometimes used for examples of written language and discourse for the spoken. Nowadays linguists accept that such a distinction based only on medium and channel is simplistic. (Christiansen 2011: 34)

A third group of scholars see discourse structure as the rhetorical organisation of a text (Mann & Thompson 1988), organisation definable as a series of "coherence relations" (Hobbs 1985) between text segments, created in the process of human communication (Brown & Yule 1983: 24–26; Widdowson 1979: 71). Widdowson (2004), who overtly criticises Harris (1952) and Stubbs for conflating the terms "text" and "discourse" (Widdowson 2004: 4-5), states more precisely:

> Discourse in this view is the pragmatic process of meaning negotiation. Text is its product. ...The discourse may be prepared, pre-scripted in different degrees. ...But whatever the degree of prescription, the text, the actual language that realizes the interaction, is immediate to it, and is directly processed on line. (Widdowson 2004: 8-9).

Seemingly inspired by Hasan & Halliday and their claim (1976: 300): "discourse ...come[s] to life as text", Christiansen (2011: 34) similarly states that "text [is] the form, discourse the content", and along the same line, Cornish (2009: 99-100), concludes his definition of the two terms in this way:

> [Text], then, refers to the connected sequences of signs and signals, under their conventional meanings, produced by the speaker ...Discourse, on the other hand, refers to the hierarchically structured, mentally represented product of the sequence of utterance, propositional, illocutionary and indexical acts that the participants are jointly carrying out as the communication unfolds ...Text, in normal circumstances of communication, on the other hand is essentially linear, due to the constraints imposed by the production of speech in real time."

Similarly, Ruiz Ruiz (2009: 4), remarks:

> [T]he two concepts [discourse and text] should not be confused or equated. Indeed, every piece of discourse has a textual form or can acquire it; the same text may include different discourses or the same discourse may adopt different textual forms.

In this paper, we shall follow this latter group of scholars and their definitions of

- "discourse" as the process and rhetorical organisation of verbal communication and
- "text" as the (oral or written) product and form.

Both discourse and text can be analysed with regard to their internal relations and structures, but methodology and terminology vary. Before proceeding with the linguistic investigation proper, we shall briefly describe the units between which such relations are created (§2.2), then define the concept of information structure (§2.3), and finally present an overall summary of structures in texts (§2.4).

2.2 Elementary Discourse Units (EDUs)

A text typically consists of more than one clause or sentence. Text segmentation has been treated in various ways in the literature, ranging from a very fine-grained division to a more general one that considers clauses as the minimal discourse unit. Such minimal units have been termed "Elementary Discourse Units", EDUs, by the Rhetorical Structure Theory (henceforth RST), a term that we shall adopt in the following.

In the "classical" RST (Mann & Thompson 1987; Mann et al. 1992; Matthiessen & Thompson 1988 and later work), EDUs are considered to be clauses with the exception of clausal subjects and objects, other clausal complements and restrictive relative clauses. In the "modern" RST (Carlson et al. 2003), EDUs are clauses – including relative clauses – as well as attribution clauses and various phrases with strong discourse cues, such as *because of, in spite of, according to.* In this paper, we shall follow these principles with the exception of not segmenting attribution clauses as distinct EDUs. Normally, as a minimal requirement, EDUs must have a verbal element, but verbless constructions ending with full stops, question or exclamation marks as well as adjectival appositions are also identified as EDUs. An example of EDU identification is reproduced in (1); the sentence comes from the English L1 part of the Europarl Corpus[2] and contains four EDUs. Satellites, i.e. rhetorically subordinated EDUs (§2.4), are shown in italics, and the nucleus in bold fonts. Each EDU is delimited by square brackets.

---

[2]See §3.1 for a description of this corpus. The numbers following each Europarl ("ep-") text are read: YY-MM-DD; "txt" indicates SPEAKER ID.

(1) [*Looking at the package of amendments to our Rules of Procedure*]₁ [*tabled
by the Committee on Constitutional Affairs,*]₂ [**I can say on behalf of my
group that we will support the thrust**]₃ [of what the Committee on
Constitutional Affairs has put forward.]₄ (ep-01-11-12.txt:56)

EDU₃ (the matrix clause), shown in bold fonts, is the nucleus of the sentence,
to which EDU₁ (a present participle phrase) is linked as a satellite expressing a
circumstantial relation. EDU₂ (a past participle phrase) is linked to EDU₁ expressing an elaboration of *the package* in question. Finally EDU₄ (a relative clause) is
linked to the nucleus EDU₄ elaborating on *the thrust*.

Other scholars use different terms for EDUs, such as "propositions" (e.g. Lehmann 1988), "abstract objects/arguments" (e.g. Prasad et al. 2008), and "discourse
segments" (e.g. Irmer 2011: 128), all terms with more or less the same meaning as
EDUs.

2.3 Information structure

Information structure is perhaps the linguistic structure that has been defined
most uniformly by scholars, starting with Halliday's (1967) "given-new" categorisation based on the Prague School's "communicative dynamism" of the single
units of a sentence (see e.g. Vachek 1966). Also subsequent and somewhat similar dichotomies such as "topic-comment" (Hockett 1958), "theme-rheme" (Firbas 1974), and "focus-presupposition" (Krifka 1993) are generally categorised as
components of the information structure of a text. Lambrecht (1994: 1), notes,
however:

> There has been and still is disagreement and confusion in linguistic theory
> about the nature of the component of language referred to in this book as
> INFORMATION STRUCTURE and about the status of this component in
> the overall system of grammar.

Regarding information density, in this paper we shall focus on the amount
of information per text span (words and sentences), thus concentrating on the
first of the four definitional elements of the term suggested by Fabricius-Hansen
(1996: 529):

> [W]e would probably say that the informational density is higher in A than
> in B if at least one of the following conditions holds, other things being
> equal: i. the average amount of discourse information per sentence is higher
> in A than in B; ...

More precisely, we shall say that the information density is higher in A than in B if both contain the same amount of information but A is shorter than B, and/or A contains more EDUs than B, other things being equal. Among such "other things", a very important issue in a comparison between Italian and Danish is sentence length, as we shall see in §3.2.

2.4 Structures in texts: An overview

The three kinds of structures in texts dealt with above all involve EDUs and the relations between them, but in different ways, as summed up in Table 1.

Table 1: Three structures in texts.

Discourse Structure	Text Structure	Information Structure
Content and process of communication:	Form and product of communication:	Information packaging in communication:
discourse relations (also called coherence or rhetorical relations) between EDUs	syntactic relations between	information density (amount of information per text span, e.g. EDUs per sentence)
rhetorical co-/subordination of EDUs	morpho-syntactic co-/subordination of EDUs	rhetorical and morpho-syntactic co-/subordination of EDUs

Although rhetorical and morpho-syntactic co-/subordination of EDUs are mentioned under discourse and text structure respectively and may therefore seem redundant with regard to information structure, they are, however, important aspects also of the "information packaging" of a text, as we shall see in §3.4.

The taxonomy of discourse relations that we follow in our work (but due to space limitations cannot pursue further in this paper) is taken from RST and consists of coordinated (multinuclear) and subordinated (nucleus-satellite) relations. We have chosen this taxonomy for the reasons also stated by Bateman & Rondhuis (1997: 6), which are particularly relevant in a cross-linguistic context:

> An important claim of this theory is that the same rhetorical relations that
> hold between spans realised by individual clauses also account for the rela-
> tionships between larger segments of text ...It is this that makes it possible
> to characterise the structure of a text in terms of a single hierarchy of rhetor-
> ical relations inter-connecting the parts drawing on only a relatively small
> number of relation-types.

Innumerable other taxonomies have been proposed, see e.g. Danlos (2008),
Irmer (2011), and Webber & Prasad (2009) for discussions.

3 Text and information structure in the Europarl corpus

At this point we shall confine our investigation to two of the three types of structures in text outlined in Table 1, i.e. the text and information structures, and
we shall commence with a brief description of our empirical basis, the Europarl
Corpus.

3.1 Corpus details and discussion

The Europarl Corpus is an open source corpus compiled by Koehn (2005) and
recently updated.[3]. It is a very large multilingual text collection with up to 50
million words per language and with source and target texts covering all 23 official languages of the European Union. The corpus was designed to train and
evaluate statistical machine translation, and it is still extensively used for this
purpose (see the corpus website for an overview). But as we shall see, it can also
serve as empirical basis for other cross-linguistic investigations.

The texts are mainly argumentative – see van Halteren (2008) for a discussion – and consist of speeches made by the members of the European Parliament
and other politicians in the years 1996–2011. Around 80 % of the speeches have
been tagged with language attributes indicating the native language (L1) of the
speaker. This made it possible for us, with the help of a Perl script, to automatically extract all Italian and Danish L1 text from the entire corpus. Since we
wanted to perform both quantitative and qualitative analyses, we compiled two
subcorpora: a subcorpus 1 with all the Italian and Danish Europarl texts from the
period 1996–2003, and a subcorpus 2 with a limited number of quasi-randomly
selected Italian and Danish texts from subcorpus 1, totalling some 15,000 words

---

[3]Europarl is available at http://statmt.org/europarl/ In this paper, we use the "v3" (third release)
of the Europarl Corpus.

in each language. We used subcorpus 1 to calculate the average sentence length of all Italian and Danish L1 texts, see §3.2, whereas subcorpus 2 served for more fine-grained and manually performed analyses, see §3.3 and §4. In order to obtain a balanced and representative subcorpus 2, our requirements for these texts, which were selected manually, concerned variety regarding "chapters" (meeting sessions), dates (so that not all texts were speeches from the same period), speakers (a certain number of different speakers was chosen) and speech length (between 200 and 700 words).

We chose Europarl as our empirical basis because it contains both parallel L1–L2 texts and comparable texts, i.e. L1 texts created in different languages but dealing with similar topics and produced in similar situations and genres for similar targets. Whereas parallel texts are clearly best suited e.g. for improving machine translation, since they permit L1–L2 text alignment and evaluation, comparable texts are generally best suited as the empirical basis for descriptive, possibly typological comparisons. In such cases, parallel texts are inappropriate because the filter of the translator and the translation strategies get in the way, and/or L2 texts may end up with a text structure very similar to that of the L1, as we shall see below. Baroni & Bernardini (2006: 260) refer to this phenomenon as "translationese":

> It is common, when reading translations, to feel that they are written in their own peculiar style. Translation scholars even speak of the language of translation as a separate 'dialect' within a language, which they call *third code* …or *translationese* … Translationese has been originally described …as the set of "fingerprints" that one language leaves on another when a text is translated between the two.

In the same vein McEnery et al. (2006: 49) state that

> source and translated texts …alone serve as a poor basis for cross-linguistic contrasts, because translations (i.e. L2 texts) cannot avoid the effect of translationese …[C]omparable corpora are a useful resource for contrastive studies and translation studies, when used in combination with parallel corpora.

3.2 Sentence length

Differences in text and information structure show themselves in many ways, one of which is the simple sentence length, measured as words per sentence[4]. Of course, many reservations should be made when conducting linguistic measurements in this way, but we find the statistical results cited below convincing enough to be taken into account and used as a first indication of profound typological differences between the two languages analysed.[5]

Table 2: Sentence length in L1 and L2 Europarl texts.

Subcorpus 1	Words	Sentences	Average words/sentence
Italian L1	1,657,592	47,405	34.97
Danish L1	546,425	22,668	24.11
Italian L2	571,115	22,154	25.78
Danish L2	1,845,951	57,574	32.06

Table 2 shows the average sentence length of all Italian and Danish L1 texts (subcorpus 1) and of the Italian L2 texts (translated from Danish) and Danish L2 texts (translated from Italian)[6]. Due to the differences of representation in the European Parliament between the two countries, there are roughly three times as many Italian L1 texts as Danish L1 texts. This, however, has no impact on the average analyses.

As the upper part of Table 2 shows, there is a considerable difference in average sentence length between the Italian L1 and Danish L1 texts, a difference amounting to 10.86 words per sentence, which means that the Italian sentences are almost 50 % longer than the Danish ones, 45.0 % to be exact. However, as the lower part of Table 2 shows, regarding sentence length, the Danish and Italian

[4]A sentence is defined as a text segment followed by a full stop, a question mark, or an exclamation mark. Colons and semicolons are defined as punctuation marks separating clauses and not sentences.

[5]Also other scholars, such as Fabricius-Hansen (1998) and Teich (2003), use sentence length to measure text complexity in CL studies.

[6]We cannot entirely exclude that some translations from Danish to Italian, or vice versa, may have been translated from another L2 text, e.g. from one of the so-called EU "relay languages" (English, French or German). The Europarl Corpus does not provide any information in this regard, but even if this were the case in some instances, the indicated differences between Italian and Danish would still be valid.

translators in the European Parliament tend to follow a rather imitative translation strategy. The Danish L2 texts are 33.0 % longer than the Danish L1 texts, while the Italian L2 texts are 35.6 % shorter than the Italian L1 texts. So regarding sentence length these L2 texts are clearly influenced by the L1 text structure, just as predicted by the scholars cited in §3.1.

The longest Danish (L1) sentence of subcorpus 1 consisted of 146 words, and interestingly enough it had been merged with the following sentence in the Italian L2 text resulting in a 226 word long sentence. Table 3 shows the lengths of the longest sentences in each group, and the overall longest Danish L2 sentence consisting of 282 words is another excellent example of "translationese".

Table 3: Longest sentence lengths in Europarl texts.

Subcorpus 1	Italian L1	Danish L1	Italian L2	Danish L2
Longest sentence words	266 ep-97-01-15.txt:97	146 ep-02-12-04.txt:17	226 ep-02-12-04.txt:17	282 ep-97-01-15.txt:97

3.3 Information density

At this point we shall return to the concept of "information density", in Table 1 defined as the amount of information per text span, e.g. EDUs per sentence. If we look at some of the numbers of Table 2 that do *not* reflect an imitative translation strategy, we see that the Danish L2 texts have 11.4 % more words and 21.5 % more sentences than the Italian L1 texts. Assuming that the source and target texts contain the same amount of information (one of the most important criteria for EU translations), a very clear "dilution" of information density both on word and sentence level has occurred in the translation process from Italian to Danish. In sections §4.1–§4.2, we supply a number of text examples that illustrate this dilution.

Also if we measure information density as the number of EDUs per sentence, there is a clear difference between the Italian and Danish Europarl texts. The count of EDUs textualised in each sentence can be a very time-consuming task, since no parser has been trained to do this convincingly. Therefore, we limited this analysis to subcorpus 2, and the results appear in Table 4:

Whereas the number of words and EDUs in the two text groups is roughly the same, the number of sentences varies considerably entailing great differences also in the average number of EDUs per sentence. Regarding sentences containing five EDUs or more, the Italian percentage is about four times the Danish

Table 4: Statistics on Europarl subcorpus 2.

Subcorpus 2	Words	Sentences	EDUs/Sentences	Average EDUs/ sentence	Percentage of sentences with five or more EDUs/sentence
Italian L1	14,708	440	1,473	3.35	21.1 %
Danish L1	14,737	678	1,455	2.15	5.5 %

Table 5: Distribution of EDUs in subordinate clauses in Europarl subcorpus 2.

Subcorpus 2	a. Subordinate clauses total	b. Relative clauses	c. Other subordinate finite clauses	d. Subordinate non-finite clauses	e. Other subordinate constructions
Italian L1	82.8 %	35.6 %	23.4 %	30.8 %	10.3 %
Danish L1	78.6 %	39.5 %	39.7 %	17.0 %	3.8 %

percentage, as shown in the last column to the right.

We then performed a finer-grained analysis of the Italian and Danish EDU textualisation and found other substantial differences in the distribution of subordinate clauses, cf. Table 5:[7]

Subordinate clauses amounted to 82.8 % of all clauses in the Italian texts as opposed to 78.6 % of the clauses in the Danish texts[8]. However, the most significant and interesting differences lie in the distribution of finite vs. non-finite subordinate clauses. The Danish texts contain 79.2 % finite subordinate clauses (columns b+c), but only 20.8 % non-finite clauses and verbless constructions (columns d+e). In the Italian texts, on the other hand, the distribution between finite and non-finite subordinate clauses is more equal: 59.0 % finite clauses (b+c) and 41.1 % non-finite and verbless constructions (d+e). In other words, subordinate non-finite and verbless constructions are twice as frequent in Italian as in Danish. Furthermore (what is not shown separately in Table 5 but included in column d), Italian speakers use the whole range of non-finite verb forms (gerunds, participles, infinitives and nominalisations) much more regularly, whereas Danish speakers generally confine themselves to infinitives (the gerund does not exist

---

[7]These constructions include complex nominal and adjectival postmodifiers (attributives and appositions).

[8]If we included clausal subjects, objects and other complements, the differences between main and subordinate clauses in the two text groups would become much more considerable.

in Danish). The majority of the subordinate constructions in (e) are complex adjectival postmodifiers, which in many cases correspond to the Danish relative clauses (column b). We shall investigate this matter in more detail in the following sections, in particular §4.1–§4.2.

3.4 EDU linkage

As just stated, morpho-syntactic linkage of EDUs differs greatly between languages and, not least, between language families and groups such as the Romance and Scandinavian. Regarding clause linkage, Lehmann (1988) can still be considered as one of the "classic" and most important papers, whereas syntactic co-/subordination has been investigated and described by many other scholars, e.g. Fabricius-Hansen & Ramm (2008: 2-3) who define these concepts in the following way:

> In what is probably their most widespread application, 'subordination' and 'coordination' – along with their adjectival cognates 'subordinate', 'coordinate', etc. – are syntactic notions denoting relations between parts of a complex syntactic unit. That is, they concern the structure of sentences or clauses and their parts. ...As far as the domain of natural discourse and texts is concerned, it is a common observation in various theoretical approaches that entities of this domain too can be organised hierarchically ('subordinating', 'hypotactically') or non-hierarchically ('coordinating', 'paratactically').

Among the many other cross-linguistic surveys on text structure are e.g. Fabricius-Hansen (1996; 1998) and Ramm & Fabricius-Hansen (2005), who investigate English, German and Norwegian, i.e. three Germanic languages, and Skytte, who investigate Italian and Danish. On grammatical shifts e.g. between finite verbs and nominalisations in translation processes between English and German, see Alves et al. (2010), and on information density and explicitness in English-German translations, see also Hansen-Schirra et al. (2007). As stated in Table 1, and like scholars such as Asher & Vieu (2005: 594), we consider EDU co- vs. subordination (both rhetorical and morpho-syntactic) as part of the "information packaging" of a text, a term suggested by Chafe (1976: 28) and later used, especially in connection with given vs. new entities and definiteness, e.g. by Clark & Haviland (1977), and Vallduví & Engdahl (1996).

In a sequence of EDUs, such as the following:

(2) EDU1: *arrive (John, in London); EDU2: go (John, home)*

EDU1 can – if interpreted as the rhetorical satellite – be textualised in different ways, as shown in the "Deverbalisation Scale" in Table 6.

Table 6: The Deverbalisation Scale

EDU1 textualised as	Textualisation EDU1 + EDU2
a. an independent sentence	*John arrived in London.* He went straight home.
b. a main clause, part of sentence	*John arrived in London* and he went straight home.
c. a subordinate finite clause	*After John arrived in London,* he went straight home.
d. a subordinate non-finite clause	*Having arrived in London,* John went straight home.
e. a nominalisation	*After his arrival in London,* John went straight home.

The scale is based on Hopper & Thompson (1984), Lehmann (1988), and Korzen (2007a; 2009), and the deverbalisation of the EDU1 increases from (a/b) to (e) together with its integration into the matrix clause. Whereas the finite verb in a main clause, levels (a/b), has its full (language specific) range of grammatico-semantic values[9] and the clause its full range of pragmatic-illocutionary possibilities, these values are gradually reduced or lost in the textualisations further down the scale. The verb in the subordinate finite clause, level (c), loses its independent tense, mood and illocution; these features will be determined and/or expressed by the matrix clause[10], in the case of for instance tense due to the so-called *consecutio temporum principle*, as in the Italian/English example (3)[b]:

(3)   a. *So che Leo è arrivato alle 9.* 'I know that Leo arrived/has arrived at 9.'

      b. *Sapevo che Leo era (*è) arrivato alle 9.* 'I knew that Leo had (*has) arrived at 9.'[11]

The non-finite verb at the (d) level loses all temporal, modal, and aspectual values, and with the exception of the constructions mentioned in footnote 13 below, it cannot render explicit its subject:

---

[9]Hopper & Thompson (1984: 708) here talk about the "prototypical verb function".

[10]Exceptions are appositive relative clauses, which may have an illocution value different from that of the matrix clause: *I brought you these books,* **which you will read for the next lesson!**, assertive (matrix) vs. directive (relative clause) illocutionary acts.

[11]In the Romance languages, the (c) level is divided into two: subordinate clauses in the indicative and in the subjunctive. The latter verbs have lost their aspect distinctions, their ability to assert an event or situation and some tense possibilities. Thus, this level can be considered as more deverbalised than the indicative level. See Korzen (2007a; 2009).

(4) *John *having arrived late, John/he went straight home.*
     *John *born into a family of musicians, John/he began studying piano at the age of ten.*

The lack of subject marking of the non-finite constructions generally entails an inherent subject/topic continuity (a topic shift normally requires a finite verb with an explicit subject), which means that the situation or event in question is evaluated and interpreted as related to the on-going topic but less important than the situation or event of the matrix clause, textualised with a finite verb.

The last of the constructions, the nominalisation, (e), is completely integrated in the matrix clause as a second order entity in Lyons's (1977: 442ff) terminology. It has lost all its verbal-morphological characteristics and its valency complements are syntactically reduced to secondary positions or simply left out, as in (5a). An NP such as (5)[b] will often appear as relatively "heavy" and tend to be avoided.

(5) a. *(The manager evaluated the performance →) The evaluation of the performance.../ The manager's evaluation...*

     b. The manager's evaluation of the performance...

In other words: The further down on the Deverbalisation Scale an EDU is textualised, the fewer grammatico-semantic features are expressed by the verb, i.e. the more "deverbalised" it is, and the more pragmatically and rhetorically subordinated and incorporated in the matrix clause is the EDU. In the case of non-finite and nominalised verbs, levels (d/e), features such as subject, tense, mood, aspect and illocution are entirely interpreted on the basis of the matrix clause[12]. Therefore, the pragmatic and semantic interpretation of non-finite or nominalised structures is entirely dependent on the matrix clause, and such structures express a particularly strong rhetorical backgrounding (explicit satellite status) of the EDU in question, as stated also by Lehmann (1988: 214):

> [A]dvanced hierarchical downgrading of the subordinate clause implies a low syntactic level for it. We will thus be justified if in the following we take advanced downgrading as a sufficient condition for high integration.

---

[12]Regarding subject, we here ignore e.g. the so-called "absolute constructions" consisting of a participle or gerund + a subject different from the subject of the main verb, e.g. **Morto il padre**, *Luca partì per Roma* '**The father [having] died**, *Luca left for Rome*'. As we saw in (5), in nominalised verb forms the subject may appear as a secondary valency complement: **The manager's** *evaluation.*

High integration of the subordinate into the main clause correlates positively with its desententialisation.

See authentic examples of (b-e) structures in §3.5.

3.5 Text (syntactic) structure and discourse (rhetorical) structure

As stated in the previous section, non-finite and nominalised structures explicitly
express the satellite status of the EDU in question. Generally – but not necessarily
– this is true also of subordinate adverbial clauses, such as the EDU1 clause of the
example in Table 6(c), *After John arrived late in London, (he went straight home).*
Exceptions to this rule can be found especially in subordinate temporal clauses,
e.g. :

(6)   *I was walking on the beach when suddenly I heard a big explosion,*

where the first (and matrix) clause is the rhetorical satellite indicating the background scene of the nucleus expressed by the syntactically subordinate circum-
stantial/temporal clause. Other exceptions are subject, object and subject complement clauses, which are valency constituents of the matrix clause and therefore
not textually backgrounded, and appositive relative clauses, which may carry
on the story line (the "continuative appositive clauses", cf. Loock 2010: 95) or
for other reasons express the most important part of the text sequence, see an
example in footnote 11 (and more details in Korzen 2007b; 2009).

On the other hand, the structures at levels (a/b) of the Deverbalisation Scale
are in themselves ambiguous as to mono- or multinuclear interpretation. Asher
& Lascarides (2003: 165-168), treat fore- and background interpretation of independent sentences in their Segmented Discourse Representation Theory (SDRT),
quoting e.g.:

(7)   *A burglar broke into Mary's apartment. a) Mary was asleep. b) A police
woman visited her the next day.*

The a) continuation is a background sequence, which permits a following
pronominal anaphorisation of the NP *a burglar: **He**stole the silver.* The b) continuation is a foreground sequence, which does not license the same pronominal
anaphor. Similar analyses (although not in a SDRT context) are found in Korzen
(2000: 484-492) and (2001: 114), where a distinction is made between primary and
secondary text topics according to the status of the text segment in which they
are located.

However, it is well known that the syndetic coordination with the connective *and* (and its cross-linguistic counterparts), as in Table 6(b), often contains an EDU1 with satellite status. The literature on the function and semantics of *and* is vast and mostly theory and/or language dependent. Important cross-linguistic studies on *and* and counterparts are found e.g. in Ramm & Fabricius-Hansen (2005), Behrens & Fabricius-Hansen (2010) and Skytte (2000: 652-660). Following Txurruka (2000), Asher & Vieu (2005: 598-599), define *and* as an unequivocal coordination marker, a viewpoint which is contrary to our analyses and those of the other scholars just mentioned. In a case like the one cited in Table 6(b), *John arrived late in London and he went straight home*, the EDU1 can very well be seen as a satellite expressing the cause of the EDU2.

To further support this viewpoint, we shall cite a few Italian and Danish examples (similar to the sentences in Table 6 but authentic, and all L1) from a corpus of comparable narrative texts, the so-called "Mr. Bean corpus", consisting of a number of retellings of two Mr. Bean episodes produced by 27 Italian and 18 Danish university students, see Skytte et al. (1999) and Korzen (2007b). The examples below reproduce a scene from the episode "The Library", in which Mr. Bean, sitting in the reading room of a library, has placed a sheet of tracing paper on a manuscript illustration that he wants to copy by hand. But then he happens to sneeze, which causes the tracing paper to fly away with the result of him drawing directly on the manuscript, thereby ruining it. Thus, the sneeze is the cause of the main event from which the following action evolves: the tracing paper that flies away, and the EDU1 indicating the sneeze is the causal satellite. The following examples show textualisations of the EDU1 (indicated with bold italics) at the following levels of the Deverbalisation Scale, (8-10): b; (11): c; (12): d; (13): e:

(8) [Danish] ***Mr. Bean kommer til at nyse,*** *og kalkerpapiret flyver væk uden han opdager det...* (Skytte et al. 1999: DSA9)[13]
[lit.] '***Mr. Bean happens to sneeze*** *and the tracing paper flies away without [that] he discovers it*'

(9) [Danish] ***Pludselig nyser han,*** *og papiret ryger væk uden at han ser det* (DSA3)
[lit.] '***Suddenly he sneezes,****and the paper flies away without that he sees it*'

---

[13]Reference indications of the Mr. Bean corpus: D = Danish, I = Italian; S = written, M = oral.

(10)   [Italian] *...dopo aver appoggiato una velina su una pagina del libro,*
        ***starnutisce fragorosamente** e sporca il libro.* (ISA13)
        [lit.] *'after having placed a tracing paper on a page of the book, **he sneezes
        loudly**and [he] dirties the paper'*[14]

As stated, all three cases are textualisations at level (b) of the Deverbalisation
Scale, but in the Italian texts, this structure is rare. Much more often the satellite
status is grammaticalised more unambiguously in other ways, i.e. as a subordinate finite (adverbial) clause:

(11)   ***poiché starnutisce** il foglio vola via e lui si ritrova a colorare sul libro
        datogli.* (ISA3)
        [lit.] *'**since he sneezes** the paper flies away and he finds himself
        colouring the book given to him'*

or – especially – as a non-finite clause, (12) or a nominalisation, (13), thus
confirming the numbers quoted in column (d) of Table 5 above:

(12)   *Poi si mette a ricalcare [...] solo che **starnutendo** il foglio gli vola via*
        (ISA1)
        [lit.] *'Then he starts to copy [...] but then **sneezing**the paper [for him] flies
        away'*

(13)   *cerca appunto di-, di di copiare il disegno, solo che eh-, **con uno starnuto**il
        foglio trasparente gli, gli vola via (IMB8)*[15]
        [lit.] *'he tries precisely to copy the illustration, however **with a sneeze**the
        tracing paper flies away from him'*

However, examples (8)–(10) are cases of syndetic coordination with *and* in
which the EDU1 plays the role of satellite, and which therefore contradict Txurruka's (2000) and Asher & Vieu's (2005) conception of *and* as an unequivocal
coordination marker. Examples like these (and others) have prompted Korzen
(2000: 87) to conclude that at least in Italian and Danish all four of the following
combinations are possible:

- rhetorically and syntactically superordinate EDUs

---

[14]Italian is a pro-drop language, and the verb form *sporca*contains the indication of the 3rd person
    singular.

[15]In the transcriptions of the oral texts, as this one, a comma indicates a short interval and a
    hyphen the extension of a vowel.

- rhetorically subordinate and syntactically superordinate EDUs

- rhetorically superordinate and syntactically subordinate EDUs

- rhetorically and syntactically subordinate EDUs

3.6 Text and information structure in Italian and Danish: An overview

The cross-linguistic Italian-Danish characteristics outlined in the previous sections are not limited to particular text types or genres. Korzen (2009) quotes a number of surveys that document the exact same situation in six other text types, including the narrative "Mr. Bean corpus" cited in §3.5. The results all confirm a higher information density and degree of deverbalisation in Italian texts than in comparable Danish texts. Italian sentences tend to be longer and to include more EDUs, of which a higher number is textualised at the lower levels of the Deverbalisation Scale, i.e. backgrounded by means of non-finite and nominalised predicates. This typically leads to EDUs containing fewer words (a finite structure will normally require at least an explicit connective and a subject) and to a multi-layered and hierarchical information structure, characterised by a high degree of topic continuity, in which the various events are evaluated with respect to their importance to the on-going topic.

On the other hand, Danish text structure tends to be more informationally linear and characterised by a higher degree of finite verbs and topic shifts. Each sentence holds fewer but longer EDUs, and different events tend to be textualised at the same and higher levels of the Deverbalisation Scale, i.e. more chronologically one after the other and with finite verb forms that permit subject/topic changes.

4 Perspectives for translation

Concerning the parallel (L2) Europarl texts cited in §3.2, Table 2, the picture was different. Regarding sentence length, we observed a general tendency towards an imitative translation strategy, i.e. a strategy whereby the target text followed the structure of the source text relatively closely.

In the following sections, we shall advocate a different translation strategy, viz. the functional strategy. This method focuses on the function of the target text with respect to the new addressees, which should be equal to the function of the source text with respect to the original addressees. The functional strategy generally requires, among other things, a particular awareness of the text structure of both source and target language; if the structure of a source text can be considered as "typical" with respect to the source language (and to the particular text type) in question, it should be "typical" also when transformed to the target language. Dealing with translations between a Romance and a Scandinavian language, two of the major text structural differences concern precisely the issues investigated above:

- Information density and sentence length, i.e. the amount for information per text span and of EDUs per sentence;

- EDU linkage, i.e. the textualisation of EDUs, particularly regarding non-finite and nominalised structures.

Very generally speaking, when translating from a Romance to a Scandinavian language, particularly long sentences should be divided into shorter ones, thereby reducing the number of EDUs per sentence, and non-finite and nominalised EDUs should be changed into finite structures, thereby rendering the text structure more linear and increasing the number of words per EDU.

In the following sections, we shall give some specific examples of how this can be done, citing a number of Europarl cases of what we would define as "felicitous translations" from Italian into Danish, "felicitous" in the sense that they respect the cross-linguistic structural differences and thereby contribute to idiomatic and "non-marked" L2 texts. Thus, they are counterexamples to the Europarl L2 tendencies cited in Table 2.

Since we are dealing with text structure, it is often necessary to quote quite lengthy passages, and given that probably not all our readers are familiar with Italian and Danish, we shall have to add an English translation of both source and target passage. So, due to the space limitations of this paper, we shall confine ourselves to relatively few examples and limit the Italian source and Danish target passages to the particular linguistic issue at play (written with bold italics) with a literal English translation of both. To those we shall add a longer co-text of the official English translation of the passage in question in order to clarify the textual content. It is interesting to see that the official English translations in some cases follow the Italian text structure, in others the Danish structure[16].

---

[16] Lexically, English can be considered a typological "hybrid language" between the Scandinavian and Romance languages, see e.g. Baron & Herslund (2005). Judging by the examples of the parallel Europarl Corpus, this seems to be true also regarding text structure.

4.1 Information density and sentence length

One way of reducing the number of EDUs per sentence is simply to divide long Italian sentences into shorter Danish ones. For instance, syndetic coordinate structures (level b on the Deverbalisation Scale) can be changed into independent sentences (level a) simply by omitting a coordinate connective and changing a comma into a full stop. Translating from Danish into Italian, the reverse manoeuvre can be applied.

(14)   [Ital. L1]*...nemmeno in altre lingue europee,**ed** è sintomatico...*
(ep-01-09-04.txt 150)
'...neither in other European languages, and it is symptomatic...'
[Dan. L2] *...heller ikke på de andre europæiske sprog.* **Man kan sige** *at det er symptomatisk...*
'...neither in other European languages. One can say that it is symptomatic...'
[Eng. L2]*...in our common language, the word 'governance' does not exist, and it may well be that it does not exist in other European languages either. **It could be said** that it is revealing ...that ...the Commission chose ...to adopt a document with an untranslatable title.*

Similarly, a subordinate clause (level c) can be changed into an independent sentence by omitting the connective and adding a full stop. The following is an example of an adversative clause, and in such cases the connective (Ital.: *mentre*, Eng.: *while*) can be changed into an adversative adverbial; in the equivalent independent Danish sentence, the adverb *ellers* 'however' has been used:

(15)   [Ital. L1]*...futuri passi **mentre, per quanto riguarda il servizio universale, l'esempio svedese dovrebbe rassicurare tutti**...*
(ep-00-12-13.txt 20)
...future steps while, regarding the universal service, the Swedish example should reassure all...'
[Dan. L2] *...de kommende skridt. **Når det gælder den universelle tjeneste, burde Sveriges eksempel ellers berolige alle** ...*
'...the future steps. When it comes to the universal service, the Swedish example should however reassure all...'
[Eng. L2] *In fact, it provides ...absolutely no certainty regarding future steps **while, as far as the universal service is concerned, the Swedish example should reassure all those who feel that privatisation will mean the end of the postal services.***

Translating from Danish to Italian, the translator should look for a text structuring adverb such as the adversative *ellers* and change it into an equivalent subordinating connective, such as *mentre*.

Even non-finite Romance clauses, level (d) on the Deverbalisation Scale, can be transformed into independent finite sentences in Danish, although this happens more rarely. Ex. (16) is a case of an Italian participle phrase:

(16)   [Ital. L1]...*ci sia stato un piccolo braccio di ferro tra i gruppi, **risoltosi nel modo che constatiamo**.* (ep-00-12-13.txt 20)
'...there has been a small tug-of-war between the groups, resolved in the way we can see.'
[Dan. L2] ...*der var lidt tovtrækkeri mellem grupperne. **Resultatet kender vi**.*
'...*there was a small tug-of-war between the groups. The result we know*.'
[Eng. L2] *I would like to start by expressing my satisfaction at the fact that this debate is being held today instead of during the January part-session, **although this is the result of a minor tussle between the groups**.*

Also EDUs without a verbal element, e.g. syntactic appositions consisting of noun, adjective, or prepositional phrases, can be translated into perfectly idiomatic Danish independent sentences. In the following example, this is done by repeating (anaphorising) the noun to which the apposition is linked and using it as the subject of an independent sentence:

(17)   [Ital. L1] ...*che garantiscano un livello minimo di garanzie e di attenzione verso il mondo degli anziani, **uguale in tutti i paesi dell'Unione**...*
(ep-02-04-11.txt 43) (see a continuation of this passage in (16))
'...that ensure a minimum level of guarantees and focus on the world of the elderly, equal in all the member states...'
[Dan. L2] ...*der sikrer et minimumsniveau af garantier og opmærksomhed over for de ældre. **Dette niveau skal være det samme i alle EU-landene**,...*
'...that ensure a minimum level of guarantees and focus on the elderly. This level must be the same in all member states...'
[Eng. L2]...Europe needs to develop policies ensuring a minimum level of guarantees and focus on the world of the elderly, **a level which is the same in all the countries of the Union**....

In case of a Danish-Italian translation, the translator should here note the repetition of the noun, which together with the modal and copula verb constitutes a segment that is really superfluous in Italian. In general, translating from Italian to Danish should imply "moving upwards" on the Deverbalisation Scale, and translating from Danish to Italian "moving downwards".

4.2 EDU linkage and deverbalisation

When translating from Italian into a Scandinavian language, the translator should be particularly aware of non-finite EDUs and in most cases, also here, seek to "move upwards" on the Deverbalisation Scale. In (18) an infinitive phrase after the preposition *da* 'to', level (d), is syndetically coordinated with the complex adjectival apposition *uguale in tutti i paesi...*cited in (17). Here, *da* + infinitive has the modal sense of *must/should* be + participle, and the Danish translator has followed the same strategy as in (17) by anaphorising the entity described, the *level of guarantees*, and using the explicit anaphor (here a pronoun) as subject of a finite form of the modal verb. Thus, the preposition + infinitive phrase has become a main clause at level (b):

(18)   [Ital. L1] *...uguale in tutti i paesi dell'Unione e **da proporre come punto d'arrivo**...*(ep-02-04-11.txt 43)
       '*...equal in all countries of the Union and to propose as a goal...*'
       [Dan. L2] *...det samme i alle EU-landene, **og det skal ligeledes opstilles som**...*
       '*...the same in all the EU countries, and it shall also be proposed as...*'
       [Eng. L2] *Europe needs to develop policies ensuring a minimum level of guarantees and focus on the world of the elderly, a level which is the same in all the countries of the Union **and must be proposed as a goal for the candidate countries too**.*

Going from Danish to Italian, the translator should again notice the repetition of the (here pronominalised) entity and be aware that a modal structure *must/should* + a passive participle can be rendered with *da* + infinitive in Italian.

The gerund does not exist in Danish, so here translators into Danish are compelled to find other solutions. Very often a Romance finite verb + a gerund will correspond to a particular coordinate Danish (and English) construction, i.e. the serial verb construction, $verb_1$ *and* $verb_2$, where the subject of $verb_2$ is the same as that of $verb_1$ but implicit[17] Normally $verb_2$ corresponds to the Italian gerund, and if a rhetorical relation can be inferred between the two verbs + complements,

---

[17]On serial verb constructions – also called complex predicates – see e.g. Lehmann (1988: 189), Herslund (2000), Choi (2003) and Aikhenvald (2005).

the Danish verb$_2$ may be adverbially specified accordingly as in the following example, where Danish *således* 'thus, in this way' expresses consequence or result:

(19)   [Ital. L1]*...dei diritti umani in quel paese..., **costruendo su tale questione**...*(ep-00-06-14.txt 176)
'*...of the human rights in that country, creating on that issue...*'
[Dan L2] *...for menneskerettighederne i Tunesien ...**og således skaber**...*
'*...for the human rights in Tunisia and this way creates...*'
[Eng. L2] *It is therefore to be hoped that the EU-Tunisia Association Council will assume the responsibility of continuously monitoring the human rights situation in Tunisia..., **and that it will create** a joint system to monitor the issue which can only bring social improvements to the human rights situation in Tunisia.*

Going from Danish to Italian, the translator should be aware of the special Italian pro-drop situation which means that a finite verb will always contain an indication of the subject's number and person (cf. ex. (10) and footnote 15 above). Therefore, the structure verb$_1$ *and* verb$_2$ is not in itself equivalent in the two languages, and in most cases, the special cohesion of the Danish verb$_1$ *and* verb$_2$ construction should be rendered differently in Italian, for instance by a finite + non-finite verb construction, as in (19), even though such a construction does not render explicit the rhetorical relation between the two verbs + complements – other than specifying the satellite status of the second and non-finite verb + complement.

Instead of by a Danish adverbial specification, like *således* in (19), the rhetorical relation between two verbs can be rendered explicit by a connective of a subordinate averbial (finite) clause, in (20) *så* 'so (that)': consequence/result. Again, going from a Danish finite clause to an Italian gerund, the explicitness of such a rhetorical relation is lost if the gerund is not particularly specified in some way:

(20)   [Ital. L1]*...sostengo la proposta di assumere ...gli obiettivi di Lisbona e di Göteborg, ...**sottraendo l'ammontare di questi investimenti**...*(ep-02-10-21.txt:49)
'*...I support the proposal to include the Lisbon and Gothenburg objectives, ...**subtracting the sum of these investments**...*'
[Dan. L2]*...et tillægsmål for stabilitets- og vækstpagten, **så udgifterne til disse investeringer bliver trukket fra**...*
'*...an additional objective of the Stability and Growth Pact, **so that the sums of these investments are subtracted**...*'

[Eng. L2] *I therefore support the proposal to include the Lisbon and Gothenburg objectives ...as an additional objective of the Stability and Growth Pact,* **subtracting the sum of these investments from the total budgetary deficit of Member States' governments.**

In many cases, an Italian gerund phrase merely expresses a concomitant (but less important) situation or event, and a frequent Danish translation will be a subordinate clause with the (semantically weak) temporal connective *idet* 'as'.

(21) [Ital. L1] *...consentire all'Unione europea di diventare...l'area più competitiva e più dinamica di una società basata sulla conoscenza, sulla piena occupazione e sullo sviluppo sostenibile,* **favorendo altresi il loro coordinamento.** (ep-02-10-21.txt:49)
'*...allow the European Union to become the most competitive and dynamic economy based on knowledge, full employment and sustainable development...* **facilitating also the coordination of these investments.**'
[Dan. L2] *...at gøre EU til verdens mest konkurrencedygtige og dynamiske videnbaserede økonomi, som bygger på fuld beskæftigelse og bæredygtig udvikling,* **idet man ligeledes fremmer samordningen af disse investeringer.**
'*...to make the European Union the most competitive and dynamic knowledge based economy, which builds on full employment and sustainable development,* **as we also facilitate the coordination of these investments.**'
[Engl. L2] *...with the objective of making the European Union the most competitive and dynamic economy based on knowledge, full employment and sustainable development in the world...,* **facilitating the coordination of these investments.**

Also EDUs textualised as attributive or appositive participle phrases are extremely frequent in Italian, and although participles do exist in Danish, they occur much more seldom. Here, a good strategy is to change the non-finite structure into a finite relative clause, as in the following example, which contains no less than four EDU participle phrases:

(22) [Ital. L1] *...quando questa è ripetitiva su ingredienti e principi attivi* **conosciuti da anni [known for years]** *e* **già immessi in commercio [already put on the market]**, *allora il sacrificio di nuovi animali è assolutamente inutile. Ma quando...nell'emendamento* **sottoscritto da oltre cinquanta parlamentari [supported by more than 50 MEPs]**, *si*

*tratta di nuovi cosmetici contenenti ingredienti nuovi, mai **testati***
***sperimentalmente prima [never tested before]**...(ep-01-04-02-txt:42)*
[Dan. L2] Når der er tale om gentagelser af forsøg med ingredienser og
*aktive bestanddele, **der har været kendt i årevis [which have been***
known for years],** og **som allerede er i handlen [which are already
***on the market],** er det absolut unødvendigt at ofre nye dyr. Men når der...i*
*det ændringsforslag, **som over 50 parlamentsmedlemmer har***
***underskrevet [that more than 50 MEPs have supported],** hr.*
kommissær - er tale om nye kosmetiske midler, der indeholder nye
*ingredienser, **hvis giftighed aldrig er blevet testet på forsøgsdyr før***
[whose level of poisonousness never have been tested on test
***animals before],**...*
[Eng. L2] I also share the public's concerns regarding animal
experimentation; when this is a matter of repeat trials on active ingredients
*and principles **which have been known for years and are already on***
***the market,** then the sacrifice of more animals serves absolutely no purpose.*
*However, Commissioner, when, as I point out in an amendment **supported***
***by over 50 Members of Parliament,** it is a matter of new cosmetics*
*containing new ingredients **which have never been tested in the past** in*
order to establish their toxicological profile in laboratory animals, then, as a
scientist, I am convinced that it is essential to carry out an initial set of
experiments on animals...

In these cases, going from Danish to Italian, the translator should be aware of relative clauses with a transitive verb in the passive voice (or which can be paraphrased with a passive verb), as in (22). In such cases the clause can be changed into a participle phrase[18].

Similarly, other lengthy Italian adjectival attributives and appositions are normally transformed into Danish finite structures, in (17) above an independent sentence. In the following (and very typical) case, we have again a relative clause:

(23)   [Ital. L1] *...un'Unione libera e indipendente, **portatrice di un progetto di***
       ***pace**...(ep-03-04-09.txt:235)*
       *'...a free, independent Union, **bearer of a project of peace**...'*
       *[Dan. L2] ...et frit og uafhængigt EU, **som er drivkraften bag et***
       ***projekt**...*

---

[18]The same is true of relative clauses with intransitive verbs in the active voice, but due to space limitations, we shall omit such examples in this paper.

'...a free, independent Union **which is the driving force behind a**
project*...*
[Eng. L2] *...the pride felt by each citizen at belonging to both their country*
and the Union: a free, independent Union **which is the author of a project**
of peace and mutual respect with regard to the rest of the world.

In such cases, the head of the Italian apposition becomes the complement of a
(finite) Danish copula verb. Going from Danish to Italian, the translator should
thus be aware of relative clauses of which the relative pronoun functions as subject of a copula verb followed by a complement.

4.3 An overview

We hope that the few text passages in sections §4.1–§4.2 will suffice as exempli-
fications of felicitous "transformations" of information density and EDU linkage
from Italian (or another Romance language) into Danish (or another Scandinavian language) and vice versa, and we believe that, in principle, the translation
rules cited in relation to each case could be implemented by human translators
as well as by machine translation systems.

In a computational context, we believe that a "pre-processing" phase could
constitute a compelling method for automatically adapting the text structure of
the source language to the text structure of the target language before the actual
translation. Scholars such as Collins et al. (2005) have demonstrated how adding
knowledge about syntactic structures can significantly improve the performance
of existing state-of-the-art statistical machine translation systems, and we see
no reason why adding knowledge about text structure should not be able to do
likewise.

In summary, the most important text structural amendments in a translational context Italian–Danish (or another Romance-Scandinavian language pair)
should be the following:

- Long sentences, e.g. containing more than four EDUs, are divided into
  shorter sentences with fewer EDUs; colons and semicolons between finite
  clauses are changed into full stops.

- Gerund phrases are changed into coordinate finite clauses with the connective *and*. In this way, the often somewhat difficult task of choosing the
  appropriate adverbial connective is avoided.

- Long appositive and attributive participle phrases are changed into finite relative clauses.

The first modification deals with information density measured as number of EDUs per sentence, the last two ones with information density as well as with clause linkage ensuring an "upward" movement on the Deverbalisation Scale and thus a more finite and paratactic L2 text structure.

Translating from Danish (or another Scandinavian language) into Italian (or another Romance language), a relatively linear text structure should become relatively more hierarchical by means of a "downward" movement on the Deverbalisation Scale. The EDUs moving down the scale should be the rhetorical satellites, for which reason a "perfect" functional translation strategy should include a rhetorical structure analysis, an analysis that probably, at the present state, could not be carried out entirely without human participation.

5 Conclusion

In this paper, we have highlighted some particularly thorny problems linked with text structure in a cross-linguistic and translational perspective. We have focused on a Romance and a Scandinavian language, Italian and Danish respectively, centring our attention on the two text structural issues that to our experience cause the greatest problems in a contrastive and/or translational context, viz. information density and clause linkage.

With the considerable theoretical and terminological confusion regarding text structure – as well as other structures in texts – we found it necessary first to clarify some definitional ambiguities and thereafter to give a fairly in-depth description of the two key issues in the two languages investigated. Serving as our empirical basis, the Europarl Corpus had a number of advantages as a combined comparable and parallel text corpus, permitting in-depth and thorough cross-linguistic L1 comparisons as well as L1–L2 comparisons and statistical counts.

The significant differences between Italian and Danish text structure that we could ascertain in our L1 comparisons, especially regarding sentence length, were not always to be found, at least not to the same extent, in our L1–L2 comparisons. We therefore believe that the two linguistic key disciplines at play here, Contrastive Linguistics and Translation Studies, are not only "neighbouring disciplines" that "would benefit from each other's insights" as Chesterman described them (see the very first paragraphs of this paper), but in fact deeply dependent on each other. Regarding information density and clause linkage, there are no easy solutions; TS, including Machine Translation, must learn about text (and discourse) structure from CL, and similarly CL should widen its horizons by including TS knowledge on translation strategies. Only that way we will be able to create for instance MT systems that can deal more efficiently than what is the case today with the two issues examined here and produce L2 texts that truly resemble L1 texts, also when it comes to the thorny information and text structure.

6 Acknowledgments

We thank our colleague Daniel Hardt for his useful comments on an earlier draft of this paper and the Danish Council for Independent Research in Humanities for financial support.

References

Aikhenvald, Alexandra Yurievna. 2005. Serial verb constructions in typological perspective. In Alexandra Y. Aikhenvald & R.M.W. Dixon (eds.), *Serial verb constructions: A cross-linguistic typology*, 1–68. Oxford: Oxford University Press.

Alves, Fabio, Adriana Pagano, Stella Neumann, Erich Steiner & Silvia Hansen-Schirra. 2010. Translation units and grammatical shifts. Towards an integration of product- and process-based translation research. In Gregory M. Shreve & Erik Angelone (eds.), *Translation and cognition*, 109–142. Amsterdam: Benjamins.

Asher, Nicholas & Alex Lascarides. 2003. *Logics of conversation* (Studies in natural language processing). Cambridge: Cambridge University Press.

Asher, Nicholas & Laure Vieu. 2005. Subordinating and coordinating discourse relations. *Lingua* 115(4). 591–610.

Baron, Irène & Michael Herslund. 2005. Langues endocentriques et langues exocentriques. Approche typologique du danois, du français et de l'anglais. In Michael Herslund & Irène Baron (eds.), *Le génie de la langue française. Perspectives typologiques et contrastives* (Langue française 145), 35–53. Paris: Larousse.

Baroni, Marco & Silvia Bernardini. 2006. A new approach to the study of translationese: Machine-learning the difference between original and translated text. *Literary and Linguistic Computing* 21(3). 259–274.

Bateman, John A. & Klaas Jan Rondhuis. 1997. Coherence relations: Towards a general specification. *Discourse Processes* 24(1). 3–49.

Behrens, Bergljot & Cathrine Fabricius-Hansen. 2010. The relation accompanying circumstance across languages: Conflict between linguistic expression and discourse subordination? In Dingfang Shu & Ken Turner (eds.), *Contrasting meaning in languages of the east and west* (Contemporary Studies in Descriptive Linguistics 14), 531–552. Bern: Peter Lang.

Brown, Gillian & George Yule. 1983. *Discourse analysis.* Cambridge: Cambridge University Press.

Carlson, Lynn, Daniel Marcu & Mary Ellen Okurowski. 2003. Building a discourse-tagged corpus in the framework of rhetorical structure theory. In Jan van Kuppevelt & Ronnie W. Smith (eds.), *Current and new directions in discourse and dialogue*, 85–112. Dordrecht: Kluwer.

Chafe, Wallace L. 1976. Givenness, contrastiveness, definiteness, subjects, topics, and point of view. In Charles N. Li (ed.), *Subject and topic*, 25–55. New York, San Francisco & London: Academic Press.

Chafe, Wallace L. 2003. Discourse: Overview. In William Frawley (ed.), *International encyclopedia of linguistics.* New York: Oxford University Press.

Chesterman, Andrew. 1998. *Contrastive functional analysis.* Amsterdam: Benjamins.

Choi, Seongsook. 2003. Serial verbs and adjunction. In *Proceedings from the first camling workshop.* Cambridge: Cambridge University Press.

Christiansen, Thomas. 2011. *Cohesion: A discourse perspective.* Bern: Peter Lang.

Clark, Herbert H. & Susan E. Haviland. 1977. Comprehension and the given-new contract. In Roy O. Freedle (ed.), *Discourse production and comprehension*, 1–40. Hillsdale: Erlbau.

Collins, Michael, Philipp Koehn & Ivona Kucerova. 2005. Clause restructuring for statistical machine translation. In *Proceedings of the 43rd annual meeting on association for computational linguistics (ACL '05)*, 531–540. Stroudsburg: Association for Computational Linguistics.

Cornish, Francis. 2009. Text and discourse as context: Discourse anaphora and the FDG contextual component. *Web Papers in Functional Discourse Grammar* 82. 97–115.

Danlos, Laurence. 2008. Strong generative capacity of RST, SDRT and discourse dependency DAGSs. In Anton Benz & Peter Kühnlein (eds.), *Constraints in discourse*, 69–95. Amsterdam: Benjamins.

Fabricius-Hansen, Cathrine. 1996. Informational density: A problem for translation and translation theory. *Linguistics* 34(3). 521–565.

Fabricius-Hansen, Cathrine. 1998. Information density and translation, with special reference to German – Norwegian – English. In Stig Johansson & Signe

Oksefjell (eds.), *Corpora and cross-linguistic research: Theory, method, and case studies*, 197–234. Amsterdam: Rodopi.

Fabricius-Hansen, Cathrine & Wiebke Ramm (eds.). 2008. *"subordination" vs. "coordination" in sentence and text: A cross-linguistic perspective* (Studies in Language Companion Series 98). Amsterdam: Benjamins.

Firbas, Jan. 1974. Some aspects of the czechoslovak approach to problems of functional sentence perspective. In Frantisek Daneš (ed.), *Papers on functional sentence perspective*, 11–37. The Hague: Mouton.

Granger, Sylviane. 2003. The corpus approach: A common way forward for contrastive linguistics and translation studies? In Sylviane Granger, Jacques Lerot & Stephanie Petch-Tyson (eds.), *Corpus-based approaches to contrastive linguistics and translation studies*, 17–30. Amsterdam: Rodopi.

Halliday, Michael A.K. 1967. Notes on transitivity and theme in English part II. *Journal of Linguistics* 3(2). 199–244.

Halteren, Hans van. 2008. Source language markers in EUROPARL translations. In *Proceedings of the 22nd International Conference on Computational Linguistics (Coling2008)*, 937–944. Manchester.

Hansen-Schirra, Silvia, Stella Neumann & Erich Steiner. 2007. Cohesive explicitness and explicitation in an English–German translation corpus. *Languages in Contrast* 7(2). 241–265.

Harris, Zellig S. 1952. Discourse analysis. *Language* 28(1). 1–30.

Hasan, Ruqaiya & Michael A.K. Halliday. 1976. *Cohesion in English*. London: Longman.

Herslund, Michael. 2000. Le participe présent comme co-verbe. In Pierre Cadiot & Furukawa Naoyo (eds.), *La prédication seconde*, 86–94. Paris: Larousse.

Hobbs, Jerry R. 1985. *On the coherence and structure of discourse. Report No. CSLI-85-37*. Tech. rep. Stanford University: Center for the Study of Language & Information.

Hockett, Charles F. 1958. *A course in modern linguistics*. New York: Macmillan.

Hoey, Michael. 1991. *Patterns of lexis in text*. Oxford: Oxford University Press.

Hopper, Paul J. & Sandra A. Thompson. 1984. The discourse basis for lexical categories in universal grammar. *Language* 60(4). 703–752.

Irmer, Matthias. 2011. *Bridging inferences*. Berlin: De Gruyter.

Koehn, Philipp. 2005. Europarl: A parallel corpus for statistical machine translation. In *MT summit*, vol. 5, 79–86.

Korzen, Iørn. 2000. Tekstsekvenser / Reference og andre sproglige relationer. In Gunver Skytte & Iørn Korzen (eds.), *Italiensk–dansk sprogbrug i komparativt perspektiv. Reference, konnexion og diskursmarkering*, vol. I–III, 65–99 / 161–619. Copenhagen: Samfundslitteratur.

Korzen, Iørn. 2001. Anafore e relazioni anaforiche: Un approccio pragmatico-cognitivo. *Lingua nostra* LXII. 107–126.

Korzen, Iørn. 2007a. Linguistic typology, text structure and appositions. In Iørn Korzen, Marie Lambert & Hélène Vassiliadou (eds.), *Langues d'Europe, l'Europe des langues: Croisements linguistiques* (Scolia 22), 21–42. Strasbourg: Université Marc Bloch.

Korzen, Iørn. 2007b. Mr. Bean e la linguistica testuale comparativa. Considerazioni tipologico-comparative sulle lingue romanze e germaniche. In Manuel Barbera, Elisa Corino & Cristina Onesti (eds.), *Corpora e linguistica in rete*, 209–224. Perugia: Guerra.

Korzen, Iørn. 2009. Struttura testuale e anafora evolutiva: Tipologia romanza e tipologia germanica. In Iørn Korzen & Cristina Lavinio (eds.), *Lingue, culture e testi istituzionali*, 33–60. Firenze: Franco Cesati.

Krifka, Manfred. 1993. Focus and presupposition in dynamic interpretation. *Journal of Semantics* 10(4). 269–300.

Lambrecht, Knud. 1994. *Information structure and sentence form: A topic, focus, and the mental representation of discourse referents* (Cambridge Studies in Linguistics 71). Cambridge: Cambridge University Press.

Lehmann, Christian. 1988. Towards a typology of clause linkage. In John Haiman & Sandra A. Thompson (eds.), *Clause combining in grammar and discourse*, 181–225. Amsterdam: Benjamins.

Loock, Rudy. 2010. *Appositive relative clauses in English: Discourse functions and competing structures* (Studies in discourse and grammar series 22). Amsterdam: Benjamins.

Lyons, John. 1977. *Semantics (Volume 1–2)*. Cambridge: Cambridge University Press.

Mann, William C., Christian Matthiessen & Sandra A. Thompson. 1992. Rhetorical structure theory and text analysis. In William C. Mann & Sandra A. Thompson (eds.), *Discourse description: Diverse linguistic analyses of a fund-raising text*, 39–78. Amsterdam: Benjamins.

Mann, William C. & Sandra A. Thompson. 1987. *Rhetorical Structure Theory: A theory of text organization. Technical report, ISI/RS-87-190*. Tech. rep. Los Angeles: C.A.: ISI.

Mann, William C. & Sandra A. Thompson. 1988. Rhetorical structure theory: Toward a functional theory of text organization. *Text* 8(3). 243–281.

Matthiessen, Christian & Sandra A. Thompson. 1988. The structure of discourse and 'subordination'. In John Haiman & Sandra A. Thompson (eds.), *Clause combining in grammar and discourse*, 275–329. Amsterdam: Benjamins.

McEnery, Anthony M., Richard Z. Xiao & Yukio Tono. 2006. *Corpus-based language studies: An advanced resource book.* (Routledge Applied Linguistics Series). London: Routledge.

Prasad, Rashmi, Nikhil Dinesh, Alan Lee, Eleni Miltsakaki, Livio Robaldo, Aravind Joshi & Bonnie Webber. 2008. *The Penn Discourse Treebank 2.0. Technical Report, IRCS-08-02.* Tech. rep. University of Pennsylvania: Institute for Research in Cognitive Science.

Ramm, Wiebke & Cathrine Fabricius-Hansen. 2005. Coordination and discourse-structural salience from a cross-linguistic perspective. *SPRIKreports* 30.

Riazi, Abdolmehdi. 2002. The invisible in translation: The role of text structure. *The Translation Journal* 7(2).

Rijkhoff, Jan. 2008. Layers, levels and contexts in functional discourse grammar. In Daniel García Velasco & Jan Rijkhoff (eds.), *The noun phrase in functional discourse grammar*, 63–116. Berlin: De Gruyter.

Ruiz Ruiz, Jorge. 2009. Sociological discourse analysis: Methods and logic. *Forum: Qualitative Social Research* 10(2).

Skytte, Gunver. 2000. Konnexion og diskursmarkering. In Gunver Skytte & Iørn Korzen (eds.), *Italiensk–dansk sprogbrug i komparativt perspektiv: Reference, konnexion og diskursmarkering*, vol. I–III, 621–793. Copenhagen: Samfundslitteratur.

Skytte, Gunver, Iørn Korzen, Paola Polito & Erling Strudsholm (eds.). 1999. *Tekststrukturering på italiensk og dansk. resultater af en komparativ undersøgelse / strutturazione testuale in italiano e danese. risultati di una indagine comparativa.* Copenhagen: Museum Tusculanum Press.

Stubbs, Michael. 1983. *Discourse analysis.* Oxford: Basil Blackwell.

Stubbs, Michael. 1996. *Text and corpus analysis.* Oxford: Basil Blackwell.

Tannen, Deborah. 1982. Analyzing discourse: Text and talk. In Deborah Tannen (ed.), *Round table on languages and linguistics*, ix–xii. Washington D.C.: Georgetown University Press.

Teich, Elke. 2003. *Cross-linguistic variation in system and text: A methodology for the investigation of translations and comparable texts.* Berlin: De Gruyter.

Txurruka, Isabel Gómez. 2000. *The semantics of 'and' in discourse. Technical Report, ILCLI-00-LIC-9.* Tech. rep. University of the Basque Country: ILCLI.

Vachek, Josef. 1966. *The linguistic school of prague.* Bloomingtion: Indiana University Press.

Vallduví, Enric & Elisabeth Engdahl. 1996. The linguistic realization of information packaging. *Linguistics* 34(3). 459–519.

Webber, Bonnie & Rashmi Prasad. 2009. Discourse structure: Swings and roundabouts. In Bergljot Behrens & Cathrine Fabricius-Hansen (eds.), *Structuring information in discourse: The explicit/implicit dimension*, vol. 1, 171–190. Oslo: University of Oslo.

Widdowson, Henry G. 1979. *Explorations in applied linguistics.* Oxford: Oxford University Press.

Widdowson, Henry G. 2004. *Text, context, pretext: Critical issues in discourse analysis.* Oxford: Blackwell Publishing.

Chapter 4

Methodological cross-fertilization: Empirical methodologies in (computational) linguistics and translation studies

Erich Steiner

Universität des Saarlandes, Saarbrücken

Recent years have seen attempts at improving empirical methodologies in contrastive linguistics and in translation studies through interdisciplinary collaboration with multi-layer corpus architectures in computational linguistics. At the same time, explanatory background for empirical results is increasingly sought in more sophisticated models of language contact in typologically based contrastive linguistics on the one hand, and in language processing in situations of multilinguality, including translation, on the other. Three attempts are discussed to narrow the significant gap between the high level of abstraction of such models, and data provided through shallow analysis and annotation of electronic corpora.

The first of these operationalizes the high level terms "explicitness/explicitation" in terms of lexicogrammatical data available in a contrastive corpus, treating them as dependent variables and attempting to explain their variation in terms of the independent variables controlled for in the corpus architecture.

The second attempt starts from the same corpus architecture, yet includes annotations about textual cohesion in its operationalizations and develops increasingly fine-grained hypotheses to limit search space and variation between independent and dependent variables so as to get closer to causal explanations rather than explanations in terms of co-variation.

The third attempt intersects corpus data of the type outlined before with data from processing studies, aiming at an integration and mutual explanation of product and process data. Our focus here is on methodological issues involved in integrating data of such different types and granularity in an overall empirical research architecture.

Erich Steiner. Methodological cross-fertilization: Empirical methodologies in (computational) linguistics and translation studies. In Oliver Czulo & Silvia Hansen-Schirra (eds.), *Crossroads between Contrastive Linguistics, Translation Studies and Machine Translation: TC3 II*, 65–90. Berlin: Language Science Press. DOI:10.5281/zenodo.1019691

1 Empirical methodologies: some issues to be addressed

Recent years have seen a few, although still limited, attempts at improving empirical methodologies in contrastive linguistics and in translation studies through interdisciplinary collaboration with projects involving multi-layer corpus architectures as developed and refined in computational linguistics. These corpus architectures provide data enriched by a variety of techniques ranging from shallow to deep processing (Vela et al. 2007, Čulo et al. 2008, Teich et al. 2008, Teich & Fankhauser 2010). They allow the posing of linguistic questions as empirical questions even in areas which until recently were considered the province of hermeneutic debates supported by – at best representative – examples. If such data and their relationship to linguistic theorizing can be clarified, linguistics and translation studies can be made much more empirical than has hitherto been the case (cf. Featherston & Winkler 2009; *ZfS Zeitschrift für Sprachwissenschaft* 2009, Hawkins 2004 for critical debates in a wider linguistic context).

As a necessary consequence of these developments, empirical methodologies have come under critical scrutiny leading to improved standards of data production, maintenance and analysis. At the same time, explanatory background for empirical results is increasingly sought in more sophisticated models of language contact in typologically based contrastive linguistics (e.g. Thomason 2001, Teich 2003, Doherty 2006, Fabricius-Hansen & Ramm 2008, Siemund & Kintana 2008, Steiner 2008, Miestamo et al. 2008, Dunn et al. 2011) on the one hand, and in language processing in situations of multilinguality, including translation, on the other (Alves et al. 2010, Carl et al. 2008). The result of these developments is a conceptual and methodological gap between the necessarily high level of abstraction of models on the one hand, and the data provided through shallow (and cheap), or else deeper (and more expensive), analysis and annotation of electronic corpora on the other. It is not immediately obvious where and how stipulated abstract and general properties deriving from models of language variation, contact and change, such as *complexity, explicitness, density, contrast, interference and shining-through etc.* show up in the data, and if so, which of the stipulated independent variables causes which (group of) properties to vary. This gap has to be narrowed through concerted efforts involving methodologies from computational linguistics, including machine translation, (contrastive) linguistics and translation studies, efforts yielding convincing operationalizations of the abstract properties involved. Abstract properties like *complexity, explicitness, density, contrast, interference* and *shining-through* can thus be linked to patterns in the data available as product data in corpora, or as process data in experimental processing studies.

Beyond this, and quite fundamentally, there is the question of "representative-ness" of data: In what sense can we claim that our data, and how much of them, represent the phenomenon we are investigating, rather than some ad-hoc varia-tion caused by any number and kind of independent variables outside the scope of our models? To take just one example, relative explicitness of textual encod-ing of meaning may be the result of different degrees of context dependence, of level of subject field expertise (of author and/or reader), of time-pressure during production, of the dialectics between economy vs. expressiveness, of the degree of training for the production of the register/genre at hand, of level of education, of formality, of the status of the text produced as an original or a translation etc. etc. If we are interested in the effects of one independent variable, say translation as a mode of text production, we must find ways of isolating it from the other potentially interfering variables. Otherwise, the effects found in our data may be said to derive from something else than the text production mode "translating".

We shall discuss three test cases of work involving linguists, translation schol-ars and computational linguists (and marginally psycholinguists): one of them investigates a key notion of translation (*explicitation*) using product-data, the other an under-researched area of language contact (*borrowing and interference phenomena on the level of cohesion*), again using product-data from a corpus, and the third investigates key aspects of language processing during translation, thus focussing on process-data. The gap to be closed exists between the notions of *explicitness/explicitation* and *contact through cohesion* on the one hand, and the level of the available data on the other. If our models of translation, for example, stipulate that translated texts are more explicit than non-translated registerially-parallel (i.e. texts of the same register) original texts in the same language, and if we want to approach this assumption empirically, then we need to operational-ize the notions of "explicitness/explicitation" with respect to the representational categories available in our data. If the categories in our data consist of

- lexical strings,

- annotation layers such as PoS, words, chunks, clauses, sentences,

- statistics on relationships between these,

- alignment phenomena between relevant units in originals and translations such as *crossing lines,* and *empty links*

we need to define, or rather operationalize, the notions of explicitness/expli-citation in terms of these categories, and we need to do so in a theoretically motivated way. Of the categories of data just mentioned the first three should be self-explanatory. *Crossing lines* as alignment phenomena occur when between aligned source-target translation units the source-target link crosses a unit boundary (non-local translations as in the translation of a syntactic subject into an object, or as the translation of a raising-verb into an adverbial). An *empty link* occurs whenever one of the source-target nodes in a translation relationship is empty at a given level of representation.

Seen relative to existing approaches, we are attempting to synthesize individual parameters of language comparison and language contact into more general dependent variables (*explicitness, cohesion*), and we suggest operationalizations in such a way as to enable empirical corpus-based (and ultimately also experimental) investigations. We shall also try to isolate causally related independent variables for the variation observed (§2). Another attempt at narrowing our search space is the formulation of increasingly fine-grained hypotheses on corpus data as illustrated in §3. This should allow us to make our observations more precise, and also to systematically reflect textual cohesion, rather than lexis and grammar only. However, this further attempt in itself does not yet solve the problem of uniquely identifying causes and effects. To that end, we shall briefly discuss an attempt at intersecting corpus data with data from processing experiments, in order to find evidence for relationships stipulated by our models of language production, and of translation more specifically (§4). Finally, an attempt is made to identify achievements as well as persistent methodological weaknesses, and implications are identified for research methodologies.

2 Explicitness of encoding, operationalization in terms of corpus-data and the task of isolating independent variables

The first attempt *CroCo*[1] departed from the assumption that translations as texts are characterized by the property of *explicitness* relative to registerially parallel original texts within the same language. Elaborate tests were conducted on corpora of translations and registerially parallel texts in the target languages English and German. A further assumption was that this explicitness is due to the translation process, taking the form of *explicitation* observable cross-linguistically between source and target text segments, so-called "translation units". Translation units were then searched for explicitation phenomena causing the observed dif-

---

[1]Cf. http://fr46.uni-saarland.de/croco/; funded by DFG 2005–2009

ferences in "explicitness" (cf. Table 3 in §4). Register and language no doubt both play their parts as independent variables causing variation in explicitness, yet the assumption here was that the translation process plays its own theoretically motivated role in this configuration. The abstract notions of *explicitness/explicitation* have their own history both in translation studies and linguistics, yet have only rarely been subjected to empirical studies (cf. Englund-Dimitrova 2005 and the literature cited therein) .

The *CroCo-corpus* is partitioned into 8 registers each in English and German (cf. Hansen-Schirra et al. 2007, Vela et al. 2007, Steiner 2008), plus one cross-register reference corpus for English and German each. The sub-corpora were compiled using sampling techniques (Biber et al. 1998) and annotated for PoS , morphology, chunks, syntactic functions, clauses and sentences (cf. Čulo et al. 2008 for an overview of the tools used). The sub-corpora of original and translated texts can be compared along all of the annotation layers, including combinations of them, both within and across English and German. A second and important source of data were alignments between originals and their translations on all of the levels annotated (i.e. word, chunk, clause, sentence cf. Čulo et al. 2011). Figure 1 shows the corpus structure.

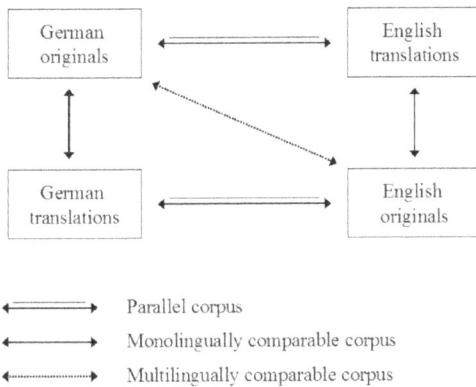

Figure 1: Bidirectional Translation Corpus (from Hansen-Schirra et al. 2012: ch.2)

The notions of *explicitness* and *explicitation* were then given a careful operationalization (cf. Table 1 for "shallow" annotation layers) in terms of the types of information contained in the different configurations of relevant sub-corpora (cf. Figure 1). It was then possible to show *whether* and *to what extent* the phenomenon of "explicitness" obtained for any of the sub-corpora compared to the others.

Table 1 uses as features low level data in the form of lexical density (LD), type-token-ratio (TTR) and part-of-speech tagging (PoS). The contrasts C1-n in the second column refer to contrasts between sub-corpora (reference corpora (ER, GR), corpora of originals (EO, GO), translation corpora (ETrans, GTrans), and register specific corpora within originals and translations as listed in footnote 2. In the third column, we list which indicator(s) in terms of the low-level data we believe to be indicative of which phenomena, and in the fourth column we posit explanations in terms of our three independent variables language, register, and status of a corpus as representing originals or translations.

The independent variables *language system, register* and *translation* can be reasonably isolated and related to the observed effects in the data. Remaining questions about representativeness of the sub-corpora can to some extent be approached with future improvements in sampling techniques and corpus size. There is the remaining question of the extent to which our corpora, especially the translation corpora, represent "competent/standard/evaluated" translations, rather than data full of opportunistic errors and mistakes. Doherty (cf. e.g. 2002: 11ff; 2006: 1ff and 159ff) strictly defends exclusively "evaluated/controlled data" as relevant for empirical work. As far as this methodological claim is concerned, we would defend the acceptance of texts as relevant data as long as they have been published as "translations", our main argument being that judgements about what counts as more or less competent language use are subject to a set of by now well-documented problems in language production generally (cf. e.g. Haider 2009), and in evaluations of translations in particular (House 2001). What our translational corpora do represent, we would claim, is the language produced in situations culturally accepted as "translating", which is not at all the same as holding that all these translations are "good" in the sense of being optimized solutions to the general problem called "translation". Furthermore, if the majority of the translated texts in the corpus can be shown to exhibit the property of "explicitness" relative to original texts, then this property is established as a distinguishing property of this subcorpus – even if in separate evaluations of these translations it can be shown that they are sub-optimal.

However, even if it can be argued that a CroCo-type architecture allows systematic studies of co-variation between variables, and even if we make a case for its "translations" to represent relevant data, we have to admit of a significant methodological problem: the third one of our variables, *translation*, if interpreted as *translation process*, is inherently complex and at present still insufficiently-understood (cf. also Becher 2010). Not only does it share all the complexities of monolingual text production, but it is text production under the additional con-

Table 1: Summary of "shallow" statistics used as operationalizations for "explicitness" (cf. Hansen-Schirra et al. 2012: ch.14)

Features	Contrast (C1-n)	Phenomenon: Indicator	Explanation
Lexical Density (LD), Type-Token-Ratio (TTR), Parts-of-Speech proportionalities (PoS)	C1 (Reference Corpora ER vs. GR)	- Experiential explicitness: LD (E>G) - Strength of lexical cohesion other than repetition: TTR (G>E) - experiential and referential density: PoS (G>E in nominal orientation)	Language System
PoS proportionalities, reflecting "nominal orientation"	C2.2 (8 Registers within languages E and G)	- Experiential density: nominal orientation English: *TOU > SHARE > WEB > ESSAY > INSTR > SPEECH > POPSCI> FICTION* German: *TOU > WEB > SHARE > ESSAY > INSTR > SPEECH > POPSCI > FICTION*	Register, Language
LD, TTR, PoS (Nominal Orientation)		- referential and experiential density: spread of language-internal variation (G>E for TTR and nominal orientation; E>G for LD)	
	C2.1 (EO vs. GO by register, with ER/GR differences factored out)	- experiential and referential density: LD, TTR, PoS	Register
LD, TTR, PoS	C3 (Translations vs. originals within a language and within a register)	Experiential explicitness: (LD) (ORI>TRANS) - lexical variation: TTR (ORI>TRANS) - referential density: nominality (ORI>TRANS, with exceptions)	Translation Process, De-Metaphoriza-tion

straints of a source text, plus usually the constraints of a professionally defined situation of production. This methodological problem can be systematically addressed by subjecting the notion of *translation process* to a more detailed analysis and by testing its effects in experimental processing studies involving the cumulation and intersecting of data from key-stroke logging, eye-tracking and post-hoc protocols (cf. Alves et al. 2010, see also §4 below). Arguing on the basis of the results of *CroCo*, we therefore feel justified in claiming that translated texts are characterized by some property, such as explicitness, and that the reason is not either the language, or the register, as these were controlled for separately. However, we are not able to convincingly show *which aspect* of the translation process is related to precisely which sub-aspect of overall explicitness/explicitation. And finally, it cannot be excluded categorically that two variables, say *translation* (independent) and *explicitness* (dependent) co-vary, but with the causing factor being located outside our model and ultimately causing the co-variation.

As a first evaluation of the *CroCo*-line of research, we would argue that the general corpus-architecture and the data processing employed can be trusted to yield more and also methodologically refined results of the type indicated here, if it is used in replications of our study. But we need improvements in the areas of *modelling* (internally over-complex variables, representativeness of data), *operationalization* of the models in terms of linguistics features, and in *processing techniques* for corpus data (processing pipelines, evaluation and significance of findings) and even more urgently for experimental data to be discussed in section 4 (amount and naturalness of data, experimental design). It is, for example, far from clear which of the product-based frequencies obtained from our corpora are the result of precisely which of the processes observed in eye-tracking or key-stroke logging experiments. There are at present no models known to us which would reliably relate corpus data to data from experiments, at least in translation studies (for a general critique of experimental data and its relationship to linguistic models cf. Schlesewsky 2009). Improvements in modelling can be expected from translation studies and/or psycholinguistics, better operationalizations should come out of (contrastive) linguistics, and improved processing techniques are under development in computational linguistics. The task at hand now, it seems, is to improve methodologically guided communication between the relevant research communities.

3 Contrasting cohesive patterns in English and German: the role of hypotheses for interpreting corpus data and the challenge of identifying contact phenomena

Our second attempt starts from the same corpus architecture as the one sketched above, yet includes annotations about textual cohesion in its operationalizations and develops increasingly fine-grained hypotheses to limit search space and variation between independent and dependent variables so as to get closer to causal explanations rather than explanations in terms of co-variation only. GECCo [2] sets out from the diagnosis that our current knowledge about English-German contrasts in cohesion is still weak. For contrastive grammar, we have reasonably comprehensive system-based accounts (Hawkins 1986; König & Gast 2007), yet these are not backed-up by empirical validation. Doherty's work (2002; 2006), which we have found very significant in its addressing phenomena of grammar, information structure and some aspects of cohesion, tests what she calls "stylistic" intuitions of competent native speakers and translators (2002: 11), based on principles of optimal integration of local textual parts into their relevant discourse context (discourse appropriate translations, Doherty 2006: 1ff). Unfortunately, her test environment is not very controlled and not critically assessed from a methodological point of view (cf. Doherty 2006: ix). Even so, she provides important intuitive and theoretically well-motivated insights into translation. Her overriding goal, however, of testing (previously trained) intuitions, rather than linguistic production and product as such, makes her work methodologically problematic as an empirical investigation.

For cohesion, not even a system-based comparison is available, much less an empirical foundation for such a comparison. The tracing of contact phenomena on the level of cohesion is therefore necessarily still in its infancy (but cf. Hansen-Schirra et al. 2007 for an early attempt; Kunz & Steiner 2013: a,b). Substantial advances in technologies using multi-layer annotated electronic corpora for text-based investigations of phenomena of cohesion hold the promise of placing constrastive accounts on an empirical basis, and beyond this comparison also allow us to trace contact phenomena in suitably configured corpora. A multi-layer representation is used, approaching tree-bank functionality and including aligned data for English and German translations in both directions as a crucial empirical base, with the exception of the spoken subcorpora. Extensive frequency in-

---

[2] http://fr46.uni-saarland.de/gecco/GECCo/Home.html; currently running and funded by DFG since 2011

formation about cohesive configurations is incorporated into what is essentially an extension and reconfiguration of the *CroCo-corpus* referred to above, tied to varieties or registers of the language concerned, and this time notably including spoken sub-corpora (cf. Table 2).

Table 2: GECCo corpus structure including spoken registers (cf. Amoia et al. 2011)

	German subcorpora	English subcorpora
	spoken	
comparable	original	original
		ELISA
	BACKBONE-DE	BACKBONE-EN
	GECCo spoken	MICASE
	collection	
parallel	translated?	translated?
	written	
comparable	original	original
	CroCo-GO	CroCo-EO
parallel	original translated	original translated
	CroCo-GO	CroCo-EO ETrans
	CroCo-GTrans	

The CroCo corpus, partitioned into 4X8 plus two reference corpora, was restructured into 4 subcorpora (GO, EO, GTrans, ETrans) with the registers no longer saved as separate sub-corpora, but as structural attributes of the 4 subcorpora. For the spoken registers, not contained in the earlier CroCo corpus, the *GECCo-corpus* does not include translations, as these registers are usually not translated. As data for the contrastive work, though, they are sufficient. The new structure allows simpler and faster query in the CQP. Searches in the corpus can still be conducted within a single register or in all registers at the same time. This modified corpus structure implements some improved processing techniques of the type mentioned as desiderata in §2 above (cf. Amoia et al. 2011).

In terms of overall explanations for the data thus obtained, one of the interesting questions is that of whether contrastive properties of cohesion in the two languages point into the same direction as some assumed generalizations in contrastive grammar (directness of mapping from semantics to grammar (G>E), different tolerance of various forms of "ellipsis" (E>G), more explicit encoding in one of the languages in the clause (G>E), possibly the opposite tendency in the verb phrase (E>G), etc.), or whether cohesion serves as a dialectic counterpart, distributing constraints not in the same direction as in grammar, but possibly in the opposite one. In the terms of Hawkins (2004: 44ff), we are ultimately interested in how the two languages cue "processing enrichment" through their different systemic options of cohesion, and ultimately also in whether or not the enrichment, and thus interpretation of discourse units, is differently affected. A further interesting object of investigation are the properties of cohesive (referential and/or lexical) chains in terms of frequency, length, distance between elements, number and kind of entailments triggered through sense relations in and between lexical chains etc.), which hitherto have hardly been accessible to empirical investigations (but cf. Hansen-Schirra et al. 2007 forthcoming for early thoughts along these lines) .

Our corpus-linguistic analysis includes the identification of various types of cohesive devices (*reference, substitution, ellipsis, coherence relations, lexical cohesion*; for some important modelling background cf. Halliday & Hasan 1976; Halliday & Matthiessen 2004: 524ff) and their lexicogrammatical realizations, the linguistic expressions to which they connect (the antecedents), as well as the nature of the semantic ties established and properties of the cohesive chains where appropriate. Including translations in the analysis should provide evidence for analogies between cohesive devices in the two languages, but also show areas where one-to-one equivalents are not preferred, or even non-existent.

The currently existing annotation requires an expansion in terms of additional layers of annotation, which are currently under construction. For instance, particular cohesive devices establishing *reference* or *substitution* can be investigated on the part-of-speech level. Other types such as *conjunctions* can be identified when examining the part-of-speech as well as the chunk level. For the investigation of *ellipsis* combined queries into different layers of annotation can be employed. For the analysis of nominal, verbal or clausal ellipsis the current annotation is too shallow and does not permit a fine-grained differentiation of types of linguistic devices. Thus, more specific cohesive categories have to be developed and annotated.

In order to narrow the gap between the concept of *contact through* cohesion and the level of our data, a structured grid of hypotheses is specified for empirical analysis as a testing ground for

- contrasts in the uses of *similar* systemic resources (e.g. the definite article in German vs. English, or the dependent variable in (H1) below)

- contrasts in the use of *different* systemic resources for similar cohesive functions/purposes (e.g. substitution vs. reference through personal pronouns vs. lexical cohesion for the function of co-reference in German vs. English)

- traces of language contact due to different usages in contact vs. non-contact varieties (categorical and/or in terms of frequency in comparisons of translated vs. original text of the same register within English or German).

Note that the formulation of hypotheses as such is not a new development in our context (cf. Steiner 1991: 141ff; Teich 2003: 143ff; Hansen 2003: 127ff; Neumann 2008: 89ff), and is, of course, standard practice in many strands of empirical work. What we are using them here for in particular is the motivated narrowing down of search space in our data for the specific purposes of our investigation.

Examples of some hypotheses are:

(H1) 3rd person singular neuter pronouns vs. masculine and feminine pronouns (frequency E(nglish)>G(erman) for originals (contrast)), in terms of PoS overall and proportionally within pronouns.

Cf. (1) and (2) for examples from our corpus:

(1) *Eine verantwortungsbewusste Politik kann diesen Prozess, der zudem von objektiven Faktoren determiniert wird, nicht nur flankieren. Sie muss **ihn** vielmehr formen.*

(2) *A responsible policy can not only accompany this process, which is additionally determined by objective factors, **it** must moreover shape **it**.*

Preliminary tests on (H1) have been run and are relatively straightforward to carry out with lexical search on our lemmatized sub-corpora. Initial results (cf. Kunz & Steiner 2013) indicate higher overall frequency as predicted, yet sensitive to register, and even unconditioned higher frequency for cohesive vs. non-cohesive usage E>G (cf. (H4)) Interpretation is less clear, because the observed differences may be due to, at least, the predominance of grammatical vs. natural gender in co-reference for 3rd person singular pronouns in German, the possible preference in German for demonstrative reference over simple personal or possessive reference (cf. (H4)), the different degrees of availability of lexical cohesion as an alternative to pronominal reference between the languages etc. So, while (H1) narrows the search space for findings, it does not in itself lead us unambiguously from the observation of co-variation to causal explanation.

(H2) GO>ETrans(lations)>EO(riginals) in locally non-ambiguous 3rd person reference within their register.

A German – English contrastive pair of (constructed) texts is given in (3) and (4) below:

(3) *Mein Freund machte seinen Abschluss, besorgte sich einen Kredit und gründete seine erste Firma. Er/ sie/ es/ der/ die/ das/ dies/ diese(r,s)/ letztere(r/s), der Versuch/ daraus …wurde ihm zum / entwickelte sich ein Verhängnis.*

(4) *My friend got his degree, obtained a loan and founded his first business. It/ this/ that/ out of this, the attempt developed (into) a disaster.*

The underlying assumption here is that English translations (versions of (4)) from German (versions of (3)) show less local ambiguity in local antecedent – pro-form relationships than English originals (not exemplified above), inheriting this (hypothesized) property from their German originals. "Local" here needs to be operationalized into "between adjacent clauses" or some such measure. It can then be tested, if ambiguity is taken to mean "number of possible antecedents for each relevant pro-form". Our assumptions here are triggered by, once more, the existence of grammatical gender in German, as well as by the higher usage of alternative and less ambiguous forms instead of *es* in German (cf. (H4)). These findings, if corroborated, should include fewer possible antecedents for German "er/sie/es" than for English "he/she/it", but certainly fewer possible antecedents for the alternative (demonstrative/ adverbial/ fully lexical) cohesive alternatives. We are referring here to the systemically conditioned availability in German of the demonstrative article, as well as "pronominal adverbs", both of which have a function of narrowing the range of plausible antecedent phrases for their occurrences if compared with personal or possessive pronouns, providing a motivation for our hypothesis (cf. Kunz & Steiner 2013: §4). As far as the cost of this analysis is concerned, we have to trace the possible antecedent – pro-form relationships within a local domain, which as such is possible on the basis of PoS annotations, combined with chunk and clause annotation. Open questions, however, arise out of the fact that co-reference relationships need not be local in the sense just introduced, thus making our measure of "ambiguity", and in that sense "complexity", one of local structure of the encoding, rather than an overall textual measure. Nor can we directly infer processing complexity from this local encoding complexity – which has to be taken for granted for any product-rather than process-based work in isolation. Local encoding ambiguities will, in fact, often be tolerated by language producers and processors in the interest of more global efficiency (Hawkins 2004: 47f).

(H3)   ETrans-T(arget)T(ext)>GO(riginals)-S(ource)T(exts) in explicitated 3rd person reference through use of fully-lexical TT-equivalent of pronominal source.

The assumption here is again that German co-reference chains in originals are locally, i.e. between adjacent members of a chain, less ambiguous than in English originals. If this is the case, then one strategy for an English translation would be to use lexically-headed phrases, possibly combined with pre-modifying demonstrative/ deictic material, to achieve a similar effect as their German source text originals. (H3) refers to one aspect of (H2), the two are thus not strictly independent. In order to obtain the relevant data, we have to retrieve co-referential chains from texts, which at this stage can only be obtained from costly hand-coded small corpora. We also consider chunk-by-chunk alignments between translationally related ST-TT units, which is why we are currently exploring improvements through increased use of tools for lexical chaining. (H3) would again successfully limit our search space, however on somewhat costly data, and with a somewhat indirect link to relevant assumptions.

(H4)   EO>GO in cohesive usage of *it vs. es* (because of alternative usage in German of demonstratives of various sorts and pronominal adverbs) between matching registers in original texts, measured both in terms of PoS overall and as proportion of cohesive vs. non-cohesive usage of *it*.

(H4) shares some of its background assumptions with (H1), but in this case we would focus on the use of *it/ es* in cohesive vs. non-cohesive usage. The production of the data is not trivial, though. Our annotation needs to cover grammatically triggered usages of 3rd person singular pronoun *it/es*, because these need to be classified into one relevant sub-class, which would then leave the relevant co-referential and thus cohesive complement class. Again, given the data can be produced at reasonable cost, the hypothesis would successfully limit the search space, even though the results obtained could be partly due to other interferring factors – though not register or the translation vs. original status, as these are being kept constant.

(H5)   In terms of the phenomena tested in H1 – H4, we predict that in a comparison of originals and translations (in this case within the same language and register), the translations will diverge from the originals in the direction of their source language.

The background for this explanation is an assumed interference, or rather, shining-through effect (cf. Teich 2003). As some initial findings indicate (cf. Kunz & Steiner 2013: §4), this is largely, but, dependent on register, not always borne out. Here it will be interesting to trace explanations for why register appears to be an influential variable on some element of the translation process.

Further hypotheses are developed for *comparisons of vagueness/ ambiguity of reference and scope*. Differences can be expected here deriving from usage of different lexicogrammatical realizations of some constant cohesive relationship, or even from different cohesive relationships altogether. An example would be the contrastive use of a generic full lexical phrase vs. a definite phrase vs. a phrase pre-modified through a determiner (possessive vs. deixis vs. demonstrative) vs. a phrase headed by a pro-form (demonstrative vs. pronoun) as tested on aligned ST-TT pairs. The interest would not be in the phenomenon as such, which has been researched under "accessibility rankings" (e.g. Ariel 1990, Hawkins 2004: 45), but in the different kinds of *ambiguity* and/ or *vagueness* associated with each case in interpretation/ enrichment. In general, we would predict that a) translations are less ambiguous and vague than their originals in SL-TL configurations (explicitation through translation), but also b) that they diverge from their original registerially-parallel counterparts in the direction of the respective source language (interference, shining-through).

A final type of hypothesis makes reference to contrastive register-specificity of cohesive configurations, and again their behaviour under contrast vs. contact conditions. For example, German written as opposed to spoken registers may be characterized by dense lexical chains with relatively low lexical repetition, whereas this distinction may be much smaller and involving more repetition for English. For translations from one of these languages into the respective other, we would then predict an interference-like "shining-through" effect (cf. Teich 2003) of source registers onto their target corpora. These configurations will be operationalized as length of lexical or referential chains, density of chains, number of chains per text sample, frequency, length, distance between elements, number and kind of entailments triggered through sense relations in and between lexical chains[3] etc. On the basis of WORDNET-type taxonomic classifications, we are investigating different levels of abstraction/ generality in chain progression language internally, but also between aligned lexical translation units. Assuming that it is a frequent translational strategy to resort to a superordinate term as a lexical equivalent in cases of lexical gaps or simply lack of knowledge, one

---

[3]I am grateful to Marilisa Amoia for emphasizing the importance and accessibility of such relationships to me in recent discussions.

might hypothesize greater generality in translations over originals. On the other hand, if contrastive registers of originals show different degrees of implicitness, possibly realized as higher generality in English of lexically realized concepts, as a register feature, as is sometimes hypothesized in comparisons of English and German texts, this might interfere with translational effects. Add to this the increased reliance of English on "general nouns" as a means of lexical cohesion (Schmid 2000, Mahlberg 2005), and we have grounds for separately exploring lexical generality as a register feature in originals, and decreasing generality relative to originals in both directions.

Another assumption on which one could base hypotheses about lexical cohesion would be that more lay-type registers, rather than expert-type registers, use topological , and often polyphyletic (non-strict inheritance), classification systems rather than typological monophyletic (strict inheritance) ones (cf. Halliday & Martin 1993: 23ff). With the help of WORDNET-based tools for lexical analysis, we can operationalize the concepts of *typology vs. topology* and of *monophyletic vs. polyphyletic* or else *historical vs. genetic*, or *hyponymy vs. meronymy* into lexically-implied sense relationships between elements of lexical chains between registers within and across languages, and between originals and translations. Note that this does not only apply to nouns and their derived adjectives, but also to preferred semantic verb classes: the often observed preference of *relational* vs. *action* verbs in English over German texts may contribute to generality and thus implicitness of the vocabulary used in lexical chains.

At this early stage of the GECCo-project, we would hypothesize shining-through effects for ST-TT configurations, and for density of chains only a possibly increasing effect of the translation process as such. We need to be aware, though, that the frequency data that can be obtained through work of the type described here is valid and interesting in research on text production in general, whether in monolingual or multilingual contexts, and is furthermore only possible through the joining of efforts from (contrastive) linguistics, translation studies, and computational linguistics.

Where in our research methodology can we trace *contact* phenomena, rather than just *contrasts* in terms of categories and frequencies? In short, where we compare originals of the same register, including the register-neutral reference corpora, across languages, we obtain cohesive contrasts. Where we compare originals and translations within the same language and the same register, any resulting differences would seem to be due to either interference, or else "normalization" in the sense of "hyper-adaptation to target-language norms". In a weak sense, these are contact phenomena. One possible causal source of these phenomena would then be the translation process, involving some form of "borrowing" (Thomason 2001: 70ff and earlier). Our research architecture is sensitive not only to classical forms of borrowing, but characteristically to shifting frequencies (i.e. over- or underuse relative to the norm established by the same register in the "originals" corpus) below the threshold of structural or lexical borrowing. The translation process in a narrower sense is not the only possible source of contact phenomena in our architecture. The cause of variation could, in fact, be any other component of the contact situation, as long as it impinges on the translation process in a wider sense. In order to make our notion of "translation" more precise, we need to appeal to process studies as shown in the following section.

4 Improving corpus architectures and relating data in corpora to data from processing experiments against relevant models

The third attempt intersects corpus data of the type outlined before with data from processing studies, aiming at an integration and mutual explanation of product and process data. Our focus here is on methodological issues involved in integrating data of such different types and granularity in an overall empirical research architecture. We shall start, though, with a few more general requirements on empirical work of the type discussed here, before concentrating on intersecting different types of data with relevant models.

There is an overall ongoing challenge in research attempts of the type discussed here: The researcher needs to be constantly aware of the cut-off point between very costly "deep" (and to some extent less reliable) annotation, and more "shallow" (and to some extent more reliable) annotation, the latter of which leaves a substantial gap between data and interpretation. Linguistically "deep" annotations, notwithstanding their disadvantages in terms of cost of production and in terms of reliability, have a clearer relationship to highly general models of language processing, whereas the cheaper and often more reliable surface annotations yield data in a very indirect and at worst spurious relationship to more ambitious and general modeling. Our annotation layers in *CroCo* (cf. §2), for example, involve lexico-grammatical information, some of it shallow and low-cost (part-of-speech-tagging, type-token-ratio, lexical density), some other annotations deeper and involving heavy checking of (semi-)automatic annotations (chunking, clause analysis, and levels of alignments), and some layers even involving annotation by hand requiring monitoring of inter-coder-consistency.

Even more challenging in our follow-up project GECCo (cf. §3), annotations involve those above plus yet more expensive annotations: referential indexing, annotating proform – antecedent configurations, chaining of referential and lexical chains. It is obvious that ways need to be found of producing these with acceptable costs and of sufficient quality, something which cannot be regarded as solved on anything but a small scale. Improved contacts between researchers in translation studies, contrastive linguistics and computational linguistics in particular are essential to make any progress here so as to improve mutual understanding of the issues involved, as well as of the possibilities and limitations of computational technologies available currently.

The question also needs to be raised of how research architectures can be made more standardized than hitherto, allowing independent repetition and (dis-) confirmation of findings. Schlesewsky (2009: 176ff) demands this for experimental data, yet the same is obviously true for corpus data. Relevant research communities need to more systematically share data and replicate each other's findings in order to arrive at methodological standards comparable to those in the more established empirical research fields. Something like "multicentric studies/ trials" may become possible for some research questions, and possibly most urgently in experimental, rather than corpus-based, studies.

As we have implied in some passages here, and elsewhere (cf. Alves et al. 2010), corpora, processing pipelines and evaluated results from corpus-based studies can be used stand-alone as sources of data to check on hypotheses of the types mentioned above. However, they will usually allow the discovery of co-variation of independent and dependent variables only, rather than a necessarily causal relationship. Even if we manage to align source-target units pair-wise within the same register and for only one hypothesis, thus excluding all but one independent variable, we may at best suspect a causal relationship. There is always in principle the possibility that our two variables in independent-dependent pairings co-vary because of some other variable outside our research design, a danger which is more or less plausible, depending on how good our model is. Graded predictions fare somewhat better than categorical predictions, as formulated e.g. in Hawkins (2004: 31ff), yet the basic methodological problem remains, at least as long as the data used are restricted to corpus i.e. product data.

Which brings us to our final point: in order to have a chance of explaining any findings we may have, we need a model, and if at all possible a model predicting the relevant behavior of our variables. The model and its derived hypotheses need to be precise enough to be falsifiable on our data. This is not always the case in (psycho-) linguistic studies generally (cf. Schlesewsky 2009: 170ff), and very hardly at this point in translation studies. And finally, we need to relate corpus data to behavioural data in the widest sense (eye tracking, key-stroke logging, think-aloud protocols, production time or reaction time studies, EEG studies, FMRI, generally to psycholinguistic and even neurophysiological data) to pave the way towards more principled explanations of the results obtained in corpus studies. This is not because psycholinguistic and neurophysiological data show us the "working of the mind" directly, but rather because they provide additional, and in some cases possibly more direct windows into the mind, even though the latter is not directly observable. Provided, that is, that we have models of translation, language contact etc. which make predictions for the data that we have.

Table 1 above shows data and interpretations from intra-lingual comparisons and inter-lingual comparisons, yet at that stage without any "parallel" corpora, i.e. source-unit into target-units mappings. Assume now that we have such additional data as shown in Table 3 (PoS-shifts in aligned translation units) and Figures 2 – 4 below[4].

The data shown in Table 3 are frequencies of PoS-shifts in source-target word alignments (not restricted to the passage shown in Figures 2 to 4), eye-fixations from a eye-tracking study (Figure 2), key-stroke logging data from the same text

---

[4]Project ProBral, funded by DAAD and CAPES 2008-2011

Table 3: Frequencies of PoS-shifts (%) (Alves et al. 2010: 116)

Type of shift	E-G	G-E
verb-noun	24.31	16.98
verb-adjective	11.69	02.80
verb-adverb	06.95	00.25
adjective-noun	17.43	09.48
adjective-verb	01.84	09.92
adjective-adverb	01.42	11.58
noun-adjective	13.89	21.63
noun-verb	05.74	16.98
noun-adverb	03.40	01.08
adverb-adjective	10.06	01.34
adverb-noun	03.05	01.59
adverb-verb	00.21	06.36

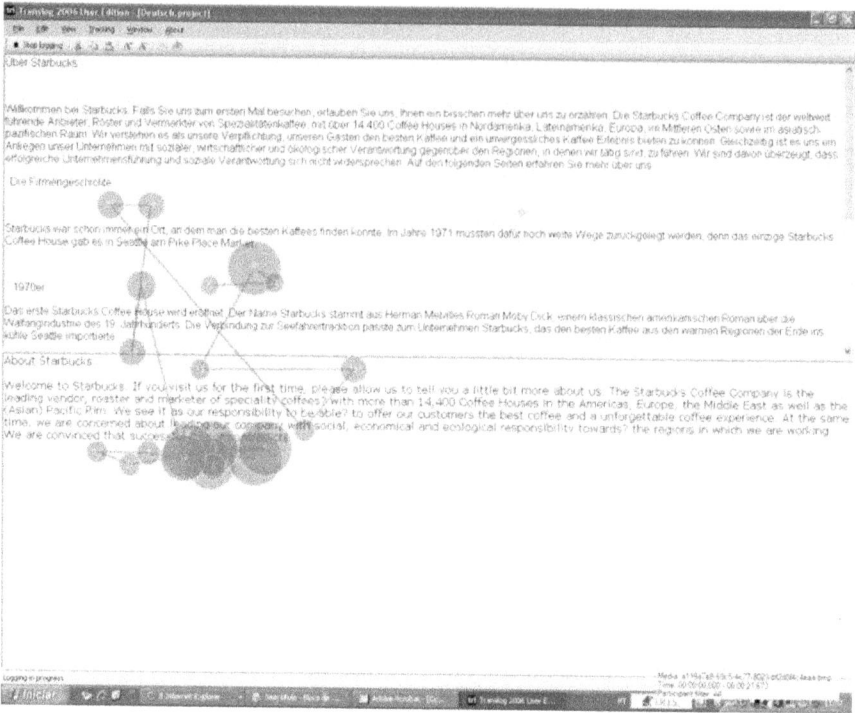

Figure 2: Eye fixations by S2 while deciding to us a noun or a verb for the translation of *sich widersprechen* in the drafting phase (Alves et al. 2010: 134)

passage in Figure 3, and process data in Figure 4 showing shifts in intermediate solutions from two subjects translating the passage shown in Figures 2 and 3. In order to interpret these data, we clearly need a type of modelling of the relevant linguistic processes (translation, language production) which makes predictions for these kinds of data. As the situation is currently, we may have models making predictions for the linguistic data, and existing models of translation procedures may even make predictions about shifts as shown in Table 3. Yet our models are still too unspecific – and models about a different domain – to make predictions about eye movements and key-stroke loggings directly. The links between cognitive processes in translations and those kinds of data are quite indirect and probably much more prone to interference by other factors, than the purely linguistic data are.

Drafting phase

★★★★We ◆are ◆conc ⬜vinced ★◆[★15.701] that ◆★★★success ★ful ◆[★44.623] do ◆not ◆contract ⬜⬜dict ★★★ion ★←←←←←←← ←←←←←←←←★⬜⬜⬜⬜⬜⬜are ◆no ←←←←←←←[★49.640] leader ⬜⬜⬜⬜⬜⬜★management ◆★★and ◆social ◆[★01:17.774] resp ★onsibilit ★y ◆★⇒. ◆

Revision phase

[∩] ★★★★★[∩] t →[ShftCtrl→] ★in ◆conc ⬜flict [★10.846] [∩] ★contradictory [★26.575] [∩]

Figure 3: Translation process data by S2 in the drafting and in the revision phase (from Alves et al. 2010: 131)

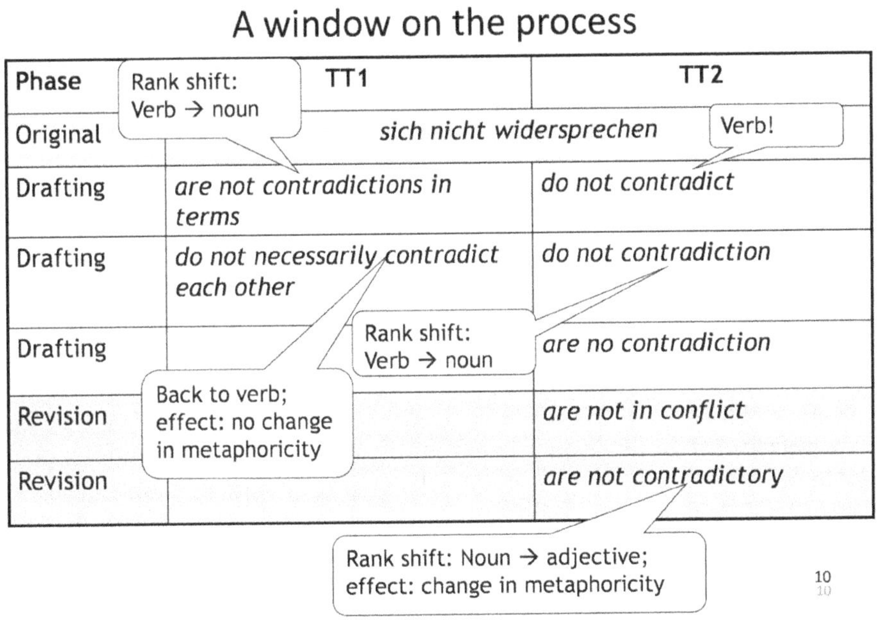

A window on the process

Phase	Rank shift: Verb → noun	TT1	TT2	
Original		*sich nicht widersprechen*		Verb!
Drafting		*are not contradictions in terms*	*do not contradict*	
Drafting		*do not necessarily contradict each other*	*do not contradiction*	
Drafting		Rank shift: Verb → noun	*are no contradiction*	
Revision	Back to verb; effect: no change in metaphoricity		*are not in conflict*	
Revision			*are not contradictory*	

Rank shift: Noun → adjective; effect: change in metaphoricity

Figure 4: Translation process data showing shifts in intermediate solutions

As an illustration of the kind of hypothesis we would suggest here, look at Hypothesis (H6) below:

(H6)   We assume that in producing a given translation unit for a trigger source-text unit, a highly metaphorized (nominalized) passage in comparison to an experientially equal less metaphorized source passage will

1. trigger a higher number of attempted intermediate word-alignments before the final solution is produced,

2. trigger more and/or longer eye fixations on the problematic unit

3. trigger longer pause units and more attempts plus more revisions in the key stroke units for that passage.

We also predict that the effects are negatively correlated to training of subjects and to length of time given for the task, but positively to direction of translation (into foreign vs. into native language). We furthermore predict a scale of relative strength of these variables training > length of time > direction of translation to be mirrored in relative frequencies of 1. to 3. above.

5 Conclusion and outlook

The significant properties of hypotheses such as our illustrative (H6) above are that it makes predictions for all of our strands of data and that it is based on a *ranking* of independent variables as to strength of effect. We would thus also be looking at *graded effects* in the data, rather than just on yes/no-effects. But note at the same time that in order to derive hypotheses such as (H6) above, we need models (of the translation process in this case) making predictions in terms of our data. And this is an area where conceptual work needs to be invested: existing models of translation are not fine-grained enough to make this sort of prediction at the moment, so these models need to be developed before studies using combinations of data from corpora and processing data can achieve the effects which they deserve. We are not claiming here that the problems involved are insurmountable, but rather that they are quite general to empirical language studies, and that we should improve communication across relevant research communities to find solutions. Empirical methodologies in contrastive linguistics and translations studies stand a lot to gain from such developments by being able to become more truly "empirical". The relevant sub-fields of computational linguistics, on their part, will find much-needed applications for (partly) existing solutions in search of relevant problems, but may even derive intelligent new solutions.

Abbreviations

TOU	Tourism text	SPEECH	Speech
SHARE	Shareholder letter	POPSCI	Popular Science
WEB	Website	FICTION	Fiction
ESSAY	Essay	ORI	Original
INSTR	Instructional text	TRANS	Translation

References

Alves, Fabio, Adriana Pagano, Stella Neumann, Erich Steiner & Silvia Hansen-Schirra. 2010. Translation units and grammatical shifts. Towards an integration of product- and process-based translation research. In Gregory M. Shreve & Erik Angelone (eds.), *Translation and cognition*, 109–142. Amsterdam: Benjamins.

Amoia, Marilisa, Kerstin Kunz & Ekaterina Lapshinova-Koltunski. 2011. Discontinuous constituents: A problematic case for parallel corpora annotation and querying. In *Proceedings of the 2nd Workshop on Annotation and Exploitation of Parallel Corpora (AEPC2 a RANLP 2011 workshop). Hissar, Bulgaria. September, 2011.*

Ariel, Mira. 1990. *Accessing noun-phrase antecedents.* London: Routledge.

Becher, Viktor. 2010. Abandoning the notion of translation-inherent explicitation: against a dogma of translation studies. *Across Languages and Cultures* 1(11). 1–28.

Biber, Douglas, Susan Conrad & Randi Reppen. 1998. *Corpus linguistics: Investigating language structure and use.* Cambridge: Cambridge University Press.

Carl, Michael, Arnt Lykke Jakobsen & Kristian Tangsgaard Hvelplund Jensen. 2008. Studying human translation behavior with user-activity data. In Bernadette Sharp & Michael Zock (eds.), *Proceedings of the 5th International Workshop on Natural Language. Processing and Cognitive Science, NLPCS 2008, Barcelona, Spain, June 2008*, 114–123. Setúbal: INSTICC Press.

Čulo, Oliver, Silvia Hansen-Schirra, Stella Neumann & Mihaela Vela. 2008. Empirical studies on language contrast using the English-German comparable and parallel CroCo Corpus. In *Proceedings of the LREC 2008 workshop "Building and using comparable corpora", Marrakesh, Morrocco, 31 May 2008*, 47–51.

Čulo, Oliver, Silvia Hansen-Schirra, Karin Maksymski & Stella Neumann. 2011. Empty links and crossing lines: Querying multi-layer annotation and alignment in parallel corpora. *Translation: Computation, Corpora, Cognition* 1(1).

Doherty, Monika. 2002. *Language processing in discourse: A key to felicitous translation*. London: Routledge.

Doherty, Monika. 2006. *Structural propensities: Translating nominal groups from English into German*. Amsterdam: Benjamins.

Dunn, Michael, Simon J. Greenhill, Stephen C. Levinson & Russell D. Gray. 2011. Evolved structure of language shows lineage-specific trends in word-order universals. *Nature* 473(7345). 79–82.

Englund-Dimitrova, Birgitta. 2005. *Expertise and explicitation in the translation process*. Amsterdam: Benjamins.

Fabricius-Hansen, Cathrine & Wiebke Ramm (eds.). 2008. *"subordination" vs. "coordination" in sentence and text: A cross-linguistic perspective* (Studies in Language Companion Series 98). Amsterdam: Benjamins.

Featherston, Sam & Susanne Winkler (eds.). 2009. *The fruits of empirical linguistics* (Studies in Generative Grammar 101). Berlin: De Gruyter.

Haider, Hubert. 2009. The thin line between facts and fiction. In Sam Featherston & Susanne Winkler (eds.), *The fruits of empirical linguistics*, vol. 1, 75–102. Berlin: De Gruyter.

Halliday, Michael A.K. & Ruqaiya Hasan. 1976. *Cohesion in English*. London: Edward Arnold.

Halliday, Michael A.K. & James R. Martin. 1993. *Writing science: Literacy and discursive power*. London: Falmer Press.

Halliday, Michael A.K. & Christian M.I.M. Matthiessen. 2004. *An introduction to functional grammar*. London: Arnold. earlier versions by Halliday in 1985/1994.

Hansen, Silvia. 2003. *The nature of translated text: An interdisciplinary methodology for the investigation of the specific properties of translations*. Saarbrucken: DFKI/Universitat des Saarlandes.

Hansen-Schirra, Silvia, Stella Neumann & Erich Steiner. 2007. Cohesion and explicitation in an English–German translation corpus. *Languages in Contrast* 2(7). 241–265.

Hansen-Schirra, Silvia, Stella Neumann & Erich Steiner (eds.). 2012. *Cross-linguistic corpora for the study of translations. insights from the language pair*

English–German (Series Text, Translation, Computational Processing). Berlin: De Gruyter.

Hawkins, John A. 1986. *A comparative typology of English and German: Unifying the contrasts.* London: Croom Helm.

Hawkins, John A. 2004. *Efficiency and complexity in grammars.* Oxford: Oxford University Press.

House, Juliane. 2001. How do we know when a translation is good? In Erich Steiner & Colin Yallop (eds.), *Exploring translation and multilingual text production,* 127–160. Berlin: De Gruyter.

König, Ekkehard & Volker Gast. 2007. *Understanding English–German contrasts.* Berlin: Erich Schmidt.

Kunz, Kerstin & Erich Steiner. 2013. Towards a comparison of cohesive reference in English and German: System and text. In Maite Taboada, Susana Doval Suárez & Elsa Álvarez González (eds.), *Contrastive discourse analysis: Functional and corpus perspectives,* 208–239. London: Equinox.

Mahlberg, Michaela. 2005. *English general nouns: A corpus theoretical approach.* Amsterdam: Benjamins.

Miestamo, Matti, Sinnemäki Kaius & Fred Karlsson (eds.). 2008. *Language complexity: Typology, contact, change.* Amsterdam: Benjamins.

Neumann, Stella. 2008. *Contrastive register variation: A quantitative approach to the comparison of English and German.* Saarbrücken: Habilitationsschrift Philosophische Fakultät II, Universität des Saarlandes.

Schlesewsky, Matthias. 2009. Linguistic data from experimental environments: A multi-experimental and multi-modal perspective. *Zeitschrift für Sprachwissenschaft* 28(1). 169–178.

Schmid, Hans-Jörg. 2000. *English abstract nouns as conceptual shells: From corpus to cognition.* Berlin: De Gruyter.

Siemund, Peter & Noemi Kintana (eds.). 2008. *Language contact and contact languages* (Hamburg Studies in Multilingualism 7). Amsterdam: Benjamins.

Steiner, Erich. 1991. *A functional perspective on language, action, and interpretation: An initial approach with a view to computational modeling.* Berlin: De Gruyter.

Steiner, Erich. 2008. Empirical studies of translations as a mode of language contact – "explicitness" of lexicogrammatical encoding as a relevant dimension. In Peter Siemund & Noemi Kintana (eds.), *Language contact and contact languages,* vol. 7 (Hamburg Studies in Multilingualism), 317–346. Amsterdam: Benjamins.

Teich, Elke. 2003. *Cross-linguistic variation in system and text: A methodology for the investigation of translations and comparable texts.* Berlin: De Gruyter.

Teich, Elke, Richard Eckart & Monica Holtz (eds.). 2008. *Workshop Linguistic Processing Pipelines. 10, July 2008, Darmstadt, Germany.* http://www.linglit.tu-darmstadt.de/index.php?id=abstracts.

Teich, Elke & Peter Fankhauser. 2010. Exploring a corpus of scientific texts using data mining. In Stefan T. Gries, Mark Davies & Stefanie Wulff (eds.), *Corpus-linguistic applications: Current studies, new directions*, 233–248. Amsterdam: Rodopi.

Thomason, Sarah G. 2001. *Language contact. An introduction.* Washington D.C.: Georgetown University Press.

Vela, Mihaela, Silvia Hansen-Schirra & Stella Neumann. 2007. Querying multilayer annotation and alignment in translation corpora. In Matthew Davies, Paul Rayson, Susan Hunston & Pernilla Danielsson (eds.), *Proceedings of the Corpus Linguistics Conference CL.Birmingham, UK, July 2007*, 27–30. http://ucrel.lancs.ac.uk/publications/CL2007/paper/97_Paper.pdf.

ZfS Zeitschrift für Sprachwissenschaft. 2009: *Linguistic data: Acquisition – evaluation – theoretical implications.*

Chapter 5

An analysis of translational complexity in two text types

Martha Thunes
University of Bergen

This article presents an empirical study where translational complexity is related to a notion of computability. Samples of English-Norwegian parallel texts have been analysed in order to estimate to what extent the given translations could have been produced automatically, assuming a rule-based approach to machine translation. The study compares two text types, fiction and law text, in order to see how these differ with respect to the question of automatisation. A central assumption behind the empirical method is that a specific translation of a given source expression can be predicted, or computed, provided that the linguistically encoded information in the original, together with information about source and target languages, and about their interrelations, provides the information needed to produce that specific target expression. The results of the investigation indicate that automatic translation tools may be helpful in the case of the law texts, and the study concurs with the view that the usefulness of such tools is limited with respect to fiction. Finally, an extension of the analysis method is proposed in order to make it relevant as a diagnostic tool for the feasibility of automatic translation in relation to specific text types.

1 Introduction

The present contribution is based on an empirical study of translational correspondences identified in selected English-Norwegian parallel texts. Two main research questions will be discussed, and the first one is about automatisation: i.e., to what extent is it possible to automatise, or compute, the actual translation relation found in the investigated parallel texts? The study attempts to answer this by analysing the parallel texts into pairs of translationally corresponding

Martha Thunes. An analysis of translational complexity in two text types. In Oliver Czulo & Silvia Hansen-Schirra (eds.), *Crossroads between Contrastive Linguistics, Translation Studies and Machine Translation: TC3 II*, 91–120. Berlin: Language Science Press. DOI:10.5281/zenodo.1019695

units, primarily at clause level, and measuring the degree of translational complexity in each such correspondence. In the investigated material, the target texts have been produced by human translators.

The second research question deals with text type. The data include two text types, fiction and law text, and these have been compared in order to find out if there is, in the empirical material, a difference in the degree of translational complexity between the two text types. In relation to this second question, an important factor is the difference in the degree of restrictedness between fiction and law text.

1.1 Key concepts

The applied notion of translational complexity is defined in terms of the types and amount of information needed when a specific translation is produced from a given source expression. Since this conception of translational complexity is related to linguistic information, the present study is seen as relevant to linguistic approaches to machine translation (MT), commonly known as rule-based MT (RBMT).[1]

In this study, 'automatisation' is understood simply as the generation of translations with no human intervention, but the investigation is not related to any particular translation algorithm or system architecture. Rather, the intention is to discuss automatisation with reference to information about languages by relating it to an assumption concerning predictability in the translational relation. I.e., we assume that there is a translational relation between the inventories of simple and complex linguistic signs in two languages which is predictable, and then also *computable*, from information about source and target language systems, and about how the languages correspond.

This means that a computable translation is *linguistically predictable*, i.e. predictable as one of possibly several alternative translations, and the basis for predicting it is the linguistic information coded in the source text, together with given, general information about the two languages and their interrelations.[2] It also means that *non-computable* translations cannot be predicted merely from these types of linguistic information, because non-computable translation tasks

---

[1] *Rule-based MT* is the classic approach to machine translation, where the translation procedure relies on information about source and target language and their interrelations, and this is in contrast to *statistical MT* (SMT), or modern machine translation, where translations are computed on the basis of statistical information about existing correspondences in large bodies of parallel texts. See Jurafsky & Martin (2009: 898).

[2] Cf. Dyvik (1998: 52) on the notion of linguistically predictable translation.

require access to additional information sources, such as various kinds of general or task-specific extra-linguistic information, or task-specific linguistic information from the context surrounding the source expression.

In order to answer the research questions given in section 1, a measurement of *translational complexity* is applied to the analysed texts. For this purpose, pairs of translationally corresponding linguistic units, primarily finite clauses, are identified as individual *translation tasks*, and 'translational complexity' is defined in the following way: in a given translation task, the degree of translational complexity is a factor determined by the types and amount of information needed to solve the task, as well as by the accessibility of these information sources, and the effort required when they are processed. The analysis to be presented is carried out within a strictly product-oriented approach; aspects related to translation methods, or to the cognitive processes behind translation, will not be considered.

In the present approach, a scale of translational complexity is assumed, and, for analytical purposes, four main types of translational correspondences are identified on this scale. The four correspondence types are organised in a hierarchy, reflecting an increase in the degree of translational complexity. Moreover, the issue of computability is closely related to the categorisation of translational correspondences. That is, a dividing line between computable and non-computable translation tasks can be drawn on a certain point across the scale of translational complexity.

1.2 Outline

This article is organised in the following way: §2 presents related approaches to the classification of translational correspondences, and discusses points of contact between the present work and, respectively, translation studies and machine translation. In §3 the correspondence type hierarchy is explained and illustrated, and some of its underlying assumptions are commented on. §4 describes how the classification model has been applied to the investigated data; it presents the analysed parallel texts, as well as certain text-typological aspects, and gives the results of the empirical analysis. §5 discusses the results in relation to the research questions given in §1, and comments further on the relevance of this study for automatic translation.

2 Related works

The type hierarchy to be presented in §3 is a fairly general classification model for translational correspondences, and its basic principles were originally defined by Helge Dyvik of the University of Bergen.[3] A further development of his model is previously published in Thunes (1998), and the approach applied in the present study is described in more detail in Thunes (2011). The model has also been adopted by several other researchers within contrastive language studies. For the purpose of analysing word-order differences between English and Norwegian, Hasselgård (1996) employs a slightly modified version of the correspondence type hierarchy as defined by Dyvik (1993), and her approach is further developed in an English-Norwegian study of thematic structure (Hasselgård 1998). Elgemark (2017) has adapted the analytical approach of Hasselgård (1998) to a contrastive study of clause-final constituents in English-Swedish. Modified versions of the correspondence type hierarchy as presented in Thunes (1998) are used by Tucunduva (2007); Silva (2008), and Azevedo (2012), all of which are studies where the model is applied for the purpose of analysing and describing translational correspondences in English-Portuguese parallel texts.

Other related approaches are found in the works of, respectively Merkel (1999); Cyrus (2006), and Macken (2010). These contributions are rooted in computational linguistics, in addition to being of relevance to contrastive language studies and translation research. Merkel (1999) presents a model for the description of structural and semantic correspondences in Swedish-English parallel texts. Cyrus (2006) develops a framework for manual annotation of translationally interrelated predicate-argument structures in a German-English parallel corpus. With reference to Dutch-English, Macken (2010) presents research on automatic alignment of translational correspondences below sentence level.

The type hierarchy model of the present study may be seen as a parallel to the topic of *shifts* in translation studies. The concept of a 'shift' in translation is defined by Palumbo (2009: 104) as "a linguistic deviation from the original text, a change introduced in translation with respect to either the syntactic form or the meaning of the Source Text (ST)."[4] The correspondence type hierarchy is not meant to be a new attempt to describe shifts in translation. Firstly, the model is designed with reference to levels of linguistic description (i.e., word forms, syn-

---

[3]The same principles are implicit in the design of the experimental machine translation system PONS, documented in (Dyvik 1990, 1995).

[4]Several researchers have presented taxonomies of the different phenomena involved in translation shifts. The model by Leuven-Zwart (1989; 1990) is frequently cited. For overviews on this topic, see §4 in Chesterman (1997; 2005), and Palumbo (2009: 104-106).

tax, semantics, pragmatics), and it is not from the outset motivated by translation research. Secondly, as will become clear in §3, the type hierarchy model aims not only at describing differences, but also to capture structural parallels, between translationally corresponding units of two languages. Thirdly, there has been a tendency in translation studies to apply the notion of 'shifts' to translation methods, whereas the perspective of the present approach is to measure translational complexity by studying relations between source expressions and their existing translations.

Insofar as the correspondence type hierarchy describes differences in linguistic structure between source and target language expressions, it is thematically connected with research carried out within the field of rule-based MT regarding divergences, and mismatches, between languages. Until the statistical paradigm became dominant, a number of rule-based approaches were developed in order to tackle translation challenges caused by various kinds of differences between languages. An overview of such rule-based translation techniques can be found, e.g., in Trujillo (1999). Barnett et al. (1991) provide a distinction between translation divergences and mismatches which is of relevance to RBMT research. Following Dorr (1990), they describe *translation divergences* as cases where "the same information is conveyed in the source and target texts, but the structures of the sentences are different" (Barnett et al. 1991: 25). Then, referring to Kameyama et al. (1991), they say that *translation mismatches* "occur when there are actually differences in the information that is conveyed" (Barnett et al. 1991: 25). On the background of these two topics, divergences and mismatches, Barnett et al. (1991) argue for the use of interlingual semantic representations in MT development, which is one example of the techniques used in RBMT. Relating to the subject of translation divergences, Dorr et al. (1998: 9-10) present an overview of types of linguistic phenomena that create what they call "mapping problems" in MT; these are basically classes of cases where source and target sentence have different predicate-argument structures, and Dorr et al. (1998: 13-18) discuss these problems in relation to various kinds of system architectures in RBMT.

The distinction between divergences and mismatches, as given by Barnett et al. (1991), is of some relevance to the present study, because it hinges on a notion of 'same information'. If we may assume that this pertains to the information which is encoded linguistically by, respectively, source and target expressions, then cases of translation divergences fall within the domain of computable, or linguistically predictable translation, whereas mismatches represent non-computable, or linguistically non-predictable, translation. E.g., the classes of divergence phenomena described by Dorr (1994) fall within the computable domain of translation, because they are ascribed to "source-language/target-language distinctions based on lexical-semantic properties" (Dorr 1994: 599), and hence they may be accounted for by information about the two language systems and about how they are translationally interrelated. Her contribution is motivated by the goal of implementing successful MT by means of appropriate techniques. As the present investigation is directed towards measuring translational complexity in existing parallel texts, issues relevant for the implementation of automatic translation will not be discussed further. Moreover, in order to describe specific types of divergences and mismatches, it would be necessary to apply more fine-grained categories than the correspondence types to be presented, and in this study the main focus will be on the distinction between computable and non-computable translation.[5]

3 Methodology

The method applied in this project involves a manual analysis of running parallel texts. In this analysis, translationally corresponding linguistic units, or *string pairs*, are identified and extracted. The chosen units of analysis will be presented in §4.1 Each string pair is analysed according to a classification model, the *correspondence type hierarchy*, which is designed to measure the degree of translational complexity in individual translation tasks.

3.1 The correspondence type hierarchy

In the following, the four main categories of the type hierarchy will be illustrated using examples of sentence pairs taken from a short story by the Norwegian author Bjørg Vik, and its translation into English.

3.1.1 Type 1

The least complex type of translational correspondence is referred to as *type 1*. An example is given in (1), where ((1a) is the source sentence, and (1b) the target sentence:

(1)   a.   Hun har vært en skjønnhet.
           'She has been a beauty.'
      b.   She has been a beauty.

---

[5]Chapter 6 in Thunes (2011) presents a further division of the two most complex correspondence types into subtypes identified by semantic criteria, and these subtypes can be seen as classes of translation divergences and mismatches.

The glossing of (1a) shows that the English target sentence corresponds word-by-word with the source sentence, and this is the characteristic of type 1. That is, in this category, the corresponding strings are pragmatically, semantically, and syntactically equivalent, down to the level of the sequence of word forms. Such correspondences are relatively infrequent in the language pair English-Norwegian.[6]

3.1.2 Type 2

In correspondences of *type 2*, there is also a very close match between the two strings, but there may be some formal differences. Firstly, the sequence of constituents may differ between source and target string; cf. example (2):

(2)   a. Dessuten virket hun overlegen.
          'Also looked she haughty.'
      b. She also looked haughty.

The glossing of (2a) illustrates the word order difference between the two strings. In the Norwegian sentence, there is subject-verb inversion: when a non-subject, such as the adverbial *dessuten*, appears sentence-initially, the verb-second restriction applies in Norwegian. In the English target sentence the subject comes first, and there is no inversion.

Secondly, in type 2 there may be differences in the use of grammatical form words, as shown in example (3):

(3)   a. Leiligheten var ufattelig rotete.
          'Flat.def was unbelievably untidy.'
      b. The flat was unbelievably untidy.

The point in example (3) is that there is no word form in (3a) matching the definite article in (3b), because Norwegian expresses the definite form of nouns by means of a suffix.

The criterion that defines type 2 correspondences is that every lexical word in the source string has a correspondent in the target string of the same lexical category and with the same syntactic function as the source word. This means that in type 2 correspondences, the two strings are pragmatically and semantically equivalent, and equivalent with respect to syntactic functions, even if there is at

---

[6]Table 2 in §4.4 presents the frequencies of the various correspondence types in this study. Similar results were found in Thunes (1998).

least one formal difference that makes the correspondence deviate from word-by-word translation. Type 2 is, like type 1, relatively infrequent in this language pair.

3.1.3 Type 3

In *type 3* correspondences there is, like in types 1 and 2, pragmatic and semantic equivalence between source and target string, but there is not syntactic functional equivalence, because there is at least one structural difference violating equivalence between the two strings with respect to syntactic categories and functions. In the pair of languages English-Norwegian, type 3 seems to be more frequent than each of the two lower types. Type 3 can be illustrated by example (4):

(4) a. Hildegun himlet lidende mot taket og svarte med uforskammet høflighet.
    'Hildegun rolled-eyes suffering towards ceiling.def and answered with brazen politeness.'
  b. Hildegun rolled her eyes in suffering towards the ceiling and answered with brazen politeness.

In this string pair, the correspondence between the Norwegian verb phrase *himlet* and the English expression *rolled her eyes* violates syntactic functional equivalence, because *himle* is an intransitive verb, whereas *rolled her eyes* consists of a transitive verb phrase and a noun phrase functioning as direct object. Also, the Norwegian adverb phrase *lidende* corresponds with the English preposition phrase *in suffering*. Still, these two sentences can be said to correspond semantically.

3.1.4 Type 4

Finally, in *type 4*, the most complex correspondence type, there is no longer semantic equivalence between source and target string. There may be pragmatic equivalence, but not necessarily. In the present study, type 4 has turned out to be very important because it is the most frequent correspondence type in the analysed texts (cf. §4.4).

The defining characteristic of type 4 correspondences is that there is at least one linguistically non-predictable semantic deviation between source and target string. This can be illustrated by example (5):

(5)   a. Her kunne de snakke sammen uten å bli ropt inn for å gå i
melkebutikken eller til bakeren.
'Here could they talk together without to be called in for to go in
milk-shop.def or to baker.def'

       b. They could talk here without being called in to go and buy milk or
bread.

Without going into detail, it may be observed that the semantic difference between these sentences lies in the correspondence between the substrings *for å
gå i melkebutikken eller til bakeren* and *to go and buy milk or bread*. These expressions do not denote the same activities, but it is inferrable from background
information about the world that both activities can have the same result, i.e. the
buying of milk or bread.

This illustrates what is involved in a linguistically non-predictable semantic
deviation: the semantic difference between source and target expression — in
the case of example (5), a difference in denotational properties — cannot be predicted on the basis of the information that is linguistically expressed in the source
string, together with information about source and target languages, and about
their interrelations. This means that in type 4 correspondences, additional information sources, such as world information, are needed in order to produce
the particular target expression. In such cases, there are normally one or more
alternative translations which *can* be predicted from purely linguistic information sources, and which can be semantically equivalent to the original expression.
With respect to (5), a linguistically predictable target expression could be *to go
to the milk shop or to the baker's*. That alternative is denotationally equivalent to
the source expression, but it does not necessarily exhibit other properties that a
translator may want to choose in a target text.

3.2 Some aspects of the classification model

The examples (1)–(5) show that the correspondence type hierarchy, as a classification model, reflects a gradual increase in linguistic divergence between source
and target string, and the analysis of translational correspondences is based on
the assumption that this increase is correlated with an increase in the degree of
translational complexity. That is, a larger amount of information, and a greater
processing effort, is required in order to solve translation tasks in correspondences of the higher types than in the lower types.

Each correspondence type covers a class of translation tasks, and in the type
hierarchy, the four classes are distinguished from each other on the basis of the

types and amount of information necessary for solving translation tasks within each class. These matters are described in detail for each correspondence type in Thunes (2011), along with discussions of the accessibility of necessary information sources, and of required processing effort, within each type.

On the scale of translational complexity defined by the type hierarchy, the division between predictable and non-predictable translation is drawn between the types 3 and 4. This means that correspondences of types 1, 2, and 3 together constitute the domain of linguistically predictable, or computable, translations, whereas type 4 correspondences belong to the non-predictable, or non-computable, domain, where semantic equivalence is not fulfilled.

A clear parallel to the increasing degree of complexity in the type hierarchy is found in Vinay and Darbelnet's set of seven translation procedures, which are presented "in increasing order of difficulty", ranging from the simplest method of translation to the most complex.[7] Although this is an interesting similarity, the present classification model is not related to Vinay & Darbelnet's categorisation of methods.[8]

Moreover, the classification of correspondences involves no evaluation of translational quality as, for instance, in terms of the model by House (1997). Among the empirical data there are occasional instances of unsuccessful translations, but translational quality is by itself no element in the classification of correspondences. Moreover, our notion of translational complexity, being based on information sources for translation, is in principle independent of grammatical complexity, and of factors that may influence the ease or difficulty with which the translator comprehends the source text.[9] Translational complexity is also distinct from the notion of linguistic complexity, as defined, e.g., by Dahl (2004).

3.3 Predictability and information sources for translation

In the present approach, the distinction between computable and non-computable translation is the same as the dichotomy between linguistically predictable and non-predictable translation (cf.§1.1), and the distinction relies further on a typology of information sources for translation, presented in Thunes (2011: 87–106). In relation to the computability issue, the most important distinctions drawn in that typology are, firstly, the division between linguistic and

---

[7]The quotation is taken from Venuti (2000: 92), where an overview of the seven procedures is presented. Pages 31–42 of Vinay & Darbelnet (1995) are reprinted in Venuti (2000: 84-93).

[8]Cf. the comments in §1.1 and §2 on the product-orientation of the present approach, and on how this study is related to translation shifts.

[9]Grammatical complexity in relation to translation is discussed by Izquierdo & Borillo (2000).

extra-linguistic information, and, secondly, the borderline between information coded inside the source language expression, and information available from the context of that expression.

Within the *linguistic information sources* for translation there is, firstly, the information supporting the translator's knowledge of source and target language systems and their interrelations. Secondly, these sources include the information that is linguistically encoded in the source expression. This covers information about the situation type described by the source text, information about the linguistic structure of the source expression, as well as information about relations of reference holding between expressions in the source text and extra-linguistic entities. The latter is derivable from the source language expression as it is interpreted in a specific context. Thirdly, the linguistic sources also include information available in the linguistic context of the source string.

The *extra-linguistic information sources* for translation comprise general background information about the world, information about particular technical domains, information about textual norms, and information derivable from previous translation training and practice. They also cover information about the utterance situation of the source text, and about the translation situation. These types may include information about the sender, about the purpose(s) of original and translation, about temporal and geographical location, etc. Another extra-linguistic information source may be information derived by applying different kinds of background information in common-sense reasoning about facts described by the SL text.

The division between linguistic and extra-linguistic information can be briefly illustrated with reference to examples (1)–(5) in §3.1.1–§4. In examples (1)–(4), which instantiate correspondence types 1–3, each target sentence can be predicted from the source sentence by means of linguistic information sources alone. That is, the translations can be computed on the basis of the information that is linguistically encoded in the source sentences, together with information about source and target language systems, and their interrelations. Then, in example (5), linguistic information sources are not sufficient in order to produce the target sentence, as background information about the world is also required.[10]

If we consider a language system to be a structure containing a finite set of components which may be combined in a limited number of possible ways, then it may be argued that information about a language system in principle constitutes a finite domain. The extra-linguistic world, on the other hand, is unlimited,

---

[10]The dichotomy between linguistic and extra-linguistic information is discussed further in Thunes (2011: 90–102).

and hence information about it can be regarded as a nonfinite domain. Then, a strategy for separating linguistic from extra-linguistic information is to delimit the given language system, and, in line with Dyvik (2003: 9), the distinction between the linguistic and the extra-linguistic is thus related to the way in which language systems are conceptually individuated. This, in turn, will be influenced by the purpose for which the language description is meant to be applied, and by empirical facts about language use; cf. Thunes (2011: 93).

The information coded in a specific source language expression is necessarily finite, delimited by the expression itself. The information available from the surrounding context is in principle unbounded, although there is in practice a limit on how much context that will be considered by the translator when producing a target expression.

Accordingly, a target expression that can be predicted from the information coded linguistically in the source string, together with information about source and target language systems and their interrelations, can be regarded as computable because there is a finite search space which contains the information needed to produce that target expression. Likewise, if a translation is non-computable, then some information falling outside the finite, linguistic domain is required in order to create that particular target expression.

For a given source expression, there is normally a number of possible translations, and the appropriateness of each alternative is typically context-dependent. A subset of all the possible alternatives in the target language will be computable, or linguistically predictable translations, determined by information about the interrelations between the two languages. In the present study, the classification of translational correspondences amounts to deciding, for each target string, whether it belongs to the set of predictable translations of the given source string, or not. If it does not, the correspondence is non-computable, and of type 4. If it does, the string pair is computable, and of type 1, 2, or 3, depending on the degree of linguistic convergence between source and target expression.

This analytical approach relies on a certain understanding of linguistic approaches to MT: automatic translation is seen as possible to the extent that the translation system has access to information about source and target languages and their interrelations, and from those information sources only linguistically predictable translations can be generated by the system. There is a principled difference between this and human translation, because the human translator chooses a predictable translation only when it appears to be the most appropriate choice also on the basis of information falling outside the finite, linguistic domain.

4 Empirical investigation

The implementation of the present methodology involves manual extraction and classification of string pairs from parallel texts. The application of the type hierarchy requires a human, bilingually competent analyst, since the classification of the compiled correspondences demands a careful linguistic analysis of each string pair.

The assignment of correspondence type to individual string pairs works like an elimination procedure where we start by testing for the lowest correspondence type and then move upwards in the hierarchy if the test fails. This may seem a fairly straightforward task, but not in every case. In particular, it can be difficult to distinguish between instances of types 3 and 4, since that may involve fine-grained semantic analyses.

4.1 Units of analysis

A limited set of syntactic units have been chosen as units of analysis, and the selection of units is influenced by the wish to make this study of translational complexity relevant to the field of machine translation. It has been an aim to find a way of segmenting text material that would be suitable for automatic translation regardless of specific algorithms for implementation. Considering the linguistic approaches to automatic translation, MT systems typically operate sentence by sentence, and hence *the finite clause* is chosen as the basic unit of analysis in this investigation. Another point motivating the choice is that in order to be of any use, an MT system must handle syntactic units at least as complex as those of the sentence level.

In this connection, 'finite clause' is understood simply as a syntactic unit containing a finite verb as its central element. Thus, occurrences of finite verbs are in practice the basis for the identification of analysis units. Whenever a word form of this category is encountered, the syntactic unit in which it fills the function of main or auxiliary predicate is identified as a unit of analysis. This means that matrix sentences and finite subclauses are typically recorded as units of analysis. Also, lexical phrases with one or more finite clauses as syntactic complement (cf. (6) in §5.2) constitute another major syntactic type among the recorded data. In such cases the finite clause is not identified as an independent unit, because the entire phrase is normally a more natural unit of translation than the syntactic complement in isolation.

The parallel texts are analysed from beginning to end. The human annotator goes through the texts in parallel in order to identify pairs of translationally related units. Notably, string pairs are extracted also when only one of the two strings is a syntactic unit satisfying the criteria by which units of analysis are identified. This is necessary because finite constructions may be translationally related to nonfinite constructions, and such correspondences are frequent in the language pair English-Norwegian. Once a unit of analysis, and its translational correspondent, are identified, the string pair is recorded and a correspondence type assigned to it. The data are stored electronically by means of the software tool Text Pair Mapper, described in Dyvik (1993).

As syntactically dependent constructions like finite subclauses occur as units of analysis, the data include nested correspondences where a superordinate string pair contains one or more embedded string pairs. E.g., if a finite subclause is embedded in a matrix sentence, as in *When he came, we could leave* (Norwegian: *Da han kom, kunne vi dra*), then two string pairs are extracted. One is the subclause and its match in the parallel text: [*When he came,*] – [*Da han kom*]; the other is the matrix sentence and its correspondent: [[CP] *we could leave*]. – [[CP] *kunne vi dra*]. In the superordinate string pair, the embedded correspondence is treated as a pair of opaque items, represented by their syntactic categories.[11]

4.2 The texts

In this study, the data are recorded from a selected set of English-Norwegian parallel texts. The texts were written during the years 1979–1996, and all translations have been produced manually. The corpus covers both directions of translation, and it includes two text types, fiction and law texts. Comparable amounts of data have been compiled for each of the text types and directions of translation. Table 1 gives an overview of text type, direction of translation, and numbers of running words for each of the text pairs that have been investigated.

4.2.1 Degree of restrictedness

In the present investigation, law texts are chosen as a representative of restricted text types, and fiction as an example of a relatively unrestricted type. The difference in restrictedness between the two text types is a direct reflection of a basic opposition between the language of the law and that of fiction: the former is strictly norm-governed in ways that the latter is not. In law-regulated societies the law is nothing less than the highest power, and this gives law texts their authority. Because of the optimally authoritative status of a law text, its production

---

[11]In the present analysis, the category label *CP* represents finite subclauses; cf. Thunes (2011: 201).

Table 1: An overview of the analysed text pairs with respect to text
type, direction of translation,and numbers of running words.

Authors and texts	Text type	Source	Target	No. of running words
Agreement on the European Economic Area, Articles 1–99	law text	Eng.		9202
Avtale om Det europeiske økonomiske samarbeidsområde artiklene 1–99			Nor.	8015
Lov om petroleumsvirksomhet §§1–65	law text	Nor.		7929
Act relating to petroleum activities, Sections 1–65			Eng.	9647
André Brink	fiction			
The Wall of the Plague		Eng.		4021
Pestens mur			Nor.	4230
Doris Lessing	fiction			
The Good Terrorist		Eng.		4008
Den gode terroristen			Nor.	4652
Erik Fosnes Hansen	fiction			
Salme ved reisens slutt		Nor.		4022
Psalm at Journey's End			Eng.	4395
Bjørg Vik	fiction			
En håndfull lengsel		Nor.		4010
Out of Season and Other Stories			Eng.	4550
Total				68681

as well as its interpretation are strongly governed by the intersubjective norms of the legal domain of society; cf., e.g., Bowers (1989: 53-54), and Cao (2007: 13-14). According to Bhatia (2010: 46-47), the primary concern in law writing is "loyalty to legislative intentions", and he describes four different norms of law writing: clarity of expression (i.e. avoiding vagueness), precision (by using as few words as possible), unambiguity, and all-inclusiveness (i.e. specifying adequately the scope of application of the law text) (2010: 38-39).

Fiction texts, then, are, like any kind of language use, subject to the linguistic norms of the language community, and there are norms of literary language use that shape the characteristics of various kinds of styles and genres.[12] Still, fiction texts are in no way as norm-governed as law texts are, and although literary norms, too, have intersubjective existence, they are not institutionalised like legal norms. As a parallel to the authority of law texts, fiction texts can acquire high status if they are particularly successful. In such cases, the status of the fiction text is determined, firstly, by the creative ability of the author to express a story, and, secondly, by the capacity of that story to create great experiences in the minds of the readers. The subjective factors attributed to the sender and recipient of a fiction text are quite different from the institutionalised norms controlling the writing and interpretation of law texts. The production of a fiction text is governed by the individual choices of the author, which may include norm violations, and its reception is determined by the subjective experiences of the readers. This is in sharp contrast to the norms of law texts, which are determined by the collective purpose of regulating society.

The text-typological differences between law and fiction are evident in relation to translation. Since the meaning of a law text expresses legal content, the translation must preserve the meaning of the original as far as possible, given differences in semantic structure between the two languages. When fiction is translated, there may be other properties than the linguistic meaning of the source text that are necessary to recreate in the target text. In particular, it will be important to preserve the literary properties of the original, and hence the choice of target expressions can be motivated by a range of other factors than the semantic content of the source text. This point is further commented on in §5 with reference to observations of semantic deviations in the empirical data of the present study.

---

[12]The kind of norms that shapes the linguistic characteristics of literary styles is described by Leech & Short (2007: 41-44) as *relative norms*.

4.2.2 Textual features

Various kinds of linguistic effects of the difference in restrictedness between the investigated text types are discussed in Thunes (2011: 279–288). The principal consequence of this opposition is that there is a greater degree of structural diversity in the fiction texts than in the law texts, and this is evident from a range of features that can be observed in the selected texts.

The investigated law texts exhibit several features which are characteristic of this text type. They contain sets of sequentially numbered sections, or articles, and are written in a formal, impersonal style, with frequent use of long, complex sentences. Mattila (2006: 98), citing Laurén (1993: 74), observes that "[s]entences in legal language are longer than those of other languages for special purposes and they contain more subordinate clauses." The texts are repetitive in the sense that specific expressions are recurrent (e.g., *with a view to, without prejudice to*). Other characteristics are heavy constituents, enumerative listing, complex coordination, no occurrences of first and second person pronouns, and numerous instances of nonfinite constructions, especially in the English texts. Another salient feature is the high frequency of headings, normally realised as noun phrases, such as *Article 1.* The texts contain a limited inventory of types of sentences and syntactic constructions, and short, syntactically simple sentences are infrequent.

The analysed fiction texts are extracts of novels, except for the text by Vik (1979), which is taken from a short story (cf. Table 1). Each extract runs from the beginning of the narrative, and none of them is a complete text. The selected fiction texts are stories evolving around a certain protagonist and other characters, and passages of dialogue are found in all of them. In comparison to law text, narrative fiction can rightly be described as unrestricted, at least in terms of the inventory of syntactic constructions that may occur. Narrative fiction texts may comprise all kinds of sentence types: simple as well as complex, declarative, interrogative, and imperative sentences.[13] Furthermore, literary texts can include direct speech and passages of other text types, which may add to the structural diversity. Moreover, as discussed in Thunes (2011: 283–284), the analysed fiction texts exhibit a larger variety of speech acts than the law texts do, and this is clearly linked with the greater degree of structural diversity in the fiction texts.

---

[13]Cf. Ochs (1997: 185–189) on the diversity of narratives. On the narrative in general, see Abbott (2002), and Toolan (2001).

4.3 Measuring translational complexity

In order to measure the degree of translational complexity in pieces of parallell texts, the classification model must be applied to running texts, without omitting any parts of them. Then, the distribution of the four correspondence types within a set of data provides a measurement of the degree of translational complexity in the parallel texts that the data are extracted from.

Calculating the distribution of correspondence types brings attention to the difference between counting the frequencies of string pairs of each type and measuring the length of text covered by each category. The reason for this is that, in the given language pair, the two least complex types (1–2) normally occur in pairs of short and syntactically simple strings of words, whereas pairs of longer and more complex strings tend to be of the two higher types (3–4). Thus, types 1 and 2 would appear as covering an unproportionally large amount of the analysed texts if the distribution of the main correspondence types would be presented merely on the basis of the numbers of string pairs (cf. Table 2 in §4.4).

Hence, the proportions of text covered by the different correspondence types will be discussed in terms of the lengths of, respectively, source and target text. More precisely, the proportions are measured by means of string lengths, i.e. by calculating the number of word forms covered by each correspondence type. The length of a recorded translational unit equals its number of word forms, and in the case of nested correspondences, the word forms in embedded strings are counted only once. That is, if a recorded unit contains any embedded strings, then each embedded unit is treated as an opaque unit in the superordinate string. The length of the matrix unit is counted as its number of non-opaque word forms, and a subordinate unit adds only 1 to the length of the superordinate string.

The most important aspect shown by the complexity measurements of this study is the division between computable and non-computable correspondences, i.e. how large is the proportion of the analysed texts covered by, on the one hand, string pairs of types 1, 2, and 3, and, on the other hand, string pairs of type 4. This division is meant to show to what extent it can be expected that an ideal, rule-based MT system could simulate the given translations, if provided with a full description of the two languages and their interrelations. Notably, this is not an estimate of how much of the given source texts that could be given *some kind of* linguistically predictable translation. Since English and Norwegian both belong to the Germanic language family, and are used in language communities which are, in cultural terms, not very far apart, the recorded data include probably only very few source expressions which have no linguistically predictable translation.[14] It should be emphasised, then, that this study tries to measure the proportion of predictable, and hence computable, translation within the specific, human-created target texts that already have been produced (cf. §3.3).

4.4 The results

Since the present investigation is based on hand-coded material, the data are of a relatively modest quantity (about 68 000 words), and it will remain a mere speculation whether the distribution of correspondence types across the total set of data may reflect the general degree of complexity in the translational relation between English and Norwegian, as instantiated in actual, human translation activity. The limited size of the compiled data prevents the detection of statistically significant results, and only tendencies may be observed within the recorded material. Hence, it is not possible to generalise about the degree of translational complexity in relation to the given language pair, the two directions of translation within this pair, or to the investigated text types. Still, on the basis of the recorded data, the results provide tentative answers to the research questions posed in §1. After a brief presentation here, the results will be further discussed in §5 with subsections.

Concerning the automatisation issue, Table 2 shows the complexity measurement across the entire collection of correspondences. By calculating the average values of the percentages given for, respectively, source and target text lengths, we find that more than half of the data are included in non-computable correspondences: string pairs of type 4 constitute 55.2% of the compiled data, whereas the computable types 1, 2, and 3 together cover as little as 44.8% of all recorded string pairs. On the basis of this result, the conclusion is that with perfect information about source and target languages, an idealised rule-based MT system could have simulated less than half of the identified correspondences.

Further, Table 2 shows that within the subset of computable correspondences, type 3 constitutes a large majority of the data. Thus, types 1 and 2 together cover a very modest proportion of the analysed texts (on average 10.0% across all data), and this strengthens the point made in §4.3 that the most important aspect shown by the data is the division between, on the one hand, types 1–3 and, on the other hand, type 4. Because types 1 and 2 are so infrequent, the distinction between computable and non-computable correspondences appears to be the most informative indicator of translational complexity, as far as the language pair English-Norwegian is concerned.

---

[14] An example could be the Norwegian noun *skiføre*, found in Vik's text (1979a). This word has no match in English, and needs to be translated by a paraphrase, such as *conditions for skiing*.

Table 2: The global distribution of correspondence types in the investigated texts.

Total results, all text pairs	Type 1	Type 2	Type 3	Type 4	All types
Number of string pairs	601	272	1 347	2 219	4 439
Percentage of string pairs	13.5	6.1	30.4	50.0	100.0
Source text length (word forms)	1 906	1 642	12 179	19 263	34 990
Percentage of source text length	5.4	4.7	34.8	55.1	100.0
Target text length (word forms)	1 926	1 741	12 940	20 547	37 154
Percentage of target text length	5.2	4.7	34.8	55.3	100.0

With respect to the text type issue, the results are summed up in table 3, which shows that the proportion of computable correspondences is on average 50.2% in the law data, and 39.6% in fiction. However, it is pointed out in Thunes (2011: 275) that these results cannot be seen as indicative of the general complexity of translating, respectively, law text and fiction between English and Norwegian. The results in Table 3 merely show that the degree of complexity is, on average, lower in the selected pairs of law texts than in those of fiction.

Table 3: Differences in translational complexity between the two text types.

Proportions of...	in law text	in fiction	in all data
computable translational correspondences (types 1, 2, 3)	50.2%	39.6%	44.8%
non-computable translational correspondences (type 4)	49.8%	60.4%	55.2%

Moreover, the results do not indicate that while the analysed fiction texts appear as clearly unsuitable for automatic translation, the law texts appear as suitable. Across the investigated material, the degree of translational complexity is found to be so high that fully automatic translation does not seem to be a fruitful option for any of the analysed text pairs, if the aim is to produce output identical to the human-created target texts of the analysed data. Furthermore, as explained in Thunes (2011: 275), the lower degree of average complexity in the chosen law text pairs is primarily due to the relatively low complexity measured in the law text translated from Norwegian into English (60.9% computable translation; cf.

Thunes (2011: 291). In the other pair of law texts, the degree of complexity is higher, and, in fact, quite similar to the average found across the four pairs of fiction texts (39.6% computable translation; cf. Table 3).

5 Discussion

In relation to the automatisation issue, the results are rather pessimistic, especially considering the fact that automatic translation tools are actually used, in particular for non-literary text types, and this is so because they do reduce the workload of manual translation. Better performance may be expected by MT systems developed for restricted domains, or subject areas, and it is also likely that some of the non-computable correspondences among the recorded data could have been maintained by translation memories.[15] The latter is highly relevant for law texts, which tend to be repetitive (cf. §4.2.2). §5.1 and §5.2 provide further comments on the automatisation issue.

Concerning the text type issue, it is an expected result to find a lower degree of translational complexity in law texts than in fiction texts. Chapter 6 in Thunes (2011) provides discussions of several kinds of recurrent semantic deviations between translationally corresponding units, and, in general, these phenomena constitute the primary factor contributing to the frequency of the most complex correspondence type. Although cases of type 4 are not infrequent within the law data, instances of semantic deviations are far more common among the fiction data than among those compiled from law text. This is in line with the high degree of restrictedness in the law texts (cf. §4.2.1). In particular, since legal translation is strongly governed by the norm of preserving the informational content of the original in the target text, the abundance of semantic deviations found in the fiction target texts would be simply unacceptable in the domain of law translation.

Given the dominance of statistical machine translation, it may appear surprising that this study assumes the traditional, linguistic approach to MT, where translations are computed on the basis of formal descriptions of source and target language systems and their interrelations. However, in recent years the general view has been formed that there is a limit to how far the purely statistical methods can reach in terms of translation quality, and for more than a decade research efforts have been put into hybrid approaches where statistical techniques

---

[15]A *translation memory* is defined by Palumbo (2009: 127–128) as "[a]n electronic database containing translated texts stored together with their originals," and the texts "are normally segmented into units one sentence long."

are combined with some kind of semantic and/or syntactic processing. If a certain level of quality is wanted, it seems unlikely that automatic translation can do without linguistic information, especially in the light of the pervasive ambiguity of natural language expressions.

Still, the general issue of computability, or linguistic predictability, which is behind the present approach should in principle also apply to statistical machine translation, because SMT, too, depends on the accessibility of relevant and sufficient information within the texts themselves in order to predict correct target expressions from available translational correspondences.

5.1 Human translations as a gold standard

With respect to the automatisation issue, translations produced by humans have been used as a gold standard for MT in this study. In relation to this, it is a point that the analysed texts provide a problematic norm for automatic translation. Since it is generally accepted that the use of machine translation requires post-editing to secure the quality of the final product, the human-created target texts represent an ideal for the end result, and not for the raw output of an MT application. The chosen norm is probably an unrealistic, and perhaps also unfair, goal for MT development, especially since high-quality translation without post-editing, or revision, is uncommon also when the translator is human. Still, manually produced target texts have been used as a standard because evaluating the products of real systems has not been an objective, and because the complexity measurements in this study aim at showing to what extent we might assume that an ideal, rule-based system could simulate the given translations.

5.2 Minimally non-computable correspondences

In order to discuss further whether it would be fruitful to apply automatic translation to the selected texts, it is interesting to consider the workload potentially involved in editing possible machine output. For this purpose, we can assume that an MT system would generate only linguistically predictable translations for the analysed source texts. This means that the recorded type 4 correspondences represent cases where the machine would produce target expressions conforming with the characteristics of one of the lower correspondence types, or possibly not generate linguistically well-formed output at all. At any rate, post-editing would be required in order to reach the gold standard represented by the human-created translations.

Of relevance here is the question whether string pairs identified as type 4 in the present study have been classified as such because of only one, or few, semantic deviations between source and target units. That is, if the semantic difference between two corresponding strings is small, then the major part of the correspondence would involve linguistically predictable translation, and it might be unproblematic for a post-editor to correct that subpart of the machine output which does not meet the standard. If post-editing amounts to simple corrections of linguistic errors that are few and easy to spot, then what Jurafsky & Martin (2009: 931), describe as the *edit cost* of post-editing would be low, and the *editing distance* between the machine output and the standard could be small, and automatic translation might be useful.[16] On the other hand, if there are many errors in the output, and, if the revision also requires syntactic and/or semantic reorganisation of the automatically generated sentences, and maybe even careful considerations of the appropriateness of various target alternatives, then the editing distance is large, and it is perhaps more cost effective to do a fully manual translation.

As mentioned in §5, a set of recurrent semantic deviations between translationally corresponding units have been identified among the recorded data, and these phenomena are likely to represent challenges that the post-editor will be faced with, i.e. types of properties that should be observed in the translation, but which cannot be predicted from the source expression without access to contextual information, and/or various kinds of extra-linguistic information. It is of significance to the question of potential edit cost that the editing distance between , on the one hand, a predictable, machine-generated translation and, on the other hand, a human-created target string with multiple semantic deviations in relation to the original will be considerably greater than the distance between a predictable translation and a target expression exhibiting only a minimal semantic difference in relation to the source string.

Thus, non-computable correspondences with only one minimal semantic deviation between source and target string are of particular interest to the question of potential edit cost. Such cases may be described as *minimally non-computable*, and in correspondences of this kind it would probably be easy to revise an automatically generated target expression to the standard of manual translation. An example can be taken from the Norwegian *Act relating to petroleum activities*.

---

[16]The term *editing distance* is borrowed from information theory. According to Jurafsky & Martin (2009: 108), "[t]he minimum edit distance between two strings is the minimum number of editing operations (insertion, deletion, substitution) needed to transform one string into another."

The noun phrase given in ((6)a) contains a relative clause, and is translated into the expression shown in ((6)b):

(6)   a.   de områder som er nevnt i tillatelsen
           'the areas which are mentioned in license.def'
      b.   the areas mentioned in the licence

The only semantic deviation in this string pair is the presence vs. absence of grammatically expressed temporal information, and because of this, example (6) is a type 4 correspondence. Here it can be assumed that a rule-based translation system would produce the semantically equivalent target expression *the areas which are mentioned in the licence*, and a human post-editor might easily choose the nonfinite alternative because he or she would know that that would be stylistically more appropriate in a law text.

In a metric for evaluating MT output, Specia (2011: 75) distinguishes between four degrees of quality, ranging from the lowest one where complete retranslation is required, to the highest degree where the output is a fully acceptable translation. Intermediate degrees on this scale are cases where the translation is not very good, but post-editing is less demanding than retranslation, and cases where very little editing is needed. Given the assumption that minimally non-computable correspondences represent translation tasks where the editing cost would be very low, there is a close affinity between this category and Specia's second highest degree of quality.

The distribution of minimally non-computable correspondences among the recorded data again puts focus on the text type issue, because such cases are far more frequent in the law texts than in the fiction texts. Within the law data, as much as 45.7% of the correspondences classified as type 4 are minimally non-computable, whereas among the fiction data, only 10.5% of the compiled type 4 correspondences are minimal ones. This primarily reflects the fact that because law text is strongly norm-governed in a way that fiction text is not (cf. §4.2.1), semantic deviations between translationally corresponding units are far less frequent in the former than in the latter. Moreover, it shows that the potential edit cost required by automatic translation would be considerably lower in the law texts than in the fiction texts.

5.3 Conclusions and a possible extension

On the basis of the data recorded in this study, the investigated pairs of law texts are tentatively regarded as representing a text type where machine translation may be helpful, if the effort required by post-editing is smaller than that of manual translation. In the case of the fiction texts, it seems clear that post-editing of automatically generated translations would be laborious and not cost effective.

The careful optimism in relation to the automatisation of law text translation is not only inspired by the findings of the present investigation, but also by the recent emergence of a research field combining insights and methods from artificial intelligence, human language technology, the law, legal informatics, and studies of legal language. E.g., under the heading *Semantic Processing of Legal Texts*, Francesconi et al. (2010) have compiled a set of contributions dealing with topics such as information extraction from legal texts, the construction of legal knowledge resources, semantic indexing, summarisation, and translation evaluation for the legal domain. Furthermore, Johnsen (2010), and Johnsen & Berre (2010) discuss the semantic modelling of law text with reference to Norwegian. Contributions like these indicate that there is progress in relation to the development of automatic analysis of law text. Moreover, since the language of law is highly specialised and norm-controlled, it is, in its own right, of interest to the field of language technology as a testing ground for applications developed for the processing of natural language, translation included.

Then, I will suggest that the correspondence type hierarchy has a potential as a diagnostic tool for the feasibility of linguistics-based machine translation in relation to specific text types. That is, by applying the method to limited selections of parallel texts of the same type, it would be possible to estimate to what extent the target text could be generated automatically. If the proportion of assumed computable correspondences would exceed a chosen threshold, it might be worthwhile to tune an MT system for the given language pair to the text type in question, for instance by developing lexicon modules covering the relevant subject domain.

Moreover, since the feasibility of MT for a given text type is determined also by potential edit cost, it would be fruitful to extend the classification model by integrating a fifth correspondence type to be assigned to the minimally non-computable string pairs. If such a fifth category could be implemented in the software used for recording translational correspondences, it would be possible to calculate automatically the proportion of minimally non-computable correspondences in terms of string length within each text pair. Such estimates could say something about the potential edit cost required by automatic translation.

Finally, we may recall that adaptations of the methodology of the present study have been put to use in several works within the field of contrastive linguistics (cf. §2). Moreover, as discussed in Thunes (2011: 446–447) the data analysed for the purposes of this investigation do not only say something about translational complexity; they also shed some light on how the language systems of English and Norwegian are interrelated, and they reveal aspects of the relation between source and target texts in the analysed corpus. Thus, the present project illustrates that the different fields of machine translation, contrastive language research, and translation studies have an important common denominator in the analysis of translational correspondences.

6 Acknowledgments

I thank the numerous authors and translators who produced the investigated texts, and for assistance in gaining lawful access to the texts, I am grateful to the Norwegian Ministry of Foreign Affairs, the Norwegian Petroleum Directorate, and the English-Norwegian Parallel Corpus (ENPC) Project, in particular to Jarle Ebeling, Knut Hofland, and the late Stig Johansson. Warm thanks are also due to the Centre for Advanced Study at the Norwegian Academy of Science and Letters, where I spent one year in the initial stage of this project. Also, I gratefully acknowledge useful comments from two anonymous reviewers on a previous version of this article. Finally, I am much indebted to Helge Dyvik for invaluable assistance, and in particular for tailoring software to the recording and processing of empirical data.

References

Abbott, H. Porter. 2002. *The Cambridge introduction to narrative.* Cambridge: Cambridge University Press.

Azevedo, Flávia. 2012. *The problem of codifying linguistic knowledge in two translations of shakespeare's sonnets: A corpus-based study.* Florianópolis: Federal University of Santa Catarina dissertation. Doctoral dissertation.

Barnett, James, Inderjeet Mani, Elaine Rich, Chinatsu Aone, Kevin Knight & Juan Carlos Marinez. 1991. Capturing language-specific semantic distinctions in Interlingua-Based MT. In *Proceedings of Machine Translation Summit III*, 25–32. Washington D.C.

Bhatia, Vijay K. 2010. Specification in legislative writing: Accessibility, transparency, power and control. In Malcolm Coulthard & Alison Johnson (eds.), *The Routledge handbook of forensic linguistics*, 37–50. London: Routledge.

Bowers, Frederick. 1989. *Linguistic aspects of legislative expression.* Vancouver: University of British Columbia Press.

Cao, Deborah. 2007. *Translating law: Topics in translation 33.* Clevedon: Multilingual Matters Ltd.

Chesterman, Andrew. 1997. *Memes of translation: The spread of ideas in translation theory* (Benjamins Translation Library 22). Amsterdam: Benjamins.

Chesterman, Andrew. 2005. Problems with strategies. In Krisztina Károly & Ágota Fóris (eds.), *New trends in translation studies: In honour of Kinga Klaudy*, 17–28. Budapest: Akadémiai Kiadó.

Cyrus, Lea. 2006. Building a resource for studying translation shifts. In *Proceedings of the Fifth International Conference on Linguistic Resources and Evaluation (LREC-2006)*, 1240–1245. Genoa.

Dahl, Östen. 2004. *The growth and maintenance of linguistic complexity* (Studies in Language Companion Series 71). Amsterdam: Benjamins.

Dorr, Bonnie J. 1990. Solving thematic divergences in machine translation. In *Proceedings of the 28th Annual Meeting of the ACL*, 127–134. Pittsburgh.

Dorr, Bonnie J. 1994. Machine translation divergences: A formal description and proposed solution. *Computational Linguistics* 20(4). 597–633.

Dorr, Bonnie J., Pamela W. Jordan & John W. Benoit. 1998. *A Survey of Current Paradigms in Machine Translation.* Tech. rep. University of Maryland, College Park. Technical report.

Dyvik, Helge. 1990. *The PONS project: Features of a translation system* (Skriftserie fra Institutt for fonetikk og lingvistikk 39, B). Bergen: University of Bergen.

Dyvik, Helge. 1993. *Text Pair Mapper.* Unpublished manuscript.

Dyvik, Helge. 1995. Exploiting structural similarities in machine translation. *Computers and the Humanities* 28(4/5). 225–234.

Dyvik, Helge. 1998. A translational basis for semantics. In Stig Johansson & Signe Oksefjell (eds.), *Corpora and cross-linguistic research: Theory, method, and case studies* (Language and Computers: Studies in Practical Linguistics 24), 51–86. Amsterdam: Rodopi.

Dyvik, Helge. 2003. *Translations as a Semantic Knowledge Source. Unpublished manuscript.* http://www.hf.uib.no/i/LiLi/SLF/ans/Dyvik/transknow.pdf. (last accessed on 22 June 2012).

Elgemark, Anna. 2017. *To the very end: A study of N-Rhemes in English and Swedish translations.* University of Gothenburg dissertation. Doctoral dissertation.

Francesconi, Enrico, Simonetta Montemagni, Wim Peters & Daniela Tiscornia. 2010. *Semantic processing of legal texts: Where the language of law meets the law of language.* Vol. 6036 (Lecture Notes in Artificial Intelligence). Berlin: Springer.

Hasselgård, Hilde. 1996. Some methodological issues in a contrastive study of word order in English and Norwegian. In Karin Aijmer, Bengt Aijmer & Mats Johansson (eds.), *Languages in contrast. Papers from a Symposium on Text-based Cross-linguistic Studies. Lund 4–5 March 1994* (Lund Studies in English 88), 113–126. Lund: Lund University Press.

Hasselgård, Hilde. 1998. Thematic structure in translation between English and Norwegian. In Stig Johansson & Signe Oksefjell (eds.), *Corpora and cross-linguistic research: Theory, method, and case studies* (Language and Computers: Studies in Practical Linguistics 24), 145–167. Amsterdam: Rodopi.

House, Juliane. 1997. *Translation quality assessment: A model revisited* (Tübinger Beiträge zur Linguistik 410). Tübingen: Gunter Narr.

Izquierdo, Isabel García & Josep Marco Borillo. 2000. The degree of grammatical complexity in literary texts as a translation problem. In Allison Beeby, Doris Ensinger & Marisa Presas (eds.), *Investigating translation. Selected papers from the 4th International Congress on Translation, Barcelona, 1998* (Benjamins Translation Library 32), 65–74. Amsterdam: Benjamins.

Johnsen, Åshild. 2010. *Forstå det den som kan. Semantisk modellering av juridisk regelverk med bruk av SBVR – en brobygger mellom jus og IT* MA thesis.

Johnsen, Åshild & Arne-Jørgen Berre. 2010. A bridge between legislator and technologist – Formalization in SBVR for improved quality and understanding of legal rules. In Thomas Eiter, Adil El Ghali, Sergio Fernàndez, Stijn Heymans, Thomas Krennwallner & François Lévy (eds.), *Proceedings of BuRO 2010: 1st International Workshop on Business Models, Business Rules and Ontologies*, 29–39. Brixen.

Jurafsky, Daniel & James H. Martin. 2009. *Speech and language processing. An introduction to natural language processing, computational linguistics, and speech recognition.* Upper Saddle River: Pearson Education. Second edition.

Kameyama, Megumi, Ryo Ochitani & Stanley Peters. 1991. Resolving translation mismatches with information flow. In *Proceedings of the 29th Annual Meeting of the ACL*, 193–200. Berkeley.

Laurén, Christer. 1993. *Fackspråk: Form, innehåll, funktion.* Lund: Studentlitteratur.

Leech, Geoffrey & Mick Short. 2007. *Style in fiction: A linguistic introduction to English fictional prose* (English Language Series). Harlow: Pearson Education Limited. Second edition.

Leuven-Zwart, Kitty M. van. 1989. Translation and original: Similarities and dissimilarities, i. *Target* 1(2). 151–181.

Leuven-Zwart, Kitty M. van. 1990. Translation and original: Similarities and dissimilarities, ii. *Target* 2(1). 69–95.

Macken, Lieve. 2010. *Sub-sentential alignment of translational correspondences.* Antwerp dissertation.

Mattila, Heikki E. S. 2006. *Comparative legal linguistics.* London: Ashgate.

Merkel, Magnus. 1999. *Understanding and enhancing translation by parallell text processing.* Dissertation No. 607.

Ochs, Elinor. 1997. Narrative. In Teun A. van Dijk (ed.), *Discourse as structure and process: Discourse studies: A multidisciplinary introduction 1,* 185–207. London, Thousand Oaks, & New Dehli: Sage Publications.

Palumbo, Giuseppe. 2009. *Key terms in translation studies.* London & New York: Continuum.

Silva, Norma Andrade da. 2008. *Análise da tradução do item lexical* evidence *para o português com base em um corpus jurídico.* Florianópolis: Federal University of Santa Catarina MA thesis.

Specia, Lucia. 2011. Exploiting objective annotations for measuring translation post-editing effort. In Mikel L. Forcada, Heidi Depraetere & Vincent Vandeghinste (eds.), *Proceedings of the 15th Conference of the European Association for Machine Translation,* 73–80. Leuven, Belgium.

Thunes, Martha. 1998. Classifying translational correspondences. In Stig Johansson & Signe Oksefjell (eds.), *Corpora and cross-linguistic research: Theory, method, and case studies* (Language and Computers: Studies in Practical Linguistics 24), 25–50. Amsterdam: Rodopi.

Thunes, Martha. 2011. *Complexity in translation: An english-norwegian study of two text types.* University of Bergen dissertation. https://bora.uib.no/handle/1956/5179.

Toolan, Michael. 2001. *Narrative: A critical linguistic introduction* (The INTERFACE Series). London: Routledge. Second edition.

Trujillo, Arturo. 1999. *Translation engines: Techniques for machine translation.* Berlin: Springer.

Tucunduva, Camila de Andrade. 2007. *Translating completeness: A corpus-based approach.* Florianópolis: Federal University of Santa Catarina MA thesis.

Venuti, Lawrence (ed.). 2000. *The translation studies reader.* London: Routledge.

Vik, Bjørg. 1979. *En håndfull lengsel.* Oslo: J.W. Cappelens Forlag.

Vik, Bjørg. 1979a. *Out of season and other stories.* London: Sinclair Browne. Translated by David McDuff and Patrick Browne.

Vinay, Jean-Paul & Jean Darbelnet. 1995. *Comparative stylistics of French and English: A methodology for translation* (Benjamins Translation Library 11). Amsterdam: Benjamins. Translated and edited by Juan C. Sager and M.-J. Hamel.

Chapter 6

Statistical machine translation support improves human adjective translation

Gerhard Kremer

Matthias Hartung

Sebastian Padó

Stefan Riezler

In this paper we present a study in computer-assisted translation, investigating whether non-professional translators can profit directly from automatically constructed *bilingual phrase pairs*. Our support is based on state-of-the-art statistical machine translation (SMT), consisting of a phrase table that is generated from large parallel corpora, and a large monolingual language model. In our experiment, human translators were asked to translate adjective–noun pairs in context in the presence of suggestions created by the SMT model. Our results show that SMT support results in an acceptable slowdown in translation time while significantly improving translation quality.

1 Introduction

Translating a sentence adequately from one language into another is a difficult task for humans. One of its most demanding subtasks is to select, for each source word, the best out of many possible alternative translations. This subtask is known, in particular in computational contexts, as *lexical choice* or *lexical selection* (Wu & Palmer 1994).

Bilingual lexicons which are commonly used by human translators contain by no means all information that is necessary for adequate lexical choice, which is often determined to a large degree by *context*. Often, dictionaries merely list a

Gerhard Kremer, Matthias Hartung, Sebastian Padó & Stefan Riezler. Statistical machine translation support improves human adjective translation. In Oliver Czulo & Silvia Hansen-Schirra (eds.), *Crossroads between Contrastive Linguistics, Translation Studies and Machine Translation: TC3 II*, 121–152. Berlin: Language Science Press. DOI:10.5281/zenodo.1019697

small number of translation alternatives, or a small set of particularly prototypical contexts is provided. The provided translations are neither exhaustive, nor do they provide distinguishing information on which contexts they require.

In this study, we ask whether the shortcomings of traditional dictionaries can be evaded by directly using a data structure used in most current machine translation (MT) systems, namely *phrase tables* Koehn (2010b). Phrase tables are merely bilingual lists of corresponding word sequences observed in parallel corpora, and thus provide a compact representation of the translation information inherent in a corpus, complemented with statistical information about the correspondences (e. g., frequencies or association measures). Together with the orthogonal information source of a monolingual language model, phrase tables build the core components of state-of-the-art statistical machine translation (SMT). While phrases serve the purpose of suggesting possible translations found in parallel data, the purpose of the language model is to fit the phrase translations into the larger context of the sentence. In our experiment, we will extract bilingual phrase pairs from the SMT output of *n*-best translations of the input sentence. In this manner, we directly deploy the information available from SMT to support human translators.

The current study focuses on one construction, namely the translation of adjectives in attributive position (preceding a noun). This task is fairly simple and can be manipulated more easily than sentence-level translation. At the same time, it is complex enough to be interesting: adjectives are known to be highly context-adaptive in that they express different meanings depending on the noun they modify (Sapir 1944; Justeson & Katz 1995). They also tend to take on figurative or idiomatic interpretations, again depending on the semantics of the noun in context (Miller 1998). Lexical choice is therefore nontrivial, and context-dependent translations are seldom given systematically in dictionaries. For example, consider the adjective *heavy*. In noun contexts like *use*, *traffic*, and *investment*, its canonical translation as German *schwer* is inappropriate. It might be translated as *intensiv(e Nutzung)*, *stark(er Verkehr)*, and *groß(e Investition)*.

Another reason for the restricted experimental setup is to control for translation complexity explicitly. While previous experiments on computer-aided translation could show a significant increase in productivity and quality for machine-assisted translation (especially for less qualified translators), they can only demonstrate a weak correlation between translation times and translation quality. This is due to the varying complexity of test examples and the varying degree of expertise of human translators. In our experiments, we aim to control the variable of translation complexity better, by restricting the task to translations of adjectives in noun contexts, and by providing machine assistance for these pairs only. Furthermore, the human translators in our experiments were all native speakers of the target language, German, with a similar level of expertise in the source language, English. The goal of our experiment is to provide a basis for re-interpretation of results by using a clear and simple experimental design which allows us to analyse the contribution of each variable.

Our experimental results show that, at least for translation from English into German by native German speakers, phrase table support results in an acceptable slowdown in translation time while significantly improving translation quality. This confirms the conclusions drawn in previous studies through evidence from a rigidly controlled experiment.

2 Related work

Interactive MT systems aim to aid human translators by embedding MT systems into the human translation process. Several types of assistance by MT systems have been presented: *translation memories* (Bowker 2012) provide translations of phrases recurring during a project. Such phrases have to be provided by the translator the first time they appear, and they are typically restricted to a document, a project, or a domain Zanettin (2002); Freigang (1998).

A closer interaction with human translators is explored in the TransType system of Langlais et al. (2000). Here, the machine translation component makes *sentence completion predictions* based on the decoder's search graph. The interactive tool is able to deal with human translations that diverge from the MT system's suggestions by computing an approximate match in the search graph and using this as trigger for new predictions (Barrachina et al. 2008).

Other types of assistance integrate the phrase tables of the MT systems more directly: Koehn & Haddow (2009) and Koehn (2010a) deploy a phrase-based MT system to display word or phrase *translation options* alongside the input words, ranked according to the decoder's cost model. Finally, full-sentence translations can be supplied for *post-editing* by the user.

Our approach is most closely related to the display of translation options alongside input words. Similarly to Koehn & Haddow (2009), we use a web applet to display options and record reaction times. However, our experiment is deliberately restricted to translations of adjectives in noun contexts, in order to explicitly control for translation complexity, an aspect that has been missing in previous work.

Gerhard Kremer, Matthias Hartung, Sebastian Padó & Stefan Riezler

3 Experimental Approach

This section presents an overview of the experimental design and describes how the set of stimulus items was assembled.

The study comprises two experiments. In the first experiment (cf. §4), participants performed a translation task with different types of supporting information provided by the machine translation system (no suggestion, best unigram translation of the adjective, best bigram translation of the adjective–noun pair). In order to test the impact of presenting phrase tables on translation speed, we measured reaction times between specific time points during each of the participants' translation tasks, using time gain/loss as a measure for the usefulness of machine-aided human translation as discussed in Gow (2003).

The second experiment complements the time aspect with a measure of the translation's quality (cf. §5).[1] We collected human judgements for all translations from experiment 1 on a simple three-point scale. This appears to be the only feasible strategy given our current scenario which focuses on local changes, i. e., the translation of individual words, which are unlikely to be picked up by current automatic MT evaluation measures like BLEU (Papineni et al. 2002) or TER (Snover et al. 2006).

Participants in the experiment were asked to translate an attributive adjective in sentential context (e. g., *bright* in "The boy's *bright* face, with its wide, open eyes, was contorted in agony."), given one of our set of translation support types. With German participants, we investigated translations from English into German, the participants' native language. This is the preferred type of translation direction in professional human translation, as the translator's experience of commonly used words in a particular semantic context is more extensive in the native language. In this experiment we assumed four factors to interact with translation speed and accuracy (cf. Table 1): adjective (30 different items), noun context (4 sentences per adjective, each sentence with a different adjacent noun), variability class (2 levels), and translation support (3 conditions), all of which are described in more detail below.

Given these considerations, each experimental item is an instance of an adjective in sentence context combined with some type of translation support. As shown in Table 1, we sampled a total of 120 experimental items for 30 adjectives. To avoid familiarity effects, we ensured that each participant saw only one in-

---

[1]Note that there have been ongoing debates on how translation quality can be assessed objectively House (1998). For example, see Reiß (1971) for a discussion on factors to consider when evaluating a translation.

Table 1: Partitions of the set of 30 adjective stimuli presented to each participant for the factors *variability* and *support*. Factor *context*: Each adjective was shown in 1 out of 4 sentences. Each context combines the adjective with a different noun.

Variability class	Translation support condition			Noun context
	None	Adjective unigrams	Adjective–noun bigrams	
High	5	5	5	} × 4
Low	5	5	5	

stance of each adjective. Consequently, we showed each participant exactly 30 experimental items. Each participant saw 3 differing sets of 10 adjectives in one of our three support conditions.

3.1 Variability classes

Stimuli for the translation experiment have been collected by examining the most frequent adjectives from the British National Corpus (BNC), many of which are polysemous, i. e., showing high context-dependent variability in translation (§1).

To verify this postulated relationship between corpus frequency and degree of polysemy, 200 high-frequent adjectives from the BNC were used in a measurement of translation variability. We defined the variability as the number of times an English adjective lemma in a two-word phrase was translated into a different German lemma[2] according to the EUROPARL v6 phrase table (see Koehn 2005). Two-word phrases should roughly account for adjectives in noun context (please note that the translated phrases were constrained to consist of exactly two words, but neither correspondence of nouns nor word order was checked). All translations that occurred only once for a given target lemma in the phrase table were considered spurious translations and thus were excluded.

The set of high-frequent adjectives from the BNC showed a highly significant correlation (Spearman's ρ = 0.5121) between corpus frequency and variability in translation (operationalised as the number of unique translations in the EUROPARL v6 phrase table). We divided adjectives into two classes and collected our targets from both extremes: one set that shows a particularly high variability in unique translations, and one set with a relatively low translation variability.

---

[2] Bernd Bohnet's parser (Bohnet 2010) was used to lemmatise the German words.

Hypothesis Highly variable adjectives are more difficult to translate, but translators will profit more from the presentation of phrase table information.

3.2 Adjectives and contexts

For each of the two variability classes (according to the phrase table) we selected 15 adjectives (see Appendix A). For each English adjective, we randomly sampled four full sentences from the BNC (Burnard 1995) parsed with the C&C parser (Clark & Curran 2007) as experimental items, with the adjective in attributive position directly preceding a noun so that the modified noun was different for each sentence.

In order to further minimise variation in translation times, we imposed some constraints on the sentences. Their length was restricted both in terms of words (15–20) and characters (80–100). Also, sentences with HTML tags were excluded and sentences were manually checked for tagging errors and cases where the noun was part of a compound expression. Selecting a set of four sentence contexts for each of the full set of 30 adjectives, our resulting set of experimental items summed up to 120 (see Table 1).

Clearly, our setup leads to a *domain difference* between the sentences to be translated (sampled from the BNC) and the phrase table (drawn from EUROPARL). This makes the task of the model more difficult, and we might fear that the BNC bigrams we want to translate are very rare or even unseen in EUROPARL.

We made the decision to adopt this setting nevertheless, since it corresponds to the standard situation for machine translation. There is only a very small number of domains (including newswire, parliamentary proceedings, and legal texts) in which the large parallel corpora exist that are necessary to train SMT models. In the translation of texts from virtually all other domains, the models are faced with new domains. Being able to show an improvement for this across-domain scenario is, in our opinion, significantly more relevant than for the within-domain setting.

3.3 Translation support

Finally, we provided three kinds of translation support to the participants: (a) no support, (b) the list of translations for the adjective unigram produced by the SMT system, and (c) the list of translations for the adjective–noun bigram produced by the SMT system. In addition to adjective translations proposed by the system in the unigram condition, suggested noun translations for the target sentence might further aid the human translator in finding the most appropriate adjective in that context, in particular for collocation-like phrases.

We presented three distinct candidate translations as supports. We chose three as a number which is high enough to give translators at least some insight into the polysemy of target adjectives but still not enough to overload them and to slow down the translation process too much. The candidate translations were shown in the order in which they were extracted from the n-best list (with $n = 3,000$) produced by the Moses[3] (Koehn et al. 2007) MT system (trained and tuned on EUROPARL v6) that decoded each target sentence. See (1) for an illustration (target adjective: *bright*).

(1) The boy's **bright** face, with its wide, open eyes, was contorted in agony.

Unigram support:	*Bigram support:*	
verheißungsvoll	verheißungsvolles	(Angesicht)
positiv	positives	(Angesicht)
gut	verheißungsvolles	(Gesicht)

Specifically, phrase alignments were looked up for each n-best sentence given as output for a target sentence, and the corresponding translated adjective and noun were used for the unigram or the bigram list, respectively. In case of phrase alignments containing multiple words (instead of just one), word alignments were looked up in the phrase table and if in this manner English target words could be uniquely paired with translated German words, these pairs were chosen. Three differing unigrams and three differing bigrams were selected in order of appearance in the n-best list and lemmatised manually.

In case this procedure yielded less than three differing unigrams, the missing adjective unigrams were chosen from the unigram list of the adjective in the other three sentence contexts. Similarly, in case less than three bigrams were found, adjective unigrams produced by the MT system for that sentence were combined with nouns in the bigram list of that sentence (in order of appearance in the list). Candidate words for unigrams and bigrams were only selected from the n-best lists if they plausibly could have been tagged as adjectives or nouns, respectively.

Hypothesis Presenting unigram translations leads to faster and more appropriate translations. Bigram phrases will produce the most appropriate translations, even if translating in this condition might be slower due to the need to read through more complex translation suggestions.

---

[3]http://www.statmt.org/moses

4 Experiment 1: The time course of machine-supported human translation

4.1 Experimental procedure

The experiment was realized as a dynamic web page, using an internet browser as our experimental platform and administering the experiment over the internet. The advantage of this method is that we have quick access to a large pool of participants. In psycholinguistics, the reliability of this type of setup for reading time studies has been demonstrated by Keller et al. (2009). Our setup is also similar to crowdsourcing, a recent trend in computational linguistics to use naive internet users for solving language tasks (Snow et al. 2008; Mohammad & Turney 2013). Unlike almost all crowdsourcing work, however, we did not use a crowdsourcing platform like Amazon Mechanical Turk and were specifically interested in the time course of participants' reactions.

The 30 experimental items were presented in three blocks of ten items each. Each block corresponded to one support condition (none, unigram, bigram). The participant could take a break between blocks, but not between items. Both the order of the blocks and the order of the items within each block were randomised.

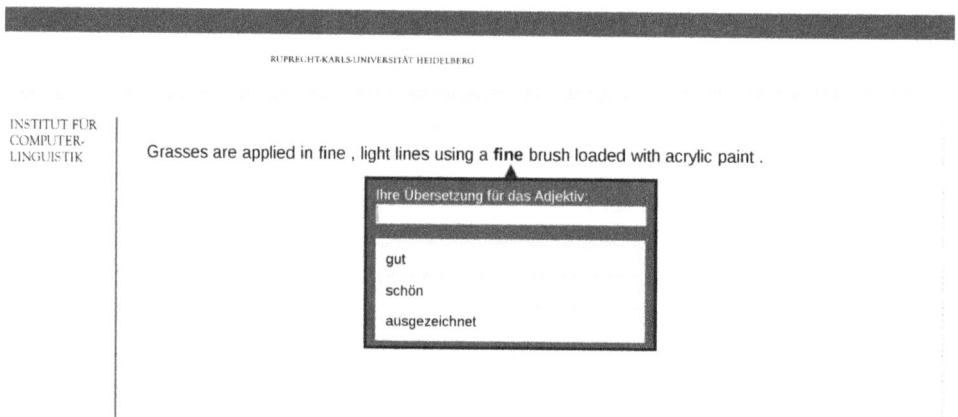

Figure 1: Screen shot of translation setup

For each item, the experiment proceeded in four steps:

1. Sentence is shown to participant (plain text, no indication of the target adjective).

2. When the participant presses a key, the target adjective to be translated is marked in boldface. Concurrently, the translation support is shown as well as a window for entering the translation (shown in Figure 1).

3. The participant starts to type the translation.

4. The participant marks the current item as finished by pressing return. The experiment proceeds directly to step 1 of the next item.

The central question in this procedure is how to measure our variable of interest, namely the length of the period that participants require to *decide on* a translation. The total time of steps 2 to 4 is a very unreliable indicator of this variable. It involves the time for reading and the time for typing. Since participants can be expected to read and type with different speeds, the total time will presumably show a very high variance, making it difficult to detect differences among the support conditions. Instead, we decided to measure the time from the start of step 2 to the start of step 3. We assume that this period, which we will call *response time*, comprises the following cognitive tasks: (a) reading the bold-faced target; (b) reading the translation suggestions; and (c) deciding on a translation. We believe that this response time, which corresponds fairly closely to the concept of *décalage* in sight translation, is a reasonable approximation of our variable of interest. This assessment rests on two assumptions. The first one is that at the time when a participant starts typing, they have essentially decided on a translation. We acknowledge that this assumption is occasionally false (in the case of subsequent corrections). The second assumption is that it is not practicable to separate translation time from reading time for the target adjective and the translation suggestions, since presumably the translation process starts already during reading (John 1996; Carl & Dragsted 2012).

To avoid possible errors introduced into the time measurements by a remotely administered experiment, all time stamps during the course of an experiment are measured by the participant's machine, similar to Keller et al. (2009). It is only at the end of each experiment that these time stamps are transmitted back to the server and evaluated. In this manner, the time measurements are as accurate as the users' machines, which usually means at least a millisecond resolution. We also applied the usual methods to remove remaining outlier participants (cf. §4.3).

4.2 Participants

We solicited native German speakers as participants mostly through personal acquaintance; no professional translators participated. Participants were not paid for the experiment. We had a total of 103 participants. 87 of these were from Germany, 13 from Switzerland, and 1 each from Luxembourg and Austria.[4] 47 were male and 56 female. The mean age was 32, and the mean number of years of experience with English (comprising both instruction and practical use) was 16.1. Thus, the participant population consisted of proficient speakers of English. This is also supported by the participants' self-judgements of their proficiency in English on a five-point scale (1: very high, 5: very low), where the mean was 1.8.

4.3 Analysis of response time

We removed outliers following standard procedure. First, 18 participants who did not complete all experimental items were completely removed from consideration. From the response times for the remaining 85 participants, we removed all measurements below the 15th percentile ($t < 2.4$ s) and above the 85th percentile ($t > 12.9$ s) for each experimental item. These outliers have a strong chance of resulting from invalid trials. Participants with a very fast response time may have used their computer's copy–paste function frequently to simply copy one of the suggested translations into the response field. Participants with very slow response times may have been distracted.

Recall that each of the 85 participants saw one instance of each of the target adjectives, and that our materials contain 12 experimental items for each adjective: 3 support conditions combined with 4 context sentences. Having further discarded 30 % of our measurements, we were left with an average of (85 / 12) * $0.7 \approx 5$ measurements for each experimental item. In our analysis, we use the mean of these individual measurements.

Our data set contains independent variables of two distinct classes (Jaeger 2008). In the first class, we have two variables (variability class and the support condition, cf. Table 1) which are *fixed effects*: we assume that these variables explain variation in the response time. The second class comprises a number of *random effects* which we expect to introduce variance but whose overall effect should be essentially random. This class includes the context sentence and the identities of adjective, participant, and context.

---

[4]One participant declined to state their country.

We therefore analysed our data with a linear mixed effects model (Hedeker 2005). Linear mixed effects models are a generalisation of linear regression models and have the form

$$y = X\beta + Zb + \epsilon \text{ with } \quad b \sim \mathcal{N}(0, \sigma^2 \Sigma), \ \epsilon \sim \mathcal{N}(0, \sigma^2 I) \tag{6.2}$$

where X is a set of variables that are fixed effects, Z a set of variables that are random effects, and ϵ an error term. The first term in the model $(X\beta)$ corresponds to a normal regression model—the coefficients β for the variables X are unconstrained. The second term, Zb accounts for the nature of random effects Z by requiring their coefficients b to be drawn from a normal distribution centred around zero. The model was implemented in the R statistical environment[5] with the package lme4[6].

4.4 Results and discussion

Table 2: Mean response times for all support conditions × translation variabilities

	Low variability	High variability	Overall
No support	5.512	5.603	5.558
Unigram support	5.885	5.335	5.615
Bigram support	6.118	6.120	6.119

Table 2 shows mean response times for the six conditions corresponding to all combinations of the levels of the fixed effects, variability and support. All conditions result in mean response times between 5.5 and 6.1 seconds. Figure 2 visualises robust statistics about the data in the form of *notched box-and-whiskers-plots* (McGill et al. 1978). The box indicates the median and the upper and lower quartiles, and the whiskers show the range of values. The notches (i. e., the "dents" in the boxes) offer a rough guide to significance of difference of medians: if the notches of two boxes do not overlap, this offers evidence of a statistically significant difference (95 % confidence interval) between the medians.

We make two main observations on these boxplots: (a) comparing Figure 2(a) with Figure 2(b), there does not appear to be a significant influence of variability; (b) comparing the different conditions in Figure 2(c), there appears to be a

---

[5]http://R-project.org
[6]http://lme4.r-forge.r-project.org

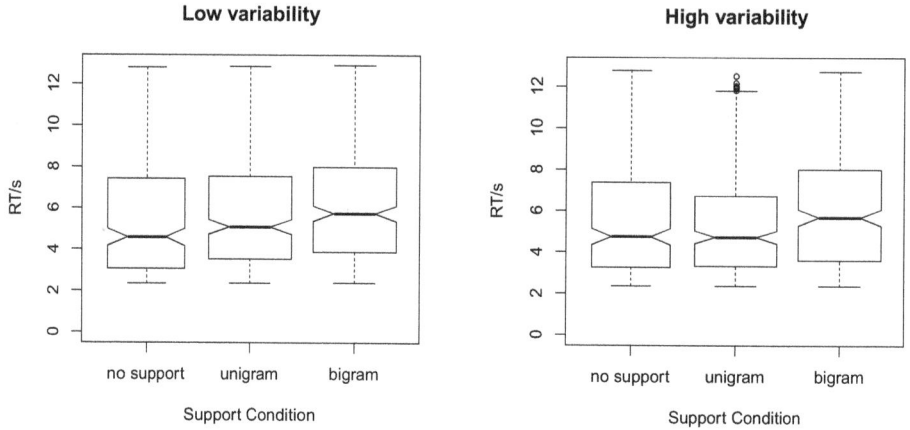

(a) low-variability adjectives

(b) high-variability adjectives

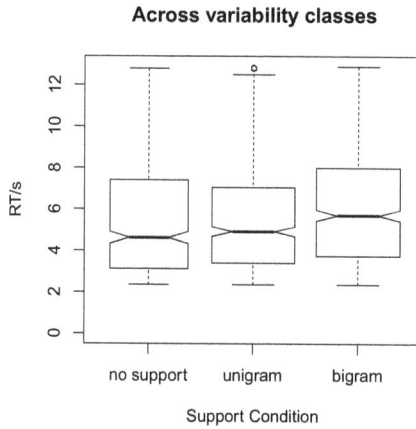

(c) across variability classes

Figure 2: Distribution of response times in all experiment conditions

significant influence of the support condition. In all three boxplots, we find that bigram support leads to significantly longer response times than no support and unigram support, which in turn are not significantly different.

These observations were validated by an analysis of our mixed effects in which we determined the significance of the individual coefficients using a likelihood ratio test. Selecting the condition "high variability/no support" as the intercept, the coefficient for bigram support (0.69, SE: 0.15) is significantly different from zero ($p < 0.001$) while the coefficient for unigram support (0.11, SE: 0.15) is not. The coefficient for low variability (0.13, SE: 0.24) is also not significantly different from zero.

In sum, one of the two hypotheses we formulated in §3 does not hold, while the other one holds at least partially. Contrary to our expectations, we do not find an effect of variability. That is, the adjectives with many possible translations are as difficult to translate as those with few possible translations. We believe that this effect is absent because we present all adjectives in a rich sentence context, as a consequence of which usually just a fairly small number of translations is reasonable, independent of whether the adjective, as a lemma, has a very large number of translation candidates or not.

Regarding the influence of the different levels of translation support, there is no significant difference between no support and unigram support: reading three additional words does not seem to interfere greatly with the time course of translation (although note that there is a tendency towards a difference between the low and high variability adjectives for this level). Bigram support, on the other hand, does add a statistically significant delay to the response time. However, the overall size of this effect, namely 0.5 to 0.6 seconds per translation, accounts for just 10 % of the response time, and only a very small percentage of the total translation time. Therefore, this effect should not be an obstacle to presenting translators with bigram support, should it be beneficial for the quality of the outcome.

5 Experiment 2: Translation quality rating

The second experiment investigates possible effects of different support conditions on translation quality. For this purpose, we elicited quality ratings from human annotators for all translations and support suggestions from the first experiment. We first describe the experimental procedure of this survey in §5.1, before we thoroughly analyse and discuss the obtained quality rating data in §5.2.

Gerhard Kremer, Matthias Hartung, Sebastian Padó & Stefan Riezler

5.1 Experimental procedure

We elicited quality ratings for all translations collected in the first experiment after eliminating the reaction time outliers (cf. §4.3). This includes the union of all translations entered by participants and all suggestions provided by the system. The full set consisted of 1,334 adjective instances to be rated, including inflected forms and incorrect spellings of the same adjective.[7] The sentences were presented to all raters in the same randomised order. For each sentence, the corresponding adjective translations and support adjectives were shown in alphabetical order alongside the sentence and the target adjective's head noun translation (which had been manually produced by one of the authors). The English target adjective was explicitly marked (surrounded by stars: '*') in the sentence context. See (3) and (4) for an illustration.

(3)   As they reached the [...] tunnel , fresh air drifted in and Devlin took a *deep* breath .
   tief   Atemzug
   tiefen   Atemzug
   tiefer   Atemzug

(4)   But after three weeks of this Potter claimed to have lost nothing but his *good* humour .
   frohe   Stimmung
   gute   Stimmung
   positiv Stimmung

Each adjective instance was judged by eight human raters who were native speakers of German with a (computational) linguistics background. They were asked to rate the quality of each adjective translation in the given sentence context and for the predefined head noun translation. For their judgements, we instructed our raters to apply a three-point Likert scale according to the following conventions:

- 3: perfect translation in context of sentence and noun

- 2: acceptable translation, while suboptimal in some aspect

- 1: subjectively unacceptable translation

---

[7]If the same adjective lemma occurred in various forms as a translation in the same sentence due to inflection or spelling mistakes, the raters were instructed to assign the same rating to all these forms.

Our notion of "suboptimal translation" (level 2 on the scale) includes two aspects: core semantic mismatches (the meaning of the adjective does not fully reflect all aspects of the best translation) and collocational incongruence (the translation of the adjective does not yield a well-formed collocation in combination with the respective noun). The second translations listed for the two following examples illustrate semantic mismatch (5) and collocational incongruence (6):

(5) But there is a *common* belief that low-rise building will increase the urban sprawl.
    verbreiteter Glaube   (3.00)
    allgemeiner Glaube   (2.67)

(6) Until now, he had managed that, with a *heavy* hand and crude peasant humour.
    harte Hand   (3.00)
    starke Hand   (2.50)

Numbers in parentheses state the average quality of the translation as given by our human raters. For our detailed rating guidelines see the appendix (Appendix B).

5.2 Analysis and discussion

The basis for all analyses in this section are the experimental items without reaction time outliers (as described in §4.3) and the quality ratings of these experimental items (as described in §5.1).

Recall that in our translation experiment translators were always free to choose a translation from the support items or, alternatively, choose a translation on their own. We will use the terms *support translations* and *creative translations* to refer to these two options. *Support suggestions* denote all support items provided in a specific experimental condition, irrespective of whether or not one of these candidates was selected by the participants as a translation. Table 3 illustrates these three terms by example for a sentence taken from the experiment data.

More specifically, for the experiment conditions "unigram support" and "bigram support", *support translations* are defined as those items that both appeared as *support suggestions* (in the respective support condition) and were also selected as translations by participants. Items that were produced by participants, but did not appear in the *support suggestions*, are considered as *creative translations*.

Table 3: Example translations of different types for the sentence: "In other words, it is a measure of the scale and likelihood of a *large* accident." Numbers in parentheses: the number of participants who produced an item.

	No support	Unigram support		Bigram support
Support suggestions	–	groß breit hoch	großer großes große	(Unfall) (Unglück) (Katastrophe)
Support transla- tions	groß (2)	groß (4)		groß (4)
Creative translations	riesig (1) schwer (1) schwerwiegend (1)	schwer (1) weitreichend (1)		schlimm (1)

The "no support" condition is a special case, as in this condition all translations were freely produced by the participants, i. e., without the possibility of relying on any support. To maintain the distinction between creative and support translations, we computed the union of all adjectives contained in the unigram support and bigram support and compared the freely produced translations against this set. Thus, the translations found in this union were considered as support translations, all the other translations as creative. Given these differences in calculation, an exact comparison of the ratio of creative translations will be possible for the unigram and bigram condition only. Nevertheless, we consider the proportion of creative translations in the "no support" condition as defined above to be meaningful in that it provides an impression of the range of the spectrum of human translations that is not covered by SMT support material.

5.2.1 Inter-rater correlation

We started by analysing the agreement among the raters. We computed an inter-rater correlation coefficient using leave-one-out re-sampling (Weiss & Kulikowski 1991). For this analysis, we first (manually) mapped all inflected word forms and incorrect spellings to the same adjective lemma. This should reduce the influence of morphological variation on the magnitude of the correlation coefficient. Second, as proposed by Mitchell & Lapata (2010), we correlated the

Table 4: Overall translation quality rating means for all experiment conditions

	Translation quality mean
No support	2.53
Unigram support	2.60
Bigram support	2.65

judgements of each rater with those of all the other raters to obtain an averaged individual correlation coefficient (ICC) for each rater in terms of Spearman's ρ. This resulted in an overall correlation coefficient of $\rho = 0.43$ for the eight raters. As we found substantial deviation of two raters from all others[8], we decided to discard their judgements. Averaging the ICCs of the remaining six raters resulted in an overall inter-rater correlation of $\rho = 0.47$. This outcome indicates that translation quality rating is a difficult task, but that our raters still produced reasonably consistent ratings. We then computed the average quality rating for each adjective instance by including the judgement scores of the best six raters. We use these averages as the basis for analysing the overall translation quality between experiment conditions in the next section and for all subsequent analyses.

5.2.2 Overall translation quality

We next consider the overall translation quality for the different support conditions. Figure 3 visualises the translation quality data as a boxplot (cf. §4.4). The medians of the quality ratings for no support and unigram support differ substantially, with non-overlapping notches, indicating a statistically significant difference in average quality ratings between these two conditions. Comparing the conditions "unigram support" and "bigram support", their medians are almost identical. However, the variance is smaller in the bigram condition (smaller box), and there are noticeably fewer outliers at the lower end (shorter whisker). Thus, although there is no significant difference in terms of average translation quality, there is a tendency of bigram support to produce fewer medium and low quality translations. The corresponding means are shown in Table 4.

These findings are corroborated by our mixed effects model analysis: analogously to the analysis of response times (see §4.3), we assumed that the factors

---

[8]Their ICCs are the only ones below 0.4, while the coefficient of their pairwise correlation is extremely low ($\rho = 0.24$; cf. the full IRC matrix in §C).

Quality Ratings

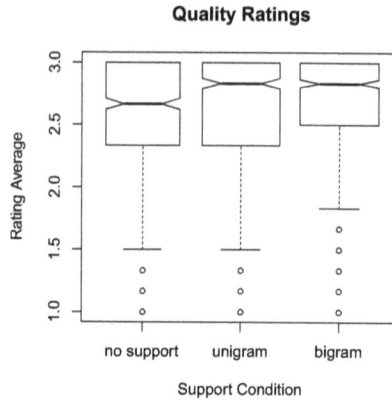

Figure 3: Distribution of averaged translation quality ratings

"variability class" and "experiment condition" are fixed effects. We used the same factors as in the response time analysis as random effects and added rater identity. But, as in the present analysis the "quality rating" (1–3) was used as the dependent variable in the model, we applied a model tailored to categorial response variables, namely the cumulative link mixed model (Christensen 2011), provided by the R package ordinal[9]. Selecting unigram support as the base level, the model yields significant differences both when compared to no support ($p < 0.001$) and bigram support ($p < 0.01$).

These results suggest that the quality of our participants' translations, while being already rather high in the absence of any support, benefits from more detailed support material. Unigram and bigram support tend to have a slightly different influence, however: unigram support primarily seems to trigger better translations as compared to no support, while there is still a number of bad translations that cannot be ruled out in this condition. Admittedly, bigram support does not yield a further quality improvement, but contributes to a reduction of poor translations.

5.2.3 Ratio of creative to support translations

An essential fact for interpreting the results of §5.2.2 is that participants were always free to forgo the support suggestions and enter their own translations. Thus, the analysis is still inconclusive, since it does not take into account how

---

[9]http://www.cran.r-project.org/web/packages/ordinal

many support suggestions were actually accepted or overridden by the participants, and what exactly contributed to the augmentation in translation quality
for unigram and bigram support. In fact, the quality gains observed under unigram and bigram support might be artefacts due to exhaustive use of creative
translations (although creativity might have been triggered by presenting support suggestions). In that case, the direct contribution of the support suggestions
to the participants' translation performance would be questionable.

For this reason, we investigate the ratio of creative translations from different
perspectives, starting from the level of participants. Afterwards, we broaden the
scope to include the levels of sentences and individual translations.

5.2.3.1 Analysis by Participants
We first investigated the proportion of par-
ticipants who produced at least one creative translation. Table 5 shows that in
the absence of any support, more than 70 % of the participants occasionally produced a translation that is not contained in the unigram and bigram support
suggestions. In the unigram condition, the proportion of creative participants
amounts to 58.8 %, decreasing with more extensive support material to 54.1 % in
the bigram condition.

Table 5: Number (and rate) of creative participants in each experiment
condition

	No. participants with $\geq$ 1 creative translation	
No support	62	(72.9 %)
Unigram support	50	(58.8 %)
Bigram support	46	(54.1 %)

Table 6: Creativity rate per participant in the "support" conditions (unigram and bigram)

	Rate of creative translations per participant							
	0 %	1–10 %	11–20 %	21–30 %	31–40 %	41–50 %	51–60 %	> 60 %
No. Participants	23	13	25	15	8	0	1	0

To obtain a more detailed picture, we also considered the individual creativity rate per participant: did participants systematically accept (or reject) the support suggestions, or did they make use of them in an intelligent manner? To address this issue, the creativity rate was measured as the number of creative translations of the respective participant in relation to all their individual translations under unigram and bigram support. Table 6 shows that 23 (about 27 % of the whole group of) participants never produced a creative translation, but always used a translation that is included in the set of support suggestions. The other participants exhibit creativity rates that are distributed within a region of moderate creativity (with one outlier, a participant who came up with creative translations in more than half of the items she translated).

Combined with the data presented in Table 5, this indicates that in both "support" conditions (unigram and bigram), only little more than half of the participants ever decided to override the support material, without individually overusing this opportunity. On the other hand, we do not observe any participants who systematically reject the support material provided.

5.2.3.2 Analysis by Sentences

On the sentence level, we are primarily interested in whether some sentences show a stronger tendency to evoke creative translations than others. Therefore, along the lines of our analysis on the level of participants, we first investigated the proportion of sentences with at least one creative translation, before taking a closer look on the creativity rate per sentence.

Table 7: Proportions of sentences with creative translations in each experiment condition

	Sentences with $\geq$ 1 creative translation	
No support	71.7 %	(86)
Unigram support	36.7 %	(44)
Bigram support	39.2 %	(47)

In the "no support" condition, our group of participants produced translations that are neither contained in the unigram nor in the bigram support in more than 70 % of the sentences (cf. Table 7). In the "unigram support" condition, 36.7 % of the sentences provoked a creative translation. Interestingly, however, this proportion is slightly higher in the "bigram support" condition.

We believe that this effect is not just random variation: we encountered 15 sentences in the data which triggered at least one creative translation in bigram support, but none in unigram support. Analysing these sentences, we discovered two major reasons for their higher disposition towards creative translations in bigram support. First, some of the support suggestions contained in the unigram set are not included in the bigram set – (7) illustrates this phenomenon, where *angemessen* would be categorised as a creative translation based on bigram support (on the right), but not based on unigram support (on the left).

(7) The show was the best it had ever been , and its *proper* length , for once.

Unigram support:	*Bigram support:*	
richtig	richtige	(Zeit)
ordnungsgemäß	richtige	(Dauer)
angemessen	ordnungsgemäße	(Länge)

Second, on the one hand, in the context of ambiguous or abstract nouns that are hard to translate when given just unigram support, some participants apparently tended towards accepting one of the unigram suggestions without reasoning too much about its collocational fit with the best translation of the context noun. On the other hand, in some cases the bigram support suggestions include a good translation of the noun in combination with an incongruous adjective suggestion. Consider (8), where all participants translated *great* as *groß* in the "unigram support" condition, while during bigram support, we also encountered the creative translation *hoch* (high), which is a better collocational match for *Genauigkeit* (accuracy) and *Präzision* (precision) in German than *groß*.

(8) Someone who hits the ball with *great* accuracy on the volley and with [...] .

Unigram support:	*Bigram support:*	
groß	große	(Genauigkeit)
großartig	große	(Sorgfalt)
riesig	große	(Präzision)

The creativity rate per sentence measures the fraction of creative translations in all translations that were collected for the respective sentence in both the conditions "unigram support" and "bigram support". Table 8 summarises the results. For about half the sentences, no creative translation was produced at all, i. e., the participants were satisfied with the support material being provided. 75 % of the sentences exhibit a creativity rate of 25 % or below. For only eight sentences, the majority of translations (> 50 %) was found to be creative. Apparently, the

Gerhard Kremer, Matthias Hartung, Sebastian Padó & Stefan Riezler

availability of support limits the need for creative translations, regarding both the number of sentences that exhibit creative translations and the creativity rate within these sentences.

Table 8: Creativity rate per sentence in the "support" conditions (unigram and bigram)

	Rate of creative translations per sentence				
	0 %	1–25 %	26–50 %	51–75 %	76–100 %
No. sentences	61	28	23	6	2

5.2.3.3 Analysis by Translations   Finally, we investigated the creativity rate on the basis of individual translations. The results of this analysis are shown in Table 9.[10] Comparing the creativity rate across the three experimental conditions, we can observe a pattern that is in line with our preceding analyses: for unigram and bigram support, only 12.3 % and 13.4 % of the translations, respectively, were found to be creative. Considering freely produced translations, we encounter a relatively high creativity rate (41.6 %). The latter percentage is also interesting from a different perspective, as it provides an estimate of the coverage of the support material: almost 60 % of the translations produced by our participants in the "no support" condition are covered either by the unigram or the bigram suggestions.

Table 9: Overall creativity ratio for experiment data without response time outliers

	No. translations	Creative translations
No support	546	41.6 %
Unigram support	614	13.4 %
Bigram support	624	12.3 %

Given that the support material in the translation experiment for each target adjective comprised only the three most likely translations as extracted from the SMT n-best list (cf. §3.3), the question arises whether support coverage would

---

[10]Note that the absolute number of translations as stated in the first column of the table differs across the experimental conditions due to the elimination of response time outliers (cf. §4.3).

improve if more suggestions from the MT system were included in the translation support. To tackle this question, we also extracted the five-best and ten-best unigram translations for the test adjectives from the Moses output.[11] As expected, the creativity rate drops from 13.4 % for the top 3 support to 10.4 % for the top 5 support (64 creative translations) and finally to 7.7 % for the top 10 support (47 creative translations).

5.2.3.4 Summary   Our creativity analysis based on participants, sentences and individual translations yields a coherent pattern: (a) translators use support translations for both unigram and bigram support in a total of almost 90 % of the cases; (b) translators use creative translations only for a subset of sentences (less than 40 %) when translation support is given; (c) about 60 % of the participants exhibit moderate individual creativity rates of between 11 % and 40 %. These findings suggest that creative translations, despite their sparsity, are used deliberately in particular cases. This leads to the question whether creative translations have an effect on translation quality, i. e., whether the quality of individual creative translations is higher compared to the corresponding support suggestions.

5.2.4 Translation quality of creative translations and support suggestions

Our latest analysis compares the overall average quality of creative translations, support translations and support suggestions in both "support" conditions. The results are shown in Table 10. Our first observation is that bigrams outperform unigrams in all the three categories, which is in line with the results of our overall quality analysis in §5.2.2.

Next, we compare the results for the different columns. The third column, "support suggestions", can be considered as a baseline of randomly picking one

---

[11] This required consulting a 50,000-best list to obtain enough distinct translations for most cases. Still, for 8 items ($\approx$ 6.7 %) we found less than five translations, and for 81 items (67.5 %) less than ten translations.

Table 10: Average quality ratings for complete data set

	Creative translations	Support translations	Support suggestions
Unigram support	2.40	2.64	2.46
Bigram support	2.42	2.68	2.52

of the support suggestions. Such a strategy would achieve an average quality of 2.46 (with unigram support) or 2.52 (with bigram support). These numbers indicate that the support material provided to our participants was of good average quality. In fact, the quality of the support suggestions is only slightly below the average of our human participants translating without support (2.53, cf. Table 4).

The "support translations" column shows that our human translators did a good job picking out the best translations from all support suggestions, increasing the quality by 0.18 (unigram condition) and 0.16 points (bigram condition). In contrast, and somewhat surprisingly, the average quality of all creative translations taken together falls slightly below the baseline in both the unigram (2.40) and the bigram (2.42) condition. Thus, it appears that creative translations cannot be assumed a priori to be of high quality.

Table 11: Average quality for experimental items that triggered creative translations

	No. instances (creative trans.)	Creative translations	Support translations	Support suggestions
Unigram support	82	2.40	2.17	1.83
Bigram support	77	2.42	2.15	1.95

A possible explanation for this finding is that creative translations were produced in particular for difficult adjectives to be translated. If this were true, we would expect that the support translations for these sentences should perform even worse. To test this prediction, we repeated our analysis for the *creativity-triggering experimental items* (i. e., the subset of experimental items for which at least one participant produced a creative translation). The results in Table 11 show that this is indeed the case: the quality of all support suggestions for these sentences is below 2, and even picking the best candidates (column "support translations") yields an average quality of below 2.2. The creative translations, with an average quality of around 2.4,[12] outperform the support suggestions and translations significantly ($p < 0.001$ for both contrasts—as determined by an approximate randomisation test, cf. Noreen 1989).[13] This means that, overall, trans-

---

[12]Note that in our experimental setting three support suggestions were provided for each experimental item. To compare the average qualities of creative translations and support suggestions, we triplicated the rating score for each creative translation.

[13]The significance analysis was performed on a slightly smaller number of experimental items (69 for unigram support, 71 for bigram support), as for some of the items, none of the participants selected a support suggestion. Average quality of the creative translations in these cases: 2.38.

lators not only use good supports when appropriate, but they are also able to recognise bad supports and replace them with better suited creative translations. For illustration, consider the following two examples where creative translations outperform the support translations (i. e., support suggestions that were actually selected by at least one participant):

(9) What does a *large* attendance at Easter communion imply?

Support translations:		*Creative translations:*	
groß	(2.00)	zahlreich	(2.17)
hoch	(1.83)		
breit	(1.83)		

(10) He delivered a *great* kick backwards at Terry's shins, the edge of his boots like iron.

Support translations:		*Creative translations:*	
groß	(1.5)	kräftig	(2.67)
		heftig	(2.50)
		großartig	(2.33)
		gut	(2.33)
		gut gelungen	(2.33)
		fest	(2.33)
		schwer	(2.17)

These examples show all support translations (left column) and creative translations (right column) for the respective sentence in all conditions (and their average qualities).

5.2.5 Summary

Across all analyses, we clearly see a positive effect of SMT support on human translation performance. Our initial hypothesis is largely confirmed, as we found a significant gain in translation quality for unigram support compared to the "no support" condition. Beyond that, bigram support does not yield a further increase in translation quality, but still tends to help excluding poor translations.[14] We found that the generally high quality of the SMT suggestions is the primary source of this effect, as our participants relied on the provided support suggestions in almost 90 % of the cases.

---

[14]Translating text segments of more than one word as natural "translation units" is exactly what is proposed in translation studies (see, e. g., Toury 1995), and which our study corroborates.

However, high quality support material is not sufficient on its own to explain the improvement in translation quality in the two "support" conditions. We found that the human translators need to review the support suggestions to (a) pick the most appropriate of the suggestions and (b) if there are no appropriate ones, suggest a creative translation. Even though the latter case occurred only for a relatively small subset of the data, in these cases the participants' creative translations turned out to be significantly superior to the support suggestions. At the same time, (b) appears to be a difficult task, given that a fraction of about a third of our participants never produced any creative translations at all. It seems, therefore, that the decision when to accept and when to override the support suggestions is the most challenging task for many participants in computer-aided translation. In contrast, (a) appears quite feasible, as the quality of our participants' selections is well beyond a "random selection" baseline and consistently so across participants.

6 General discussion and conclusion

In this study, our goal was to investigate the usefulness of adjective–noun translations generated by MT systems and presented to non-professional human translators as unigram or bigram suggestions during the translation of individual adjectives in sentence context. This choice makes for an interesting translation task, due to the meaning variation of adjectives in context, while allowing us to control translation variability fairly strongly.

The first variable we measured was translation time. In presenting three suggestions in both the unigram and bigram conditions, we found a statistically significant increase in response times for the bigram support condition but not the unigram support condition. Even for the bigram condition, however, the mean response time increased only by around 0.6 seconds (i. e., by $\approx 10\,\%$) compared to no support. Contrary to our intuitions, the level of translation variability as defined by phrase table counts had no statistically significant influence on response times. However, in interaction with the support condition "unigram" we partly observed an effect we had predicted: highly variable adjectives were translated faster than low-variability adjectives in the unigram condition.

The second variable of interest in the translation process was translation quality. We elicited judgements on a three-point scale from human annotators. Although the inter-rater correlation in the judgement experiment was mediocre, the average quality ratings in the two support conditions were statistically significantly higher than without support. Furthermore, in the bigram condition, participants produced the least amount of low-quality translations. Further analysis established that the SMT-produced support suggestions were generally of high quality, and were accepted well by human translators, who were consistently able to pick the best translations from among the candidates.

In summary, we found a strong case in favour of supporting non-professional translators with SMT support, provided that the quality of the support material is high enough that just choosing between support suggestions is a reasonable strategy. In terms of the choice between unigram and bigram support, there is a substantial improvement in quality already for unigram support without a significant accompanying translation delay. For bigram support, the time to read through the suggestions becomes a significant (although still small) factor, but pays off with a further reduction in poor translations.

Recall that we obtained these results by presenting three support candidates for each adjective to be translated. This is of course not the only possible choice. We found that longer n-best lists will cover a larger fraction of translations (90 % for 5 suggestions), but we would expect that more suggestions will slow down the translation process considerably, clutter the translation interface, and make translators even more reluctant to dismiss poor suggestions.

Machine-supported human translation is an open field with ample potential for creative strategies to combine the complementary strengths of man and machine. In future work, we would like to explore ways to generalise our experimental setup to larger phrases without giving up the control over translation complexity that we have utilised in this experiment.

Gerhard Kremer, Matthias Hartung, Sebastian Padó & Stefan Riezler

Appendix

A Adjective stimuli set

Table 12: The set of 30 adjectives used as stimuli in the translation support experiment

Low variability	High variability
lovely	final
bright	essential
formal	hard
dark	large
complex	common
fresh	proper
ordinary	real
rich	main
deep	present
recent	strong
heavy	serious
immediate	major
domestic	clear
separate	great
likely	good

B Guidelines for quality rating

- If more than one inflected form of the same adjective lemma occurs as a translation in the same sentence: assign the same rating.

- In case of spelling mistakes: rate the adjective as if it was spelled correctly.

- If more than one word has been produced as a translation: consider only the (first) adjective.

- If the only translation produced is not an adjective, but a noun: rate the appropriateness of the noun as a translation for the adjective in the given context (e. g.: _major_ → _Haupt-_).

- Rate the appropriateness of each adjective only in combination with the translation given for its head noun.

- Try to use the full scale (1–3) to rate the quality of all adjective translations per sentence. However, in case of sentences with only a few different adjective translations: if all of them are bad, it is not necessary to exhaust the full scale.

- Try to work swiftly.

C Quality rating: inter-rater correlation matrix

Table 13: Inter-rater correlation matrix for our full set of raters in the judgement experiment

	R1	R2	R3	R4	R5	R6	R7	R8	ICC
R1	1.00	0.40	0.36	0.24	0.38	0.38	0.36	0.41	0.36
R2	0.40	1.00	0.49	0.42	0.50	0.47	0.41	0.48	0.45
R3	0.36	0.49	1.00	0.38	0.44	0.47	0.51	0.45	0.44
R4	0.24	0.42	0.38	1.00	0.41	0.42	0.37	0.43	0.38
R5	0.38	0.50	0.44	0.41	1.00	0.50	0.39	0.49	0.44
R6	0.38	0.47	0.47	0.42	0.50	1.00	0.49	0.49	0.46
R7	0.36	0.41	0.51	0.37	0.39	0.49	1.00	0.47	0.43
R8	0.41	0.48	0.45	0.43	0.49	0.49	0.47	1.00	0.46

Acknowledgements

Credit for the implementation of the experiment GUI goes to Samuel Broscheit. We are grateful to our significant others for participating in the quality ratings.

References

Barrachina, Sergio, Oliver Bender, Francisco Casacuberta, Jorge Civera, Elsa Cubel, Shahram Kadivi, Antonio Lagarda, Hermann Ney, Jesus Thomas, Enrique Vidal & Juan-Miguel Vilar. 2008. Statistical approaches to computer-assisted translation. *Computational Linguistics* 35(1). 3–28.

Bohnet, Bernd. 2010. Top accuracy and fast dependency parsing is not a contradiction. In *Proceedings of COLING*, 89–97. Beijing.

Bowker, Lynne. 2012. *Computer-aided translation technology – A practical introduction*. Ottawa: University of Ottawa Press.

Burnard, Lou. 1995. *User's Guide for the {British National Corpus}*. British National Corpus Consortium, Oxford University Computing Services.

Carl, Michael & Barbara Dragsted. 2012. Inside the monitor model: Processes of default and challenged translation production. *Translation: Computation, Corpora, Cognition* 2(1).

Christensen, Rune Haubo Bojesen. 2011. *Analysis of Ordinal Data With Cumulative Link Models – Estimation with the ordinal package*. http://www.cran.r-project.org/web/packages/ordinal. R package version 2011-09-14.

Clark, Stephen & James R. Curran. 2007. Wide-coverage efficient statistical parsing with CCG and log-linear models. *Computational Linguistics* 33(4). 493–552.

Freigang, Karl-Heinz. 1998. Machine-aided translation. In Mona Baker (ed.), *Routledge encyclopedia of translation studies*, 134–139. London: Routledge.

Gow, Francie. 2003. *Metrics for evaluating translation memory software*. University of Ottawa MA thesis.

Hedeker, Donald. 2005. Generalized linear mixed models. In *Encyclopedia of statistics in behavioral science*. New York: Wiley.

House, Juliane. 1998. Quality of translation. In Mona Baker (ed.), *Routledge encyclopedia of translation studies*, 197–200. London: Routledge.

Jaeger, T. Florian. 2008. Categorical data analysis: Away from ANOVAs and toward logit mixed models. *Journal of Memory and Language* 59(4). 434–446.

John, Bonnie E. 1996. TYPIST: A theory of performance in skilled typing. *Human-Computer Interaction* 11(4). 321–355.

Justeson, John S. & Slava M. Katz. 1995. Principled disambiguation: Discriminating adjective senses with modified nouns. *Computational Linguistics* 21(1). 1–27.

Keller, Frank, Subahshini Gunasekharan, Neil Mayo & Martin Corley. 2009. Timing accuracy of web experiments: A case study using the WebExp software package. *Behavior Research Methods* 41(1). 1–12.

Koehn, Philipp. 2005. Europarl: A parallel corpus for statistical machine translation. In *Proceedings of the tenth machine translation summit*, 79–86. Phuket. http://mt-archive.info/MTS-2005-Koehn.pdf.

Koehn, Philipp. 2010a. Enabling monolingual translators: Post-editing vs. options. In *Proceedings of the human language technologies: The 2010 annual conference of the north american chapter of the ACL*, 537–545. Los Angeles.

Koehn, Philipp. 2010b. *Statistical machine translation.* Cambridge: Cambridge University Press.

Koehn, Philipp & Barry Haddow. 2009. Interactive assistance to human translators using statistical machine translation methods. In *Proceedings of machine translation summit XII.* Ottawa.

Koehn, Philipp, Hieu Hoang, Alexandra Birch, Chris Callison-Birch, Marcello Federico, Nicola Bertoldi, Brooke Cowan, Wade Shen, Christine Moran, Richard Zens, Chris Dyer, Ondrej Bojar, Alexandra Constantin & Evan Herbst. 2007. Moses: Open source toolkit for statistical machine translation. In *Proceedings of the ACL 2007 demo and poster sessions.* Prague.

Langlais, Philippe, George Foster & Guy Lapalme. 2000. TransType: A computer-aided translation typing system. In *Proceedings of ANLP-NAACL workshop on embedded machine translation systems.* Seattle.

McGill, Robert, John W. Tukey & Wayne A. Larsen. 1978. Variations of box plots. *The American Statistician* 32(1). 12–16.

Miller, Katherine J. 1998. Modifiers in WordNet. In Christiane Fellbaum (ed.), *WordNet: An electronic lexical database,* 47–67. Cambridge: MIT Press.

Mitchell, Jeff & Mirella Lapata. 2010. Composition in distributional models of semantics. *Cognitive Science* 34. 1388–1429.

Mohammad, Saif & Peter Turney. 2013. Crowdsourcing a word–emotion association lexicon. *Computational Intelligence* 29(3). 436–465.

Noreen, Eric W. 1989. *Computer intensive methods for testing hypotheses: An introduction.* New York: Wiley.

Papineni, Kishore, Salim Roukos, Todd Ward & Wei-Jing Zhu. 2002. BLEU: A method for automatic evaluation of machine translation. In *Proceedings of the 40th annual meeting on association for computational linguistics,* 311–318. Philadelphia.

Reiß, Katharina. 1971. *Möglichkeiten und Grenzen der Übersetzungskritik: Kategorien und Kriterien für eine sachgerechte Beurteilung von Übersetzungen* (Hueber Hochschulreihe 12). München: Max Hueber.

Sapir, Edward. 1944. Grading: A study in semantics. *Philosophy of Sciences* 11. 83–116.

Snover, Matthew, Bonnie Dorr, Richard Schwartz, Linnea Micciulla & John Makhoul. 2006. A study of translation edit rate with targeted human annotation. In *Proceedings of amta,* 223–231. Cambridge.

Snow, Rion, Brendan O'Connor, Daniel Jurafsky & Andrew Ng. 2008. Cheap and fast – But is it good? Evaluating non-expert annotations for natural language tasks. In *Proceedings of the 2008 conference on empirical methods in natural language processing*, 254–263. Honolulu. http://www.aclweb.org/anthology/D08-1027.

Toury, Gideon. 1995. *Descriptive translation studies and beyond*. Vol. 4 (Benjamin Translation Library). Amsterdam: Benjamins.

Weiss, Sholom M. & Casimir A. Kulikowski. 1991. *Computer systems that learn: Classification and prediction methods from statistics, neural nets, machine learning and expert systems*. San Mateo: Morgan Kaufman.

Wu, Zhibiao & Martha Palmer. 1994. Verb semantics and lexical selection. In *Proceedings of the 32nd annual meeting on association for computational linguistics*, 133–138. Las Cruces.

Zanettin, Federico. 2002. Corpora in translation practice. In *Proceedings of the LREC workshop language resources for translation work*, 10–14. Las Palmas de Gran Canaria.

Chapter 7

Abstract pronominal anaphors and label nouns in German and English: Selected case studies and quantitative investigations

Heike Zinsmeister

University of Stuttgart

Stefanie Dipper

Ruhr-University Bochum

Melanie Seiss

University of Konstanz

Abstract anaphors refer to abstract referents, such as facts or events. This paper presents a corpus-based comparative study of German and English abstract anaphors. Parallel bi-directional texts from the Europarl Corpus were annotated with functional and morpho-syntactic information, focusing on the pronouns 'it', 'this', and 'that', as well as demonstrative noun phrases headed by "label nouns", such as 'this event', 'that issue', etc., and their German counterparts. We induce information about the cross-linguistic realization of abstract anaphors from the parallel texts. The contrastive findings are then controlled for translation-specific characteristics by examination of the differences between the original text and the translated text in each of the languages. In selected case studies, we investigate in detail "translation mismatches", including changes in grammatical category (from pronouns to full noun phrases, and vice versa), grammatical function, or clausal position, addition or omission of modifying adjectives, changes in the lexical realization of head nouns, and transpositions of the demonstrative determiner. In some of these cases, the specificity of the abstract noun phrase is altered by the translation process.

Heike Zinsmeister, Stefanie Dipper & Melanie Seiss. Abstract pronominal anaphors and label nouns in German and English: Selected case studies and quantitative investigations. In Oliver Czulo & Silvia Hansen-Schirra (eds.), *Crossroads between Contrastive Linguistics, Translation Studies and Machine Translation: TC3 II*, 153–195. Berlin: Language Science Press.
DOI:10.5281/zenodo.1019699

1 Introduction

Abstract *anaphora* denote an anaphoric relation between an anaphoric expression (i.e., the abstract *anaphor*) and an *antecedent* that refers to an abstract object, such as an event or a fact (Asher 1993). In the well-known example given by K. Byron (2002), the pronoun *it* (underlined in (1a)) refers to an *event*: namely, the migration of penguins to Fiji. In the alternative sequence (1b), the demonstrative pronoun *that* refers to the *fact* that penguins migrate to Fiji in the fall. In both examples, the antecedent is expressed by a clause in the preceding sentence.

(1)   a.   Each fall, penguins migrate to Fiji. It happens just before the eggs hatch.
      b.   Each fall, penguins migrate to Fiji. That's why I'm going there next month.

Our method consists of a contrastive, corpus-based approach to investigate the properties that characterize different instantiations of abstract anaphora in English and in German. In the future, we plan to derive features from the corpus annotation that will facilitate automatic resolution of abstract anaphora.

In this paper, we focus on the realization of the anaphoric element, i.e., the *anaphor*. We restrict our investigation to a well-defined set of pronouns and lexical NPs (e.g., *this issue, this directive*, etc.).

We present the results of a comparative corpus study on the realization of abstract anaphors in a parallel bi-directional corpus of English and German. In addition to comparing the cross-linguistic realizations, we also examine these differences between original text and translated text in each of the languages. For a more detailed study on the latter differences, see Dipper et al. (2012).

In previous studies, we focused on the use of pronouns as abstract anaphors (Dipper et al. 2011; Dipper & Zinsmeister 2009). In this paper, we take into account both pronouns and a selection of full NPs. The NPs under consideration here contain a demonstrative determiner, because demonstrative NPs are likely to be used anaphorically. In addition, the NP's head must be an abstract noun such as *issue, effect*, or *process*. We contrast quantitative results from our previous studies with results from our more recent annotations of full NPs.

Furthermore, we investigate selected samples of "translation mismatches" in detail. These mismatches can include anaphors that are not translated word-for-word, but that involve *edit operations*, i.e., addition, deletion, or substitution of words. However, some such mismatches also concern *specificity*, i.e., translation mismatches that affect the amount of information available to the hearer for the resolution of the reference of the abstract anaphor – for example, when an anaphor is not translated by the most obvious translation candidate, but instead by a target word that is more or less specific than its source word.

The annotated corpus thus far only permits tentative conclusions. We consider the research reported here to be a pilot study that highlights aspects that appear worthy of investigation on a large scale in the future.

The paper is organized as follows: §2 addresses related research; §3 introduces the corpus and the annotations upon which the study is based. In §4, we present quantitative investigations concerning selected properties of the abstract anaphors, such as grammatical category, grammatical function, and position. §5 introduces a range of case studies that address translation mismatches.

2 Related work

The majority of projects that analyze abstract anaphora deal with monolingual data. This section begins with a short, general overview of relevant projects, and then addresses in more detail projects that have examined multilingual corpora.

General studies Most annotation projects that analyze abstract anaphora are limited to pronominal markables (e.g., Byron 2003; Hedberg et al. 2007; Müller 2007). Some also annotate full NP markables, often restricted to demonstrative or possessive NPs (e.g., Vieira et al. 2002; Pradhan et al. 2007; Poesio & Artstein 2008). In projects that have analyzed pro-drop languages, zero anaphora have also been considered (e.g., Recasens 2008; Navarretta & Olsen 2008). A recent overview of projects concerned with the annotation of abstract anaphora is provided by Dipper & Zinsmeister (2010).

Multilingual studies Multilingual corpora have been annotated in Recasens (2008); Navarretta & Olsen (2008); Navarretta (2008); Pradhan et al. (2007); Weischedel et al. (2010). In contrast to the present work, these projects utilize "comparable" rather than parallel corpora (see §3).

Recasens (2008) compares the use of pronominal and NP abstract anaphors in Catalan and Spanish, determining that Spanish prefers personal over demonstrative pronouns, whereas no such preference is found in Catalan. In both languages, full NPs account for half of the abstract anaphors. The heads of these full NPs largely overlap with the "label nouns" reported by Francis (1994): Francis's list is also used in our study (see §3).

Navarretta (2008) and Navarretta & Olsen (2008) compare pronominal abstract anaphors in Danish and Italian. They find that Italian generally avoids the use of pronouns as abstract referents, preferring to use full NPs instead.

Pradhan et al. (2007) and Weischedel et al. (2010) annotate information at various linguistic levels in English, Chinese, and Arabic; a subset of the English and Chinese data consist of parallel (translated) texts. In addition to annotating nominal coreference, they also mark verbs that are coreferenced with an NP (e.g., *grew* and *the strong growth*).

Parallel studies   Annotation of parallel texts has been conducted by Vieira et al. (2002), using a subcorpus from the parallel MLCC corpus.[1] The researchers investigate demonstrative NPs in French and Portuguese, finding similar attributes: In both languages, demonstrative NPs predominantly use abstract head nouns. Vieira et al. (2002) do not distinguish between texts in original and translations.

Characteristics of parallel corpora   Parallel corpora, such as MLCC (see above) or Europarl (Koehn 2005), consist of original and translated texts. There has been a long-standing debate over the extent to which translated language deviates from comparable original language due to influences from both the original source language and the translation process; some arguing that such material should therefore not be used as a base for linguistic investigations (other than those focusing on translation issues such as, e.g., Čulo et al. 2008); see the related discussion in §4.

For instance, Cartoni et al. (2011) investigate the use of discourse connectives in original and translated French texts from Europarl, finding that translated texts contain significantly more discourse connectives than original texts. Halteren (2008) shows that based on word *n-grams* it is possible to identify the source language in Europarl translations with accuracies between 87.2 and 96.7%.

3 The corpus

For our study, we used parts of the Europarl Corpus (release v3, 1996–2006, Koehn 2005). The Europarl Corpus consists of transcripts of European Parliament debates. Individual contributions by speakers ('turns') in the debates were

---

[1]The MLCC corpus includes written questions asked by members of the European Parliament and the corresponding answers from the European Commission, cf. http://catalog.elra.info/product_info.php?products_id=764.

delivered (for the most part) in the speaker's native language. Professional translators provided official EU translations into the other EU languages.

The original contributions were spoken, but might have been based on written
scripts. Speakers had the option to edit the transcripts before publication. As a
result, the register of these turns is of a mixed character, varying between spoken
and more standardized written language.

We created subcorpora by extracting German and English turns (contributions
by German and English speakers), along with their sentence-aligned translations.
This provided us with four different subcorpora; the German original turns (DE_o)
and their English translations (EN_t), and the English original turns (EN_o) and
their German translations (DE_t).

These four subcorpora stand in different relations to each other (see Figure 1).
EN_o and DE_t (and DE_o and EN_t) are *parallel* corpora, i.e., they consist of original
texts and their translations. The subcorpora DE_o and EN_o (and similarly, DE_t and
EN_t) are comparable corpora, i.e., corpora in different languages that deal with
the same overall topic and come from the same overall register. This notion of
comparable corpora is often used in corpus-linguistic research; we therefore call
this type of relation *comparable$_{corp}$*. Finally, the subcorpora DE_o and DE_t (and
EN_o and EN_t) are also comparable corpora, in that they represent varieties of the
same language. Translation studies generally refer to such corpora as comparable, thus we call this type of relation *comparable$_{trans}$*. We based the investigations presented in this paper on these various relations between the subcorpora.

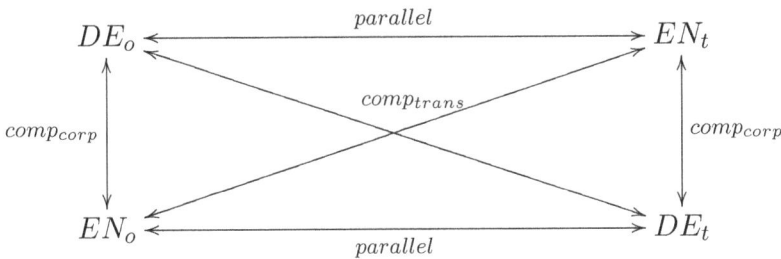

Figure 1: There are three types of relations between the four subcorpora: parallel, comparable in the corpus-linguistic sense (*comp$_{corp}$*),
and comparable in the translation-studies sense (*comp$_{trans}$*)

Anaphora Corpus   We created a small manually annotated corpus, which we
call *Anaphora Corpus*. For this, we randomly selected about 100 turns from DE_o

and EN_o, respectively, for our manual annotation study; our goal was to investigate the properties of abstract anaphors, in particular their realization as pronouns or full lexical NPs, but also in terms of function, position, etc. To this end, a number of pre-processing steps were applied. These included verifying the native language of the speakers.[2] After this step, we were left with 94 German original turns and 95 English original turns. Further pre-processing of the data included tokenizing, POS tagging, and chunking by means of the TreeTagger (Schmid 1994). For the manual annotation of the German and English turns, we used MMAX2 (Müller & Strube 2006).

The various processing steps and manual annotations implemented are described in the following sections.

3.1 Annotating pronominal abstract anaphors

We adopted a cross-linguistic bootstrapping approach for the annotation of abstract pronouns. Starting with a well-defined set of markables in the original language, we collected all translation equivalents on the side of the "target" language (the translation of the original language).

In the first round of annotation, we chose original texts from German (DE_o), because German, unlike English, has a pronoun that is unambiguously used as an abstract anaphor: the uninflected singular demonstrative pronoun *dies* 'this'. In addition, we defined as markables the (ambiguous) demonstrative pronoun *das* 'that' and the (ambiguous) third-person neuter pronoun *es* 'it'. For all instances of these pronouns, the annotators first determined whether they were in fact being used as abstract anaphors by specifying their antecedents. In a further annotation step, the annotators had to determine how the German abstract anaphors were translated in the English data (EN_t).

For the second round of annotation, we considered the reverse translation direction: English original texts (EN_o) and their German translations (DE_t). We extended our set of markables to include the adverbs *as, so,* and *likewise*, because it was determined in the first annotation round that these adverbs often served as translations of German anaphors.[3]

In total, 871 instances of neuter pronouns were found in DE_o, and 1,224 instances of pronouns and adverbs (= the extended set) in EN_o. Of these, 203 (DE_o) and 297 (EN_o) were determined to be abstract anaphors.

---

[2]The language markers provided in release v3 turned out to be incomplete and partially incorrect. We therefore looked up each speaker's origin in a database of EU members of parliament.
[3]Because we used different sets of markables in the different annotation rounds, the figures from different rounds cannot be easily compared, see below.

For further details of the annotation process and the annotated features, see Dipper et al. (2011).

3.2 Annotating abstract NPs

In addition to pronominal abstract anaphors, we also annotated abstract full NPs. To accelerate the annotation process, we carefully preselected a set of NPs that seemed likely candidates for abstract anaphors by applying two constraints: First, only NPs with a demonstrative determiner were selected, because such NPs are generally used anaphorically. Second, we defined a list of admissible head nouns that refer to abstract entities.

For English, abstract nouns (such as *report, arrangement*, and *fact*) were selected. The list of nouns, which was heavily influenced by the *label nouns* defined by Francis (1994), comprised 211 abstract nouns. Table 1 provides some examples. In total, 132 instances of these nouns (in singular and plural form) occurred in EN_O of the Anaphora Corpus.[4]

We chose the most common translations for the English label nouns to create a list of German label nouns[5] and excluded non-abstract translations. This resulted in between one and ten German translations per English noun, with an average of 3.6 translations per English noun. Some example translations are provided in Table 1. The large number of German label nouns can be explained by the fact that we started out with a predefined set of English label nouns, and that these nouns are quite general in meaning; thus, depending on the context, they can be translated with a variety of German abstract nouns.

Table 1: English label nouns and their German translations

English noun	German translations
problem	*Problem* 'problem', *Fragestellung* 'question', *Problemstellung* 'problem'
activity	*Aktivität* 'activity', *Aktion* 'action', *Handlung* 'act'
subject	*Gegenstand* 'object', *Gesprächsgegenstand* 'topic'
topic	*Gegenstand* 'object', *Inhalt* 'content', *Thematik* 'subject matter', *Thema* 'matter', *Themengebiet* 'topic area'

Table 1 also shows that our method yielded multiple English translations for German label nouns as well. For example, *Gegenstand* 'object' can be translated

---

[4]EN_O: 132 instances of 45 different label noun types.
[5]Translations based on LEO, http://www.leo.org/.

as *subject* or *topic*. The final list consisted of 452 types of German label nouns. Of these, 134 (inflected) instances occurred in the German Anaphora Corpus DE_o.[6] Of course, not all of these were true instances of abstract anaphors (see below).

In a pre-processing step, the data was split into individual original *alignment units* as provided by the Europarl Corpus, each followed by its translation. In the units of the original text, all noun chunks with a label-noun head were pre-marked as *markables* (English label nouns in EN_o, and German label nouns in DE_o). In the translated units, noun chunks were generally pre-marked as potential translation equivalents.

In the annotation procedure, the annotators were first asked to check whether the label noun occurrences were in fact abstract. This was important because some label nouns can be ambiguous between an abstract and a non-abstract interpretation. For example, *area* can also refer to an actual geographic area, and *report* can refer to a copy of a report. This procedure resulted in 130 English and 117 German abstract NPs for further manual annotation.[7]

Annotators were next asked to align the original noun chunk with its translation. After this step, both the original label noun and the corresponding material in the translation were annotated for category, function, and position.[8] Figure 2 shows screenshots of the MMAX2 annotation windows.

In sum, for the analysis of both pronominal and NP anaphors, the same data and similar strategies were used. In both cases, we started out with a well-defined set of markables, although the set of markables for pronominals was naturally considerably smaller than the set of label nouns. In both cases, we considered how the markables had been translated and whether we could induce new markables for the next annotation round. We believe that this kind of bootstrapping approach provides a faster and more efficient method of extracting anaphors in two languages in comparison to processing contiguous text without predefined markables. Working without predefined markables would also present the risk

---

[6] DE_o: 134 instances of 51 different label noun types.

[7] This demonstrates that our pre-selection was highly successful in the case of abstract NPs. In contrast, occurrences of the pronominal anaphors *this, that, it,* and *das* 'that' and *es* 'it' in German most often refer to concrete referents.
Annotators did not need to determine the antecedents in the case of abstract NPs, because we could assume that most of the label nouns were abstract *per se*. In ambiguous cases, annotators did a quick check of the previous context to determine whether the noun was abstract.

[8] Admissible values were:
– Category: 'noun phrase', 'pronoun', 'pronominal adverb', 'genauso/likewise', 'sentence', 'other'
– Function: 'subject', 'object', 'object of a preposition', 'noun phrase attribute', 'other'
– Position: 'topic/prefield', 'matrix', 'embedded', 'other'.

that annotators would disagree on the set of types under consideration or, more likely still, on the markables themselves.

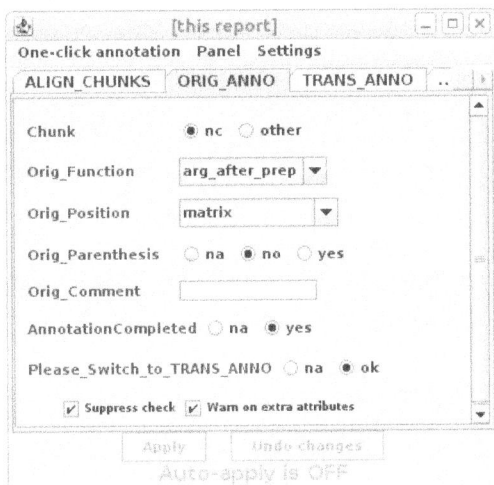

Figure 2: MMAX2 annotation windows: The upper panel shows English alignment units, along with their German translations. Noun chunks with label nouns to be processed by the annotators are highlighted in yellow. Translation candidates are marked in red. In the first alignment unit, the anaphoric abstract noun chunk 'this report' has been aligned with its German equivalent 'diesem Bericht'. The lower panel displays features that have been annotated to the English noun chunk. Similar features have also been annotated to the translated noun chunk (not displayed in the figure).

Heike Zinsmeister, Stefanie Dipper & Melanie Seiss

4 Quantitative investigations

This section presents our quantitative results from investigation of the Anaphora Corpus. For selected cases, findings based on our manually annotated data are complemented by evaluations of data from the entire German and English Europarl Corpus.

An obvious advantage of using parallel texts for cross-linguistic research is that the aligned units convey the same meaning and allow us a direct comparison of how this meaning is expressed linguistically in the two languages. This cross-linguistic use of parallel texts also has limitations, as many studies in translation studies have shown. The most troublesome for our research purposes are:

(i) The problem of *translation shifts* (cf. Vinay & Darbelnet 1958/1995; Dorr 1994); this refers to the fact that translated texts systematically differ from their source texts due to language-inherent differences. Further factors that can result in language-specific differences in translations are stylistic preferences (e.g. language-specific conventions that apply to parliamentary debate protocol and its translation) and cultural differences, for which the background knowledge of the hearers plays a role (Klaudy 2008).

(ii) Effects inherent to the translation process, which can affect the characteristics of translated texts in various ways. There are two subtypes that are particularly relevant for us: the *shining-through* of source-language preferences when a translation is too faithful to its source text (cf. Teich 2003), and the tendency of translated texts to be more *explicit* than their sources (Vinay & Darbelnet 1958/1995; Blum-Kulka 1986).[9] Both of these characteristics might directly affect how anaphoric links are expressed,

---

[9]Vinay & Darbelnet (1958/1995: 342) were the first to define the concept of *explicitation*, "a stylistic translation technique which consists of making explicit in the target language what remains implicit in the source language because it is apparent from either the context or the situation".

Blum-Kulka (1986) formulated the explicitation hypothesis: "The process of interpretation performed by the translator on the source text might lead to a TL [target language] text which is more redundant than the SL [source language] text. This redundancy can be expressed by a rise in the level of cohesive explicitness in the TL text. This argument may be stated as 'the explicitation hypothesis', which postulates an observed cohesive explicitness from SL to TL texts regardless of the increase traceable to differences between the two linguistic and textual systems involved. It follows that explicitation is viewed here as inherent in the process of translation" (Blum-Kulka (1986: 19); both citations from Klaudy 2008).

For a recent survey and critical assessment of the explicitation hypothesis, see Becher (2011: Ch. 2).

such that translated texts could end up quite different from comparable original texts.

We expect the aspects listed in (i) to result in differences between languages (*parallel* and *comparable$_{corp}$* corpora, cf. Figure 1), and those effects in (ii) to result in differences between original and translated texts (*comparable$_{trans}$* corpora). These differences – even if only in form and not in meaning – pose problems for approaches that target the automatic resolution of anaphora.

Having outlined the specific characteristics of translated texts, we then pursued a two-step approach. First, we compared the expression of abstract anaphors in the aligned units of the *parallel* resources. Second, we checked our results — when possible — with the *comparable$_{trans}$* part of the corpus. This process required a number of steps, explained below in greater detail.

Step 1: We first examined parallel (translated) texts. A naïve assumption would be that in aligned units of parallel texts, abstract anaphors would be realized in the same way in both languages (e.g., with the same category and function). When we found differences between the parallel texts (e.g., a transposition,[10] as described in (a)), there were two possible explanations: either the differences were due to (i) language-specific preferences, or to (ii) effects of the translation process.

> (a) *Observation of transposition*: German pronouns tend to be translated by English NPs.

To determine which explanation was applicable, we pursued various methods.

Step 2: We next checked whether the tendencies also appeared in the reverse translation direction (b).

> (b) *Reverse translation direction of (a)*: English pronouns would tend to be translated by German NPs.

If (b) were true, observation (a) would likely represent an effect of the translation process. If the tendencies only showed up in one translation direction, it would indicate a language-specific effect.

Moreover, we could check whether the tendency was also observed in the reverse direction of the *transposition* (c).

---

[10]We use the term *transposition* to refer to changes in the grammatical category, function, etc., that occur as the result of translation.

(c) *Reverse transposition of (a)*: German NPs would tend to be translated by English pronouns.

If this were the case, the transpositions in question would seem to occur at random, and no general "rule" could be deduced from the observations.

Step 3: In addition, we checked the ratios in a *comparable$_{trans}$* corpus (e.g., by comparing the numbers of pronouns and NPs in DE_o and DE_t, and in EN_o and EN_t). If we observed differences between original and translated texts for both German and English, this would indicate an effect of the translation process. If these differences were observed in one language only, it would indicate a language-specific effect.

We applied Steps 1 to 3 in order to shed light on the *linguistic similarity* of abstract anaphors in German and English, and in original texts and translated texts.

The following sections present quantitative results for abstract anaphors with regard to lexical choice (§4.1), grammatical category (§4.2), grammatical function (§4.3), and position in the clause (§4.4). For each of these properties, we examined pronominal anaphors (cf. §3.1) and label noun NP anaphors (cf. §3.2) annotated in the Anaphora Corpus. More detailed, qualitative discussions of translation equivalences are provided in §5.

4.1 Lexical choice

Pronominal abstract anaphors We first focused on the different lexical realizations of abstract anaphors in the original and translated texts, and compared their frequencies.

Table 2 provides a comparison of the frequency rankings in the comparable$_{trans}$ corpora (DE_o–to–DE_t, and EN_o–to–EN_t; the table is organized in accordance with the corpus scheme from Figure 1).

The table illustrates that the lexical choices lead to distributions in the translated corpora that correspond to those in their comparable$_{trans}$ counterparts: The top-ranked pronouns are equivalent in both comparable$_{trans}$ pairs. For the German corpora, *das, dies, es* are top-ranked, with *wie* 'as' intervening in DE_t; as this word was not part of the original markable set, its frequency cannot be compared. For the English corpora, *this, that, it, as* are top-ranked. The re-ranking of *it*, and *as* (in EN_t vs. EN_o) can probably be explained by the fact that *wie* (the German equivalent of *as*) was not included in the first annotation round, as just noted. A remarkable deviation is the relative overuse of *dies* 'this' in DE_t in comparison to

Table 2: Frequency rankings of original pronominal abstract anaphors
and translation equivalents

Rank	DE_o pronouns	Freq	Rank	EN_t most frequent equivalents	Freq
1.	*das* 'that'	123	1.	*this*	55
2.	*dies* 'this'	45	2.	*that*	52
3.	*es* 'it'	35	3.	*it*	22
			4.	*as*	9
			5.	*which*	5
			6.	*they, these things, likewise, what, to do so, this threat*	< 5
				...	

Rank	EN_o pronouns	Freq	Rank	DE_t most frequent equivalents	Freq
1.	*this*	108	1.	*das* 'that'	71
2.	*that*	103	2.	*dies* 'this'	48
3.	*as*	42	3.	*wie* 'as'	31
4.	*it*	36	4.	*es* 'it'	13
5.	*so*	8	5.	*deshalb* 'therefore'	8
			6.	*damit* 'with that'	6
			7.	*was* 'what', *so* 'so', *hier* 'here', *davon* 'thereof', *dieser Prozess* 'this process', ...	< 5

DE_o if we only take into account occurrences of *das, dies,* and *es*.[11] This might be an example of *shining-through* of the frequently occurring English *this* in EN_o.

Table 3 provides a detailed view of the anaphors by aligning them with their actual translations. For each pronominal abstract anaphor, its absolute frequency in the original data and the number of different equivalence types is given. In addition, the most frequent equivalence types are listed, together with their absolute frequencies in the translated text.

---

[11]Chi-squared test: χ^2 = 7.3459, *df* = 1, $p < 0.01$ based on R's *prop.test(c(45,48),c(203,132))*.

Table 3: Pronominal markables and their most frequent translation equivalents. The pronominal frequencies include cases in which the pronoun could not be aligned to corresponding material in the translation.

DE original			EN translations	
Pronoun	Freq	Types	Top equivalents	Freq
das 'that'	123	25	*that*	44
			this	27
			it	12
			which	5
			as	3
dies 'this'	45	9	*this*	23
			that	4
			as	3
			it	3
es 'it'	35	8	*it*	8
			this	5
			that	4
			as	3
EN original			DE translations	
Pronoun	Freq	Types	Top equivalents	Freq
this	108	42	*dies* 'this'	32
			das 'that'	21
			damit 'so that'	4
			hier 'here'	4
that	103	39	*das* 'that'	43
			dies 'this'	9
			deshalb 'therefore'	8
as	42	11	*wie* 'as'	31
it	36	16	*es* 'it'	9
			das 'that'	7
so	8	4	*dies* 'this'	4

Comparison of the anaphors with their translation equivalences in Table 3 demonstrates that in almost all cases, the literal translation is observed most frequently. *Das* 'that' is most often translated as *that*, *that* as *das*, and so forth. The only exception is the English *so*, which most often translates into *dies* 'this' — the German pronoun that unambiguously refers to abstract objects.[12]

Abstract anaphors with demonstrative label nouns An overview of the most frequent label nouns occurring in the Anaphora Corpus is provided in Table 4.

The ten most frequent types listed in Table 4 account for 59% of all instances in the original corpora, and for the considerably smaller proportion of 46% in the translated corpora.[13] This could be an effect of style in the translations, as translators might tend to show more diversity than the original authors. However, this conclusion does not hold when evaluating larger parts of the Europarl Corpus as discussed on page 171.

Examining individual translation pairs confirms the same tendency of literal translation preference as was observed with the pronominal anaphors. Most of the nouns are translated by only one or two different translation equivalences. Exceptions with greater translational variance include *agreement* (five equivalent types: *Abkommen, Einigung, Vereinbarung, Übereinkommen, Übereinstimmung*), *issue* (four types: *Angelegenheit, Erweiterung, Problem, Thema*), *Thema* (four types: *area, issue, subject, topic*), and *Frage/Fragen* (four types: *area , issue, situation, questions*).

Comparing the rankings in Table 4, the *parallel* rankings (horizontal neighbors, e.g., DE_o and EN_t) are more similar to each other than to the *comparable*$_{trans}$ rankings (diagonal neighbors, e.g., DE_o and DE_t).[14] It seems that in the case of label noun anaphors, the topic of the individual texts has a greater effect on the choice of the lexical items than language-specific conventions. This is in correspondence with findings reported in the literature.

---

[12] The preferences of the literal translations are significant according to a Chi-squared test for *das* ($\chi^2 = 5.0685, df = 1, p < 0.05$), *dies* ($\chi^2 = 17.1429, df = 1, p < 0.001$), *that* ($\chi^2 = 28.0137, df = 1, p < 0.001$), and *as* ($\chi^2 = 39.1301, df = 1, p < 0.001$). There is no significant difference for the translation of *this* as either *dies* or *das*. The other anaphors' frequencies are too low to be conclusive.

[13] The proportion of instances associated with the top-ten most frequent types, broken down by language, are: DE_o: 56%, EN_t: 44%, EN_o: 62%, DE_t: 48%.

[14] Some of the differences are artificial, related to the selection of label nouns that were premarked as markables. *Directive*, for example, was not in the list of English label nouns and is therefore missing from EN_o. See the discussion of the nouns *Bereich* 'area' and *directive* below.

Table 4: Frequency rankings for the most common label nouns

Rank	DE_o label nouns	Freq	Rank	EN_t label nouns	Freq
1.	*Bericht* 'report'	13	1.	*report*	13
2.	*Richtlinie* 'directive'	12	2.	*directive*	10
3.	*Thema* 'issue'	10	3.	*issue*	7
4.	*Prozess* 'process'	6	4.	*process*	5
5.	*Frage* 'question/ issue'	5	5.	*debate*	4
	Punkt 'point'	5	6.	*area*	3
7.	*Debatte* 'debate'	4		*questions*	3
	Fragen 'questions/ issues'	4		*subject*	3
	Zusammenhang 'context'	4	9.	*basis*	2
10.	*Ergebnis* 'result'	3		*connection*	2

Rank	EN_o label nouns	Freq	Rank	DE_t label nouns	Freq
1.	*report*	19	1.	*Bericht* 'report'	15
2.	*proposal*	10	2.	*Thema* 'issue'	8
3.	*area*	9	3.	*Vorschlag* 'proposal'	7
4.	*agreement*	8	4.	*Bereich* 'area'	6
5.	*issue*	7	5.	*Fall* 'case'	5
	point	7		*Punkt* 'point'	5
7.	*context*	5	7.	*Angelegenheit* 'issue'	4
	subject	5		*Berichts* 'report' (genitive)	4
9.	*debate*	4		*Gebiet* 'area'	4
	problem	4		*Problem* 'problem'	4

Usage preferences for selected nouns In addition to using the comparable corpora that form part of the Anaphora Corpus, we also took advantage of the huge amount of comparable data provided by the Europarl Corpus: 12,800 German original turns with 4.9 M tokens, and 11,500 English original turns with 3.4 M tokens. In this section, we illustrate how this data can be used to detect interesting cases that seem worthy of closer examination. Note that in this subsection, the abbreviations DE_o, DE_t, etc., are also used to refer to the respective subcorpora of the Europarl Corpus. In most other sections in this paper, these abbreviations refer exclusively to the Anaphora Corpus.

Our starting point was the considerable divergence we found in the frequencies of certain label nouns in comparisons of original and translated turns in our Anaphora Corpus. We selected all label nouns with "considerable" differences (greater or equal to four) between the frequencies of original and translated turns, see Table 5. The columns labeled 'Anaphora Corpus' list the respective figures. A

Table 5: Label nouns with difference greater of equal four between the frequency of original and translated turns. '#' indicates absolute frequencies (as occurring in the annotated corpora): 'Diff' represents the difference between the two frequencies. 'Freq' refers to frequencies relative to the total number of nouns, multiplied by 1,000 (calculated on the basis of all Europarl turns). DE_o/DE_t etc., is the proportion of the label noun's frequency in the original turns compared to its frequency in translated turns. The entries are sorted according to the differences in frequency in the Anaphora Corpus; notable figures are printed in boldface. (For nouns marked with '*', see the remarks in the text.)

| Label noun | Anaphora Corpus | | | Europarl Corpus | | |
	$\#DE_o{:}\#DE_t$	Diff	Freq DE_o	Freq DE_t	DE_o/DE_t	DE_t/DE_o
*Richtlinie** 'directive'	12 : 0	12	2.656	3.282	0.809	1.236
Vorschlag 'proposal'	1 : 7	−6	3.272	3.835	0.853	1.172
*Bereich** 'area'	0 : 6	−6	4.020	2.714	1.481	0.675
Frage 'question/issue'	5 : 0	5	6.695	5.440	1.231	0.813
Fall 'case'	0 : 5	−5	2.260	2.362	0.957	1.045
Prozess 'process'	6 : 2	4	0.482	0.776	0.621	1.611
Debatte 'debate'	4 : 0	4	2.355	1.523	1.546	0.647
Fragen 'questions/issues'	4 : 0	4	2.349	2.820	0.833	1.200
Angelegenheit 'issue'	0 : 4	−4	0.287	1.375	0.209	4.797

| Label noun | Anaphora Corpus | | | Europarl Corpus | | |
	$\#EN_o{:}\#EN_t$	Diff	Freq EN_o	Freq EN_t	EN_o/EN_t	EN_t/EN_o
*directive**	0 : 10	−10	4.900	4.579	1.070	0.934
proposal	10 : 1	9	5.436	5.690	0.955	1.047
agreement	8 : 1	7	4.868	4.116	1.183	0.845
*area**	9 : 3	6	3.480	4.361	0.798	1.253
point	7 : 1	6	5.885	6.668	0.883	1.133
report	19 : 13	6	18.881	13.438	1.405	0.712
context	5 : 0	5	1.292	1.506	0.858	1.165

negative number in the 'Diff' column indicates that the label noun occurs more often in the translated turns. For example, Table 5 shows that the noun *Angelegenheit* 'issue' (ranked last in the top table) never occurs in a German original turn, but occurs four times in translations from English turns (i.e., a difference of four occurrences). In contrast, the noun *report* (see the lower table) occurs considerably more often in original English turns (19 times) than in translated turns (13 times).

Similarly, the nouns *Bereich* 'area' and *directive* (marked with '*' in the table) were only annotated in translated turns. However, this is because *Bereich* and *directive* were not included in our original set of label nouns, and thus their occurrences were not pre-marked and annotated in the MMAX2 files, although they appear quite frequently as translation equivalents in the annotated translations. In the next round of annotations, they will be included in our set of label nouns, in accordance with our general bootstrapping approach. The fact that the EN_o noun *directive* was not included in the first annotation round also had an impact on the frequency of its DE_t translation *Richtlinie* 'directive' (ranked first), which was never found in German translations for this reason. The same holds true for the frequency of the EN_t noun *area*: Its literal DE_o counterpart *Bereich* was not annotated in the original texts.

For each of the label nouns with considerable differences, we calculated its frequency in *all* original and translated turns of the Europarl Corpus (release v3).[15] We found that these frequencies differed significantly for all nouns, except for *Fall* 'case' in German and *directive* and *proposal* in English.[16]

In general, certain label nouns seem to be overused in translated texts in comparison to original texts. This can be seen in the last four columns in the tables, which list the relative frequencies of the label nouns in original and translated turns (multiplied by one thousand) and the ratio of these frequencies. For instance, the first noun is *Richtlinie* 'directive', which occurs with a relative frequency of 2.656 in original turns and of 3.282 in translated turns. This indicates that the noun occurs more often in translated turns. This is reflected by the fact that the proportion DE_o/DE_t is less than one and, consequently, the proportion DE_t/DE_o is greater than one. The last two columns show that in six instances (out of nine) in the German data, the proportion DE_t/DE_o is greater than one, and that in four times (out of seven) in the English data the proportion EN_t/EN_o is greater

---

[15]Only translations from original turns in German and English were considered.

[16]Chi-squared test with continuity correction, using the label noun vs. the class of all other nouns as features. With the noun *context*: $\chi^2 = 8.39, df = 1, p < 0.01$; all remaining nouns: $\chi^2 > 25, df = 1, p < .001$. Significant effects are easily achieved in large corpora. In Dipper et al. (2012), we discuss the results on the basis of their effect size (as suggested by Gries 2005).

than one as well. We tentatively conclude from this that the translations possibly have a more restricted vocabulary than the comparable original texts, and that individual common types thus occur with a higher relative frequency in the translated texts than in the originals.

A strikingly large frequency difference can be observed for the German noun *Angelegenheit* 'issue', which occurs 4.8 times more often in the translated turns of the Europarl Corpus; the second-ranking noun in translations is *Prozess* 'process', which occurs 1.6 times more often. Conversely, the nouns *Debatte* 'debate' and *Bereich* 'area' top the list of nouns that occur more often in the original turns — approximately 1.5 times more often. The differences in the English data are less pronounced. The top-ranked noun is *report*, which occurs 1.4 times more often in the original data.

The top-ranked nouns, i.e., those that demonstrated considerable frequency divergence both in the Anaphora Corpus and in the Europarl Corpus (indicated by figures printed in boldface in Table 5), were subject to further investigation.

Angelegenheit 'issue': The striking frequency differences that occur with *Angelegenheit* 'issue' might be attributable to the fact that the word seems to be used as a kind of "dummy" translation for English nouns that are highly unspecific, such as *issue, matter*, or *matter of concern*. (2) shows such an example.[17]

(2) EN_o: But, on this issue, I do not see any room for soft law which is why in the transition period there will be total adherence to the current financial regulation until that law is changed by due democratic process in this House and in the Council.

     DE_t: Aber in dieser Angelegenheit sehe ich keinen Raum für "soft law", weshalb es im Übergangszeitraum eine strikte Befolgung der aktuellen Haushaltsordnung geben wird, bis diese Rechtsvorschrift durch das erforderliche demokratische Verfahren in diesem Hohen Hause und im Rat geändert worden ist.   (ep-00-03-01/28)

Prozess 'process': Interestingly, in the Europarl Corpus, the noun *Prozess* 'process' occurs much more often in translated turns than in original ones—contrary to the ratios observed in the Anaphora Corpus. *Prozess* is always translated by its closest equivalent 'process' in the Anaphora Corpus, and vice versa: *process* is always translated by *Prozess* in this data. Our data do not permit any tentative conclusion that would explain the observed frequency differences.

---

[17]We mark the examples taken from the Europarl corpus with the name of the file (e.g., ep-00-03-01) and the speaker ID, as provided by release v3 of the Europarl Corpus.

Debatte 'debate': occurs more often in original German turns (no occurrence in DE_t in the Anaphora Corpus). A highly speculative explanation is that the German *translators* — in contrast to the German *speakers* — prefer the noun *Aussprache* as the translation of *debate*. *Aussprache* can mean 'discussion' but also 'interlocution, talk', whereas *Debatte*, as used in every-day language, means 'dispute, argument'. Used in the sense of 'parliamentary debates', the negative connotation is absent, the meaning being 'discussion, debate'. However, translators could be avoiding the use of the noun *Debatte* due to its negative connotations in other contexts.

Bereich 'area': As mentioned above, the noun *Bereich* 'area' was not annotated in original German turns in the first annotation round. The six examples that appeared in the translations (see Table 5) are translations of *area* (five times) and *question* (one time). In an extra step, we looked up all occurrences of *Bereich* in DE_o: this resulted in six instances that are translated in six different ways, e.g., by *area, sphere*, etc. (cf. (3)). This means that in the translation direction DE_o-to-EN_t, we observe a vast variety of English expressions that correspond to German *Bereich* 'area', whereas in the reverse direction (EN_o-to-DE_t) *Bereich* is only used as a translation of *area* (and, in one instance, of *question*).

(3) DE_o: Deswegen brauchen wir ein gemeinsames
     Satellitenaufklärungssystem der Europäischen Union und gemeinsame
     Standards für die Telekommunikation in <u>diesem Bereich</u>.
     EN_t: That is why we in the European Union need a single satellite
     reconnaissance system and common standards for telecommunications in
     <u>this sphere</u>.   (ep-06-05-17/20)

Report 'report': Finally, the noun *report* occurs extremely frequently in the Anaphora Corpus, both in EN_o and EN_t (and with similar frequencies in the Europarl Corpus). Some of these occurrences can be explained by the fact that in their turns, speakers often refer to reports that are up for discussion, see (4).

(4) EN_o: Madam President, I would like to thank the rapporteur for
     producing <u>this report</u> because it is a very important one.
     DE_t: Frau Präsidentin, ich möchte dem Berichterstatter für <u>seinen Bericht</u>
     danken, denn es handelt sich um einen wirklich wichtigen Bericht.
     (98-11-17/284)

4.2 Grammatical category

Pronominal abstract anaphors   In addition to lexical choice, we also investigated the grammatical properties of the anaphors. We evaluated whether pronouns were translated by pronouns — as our initial "naïve assumption" would predict (see Step 1 in §4) — or by another category (e.g., full NP, adverbial, or clause). This investigation was motivated by findings on cross-linguistic differences (e.g., between Danish and Italian and between Spanish and Catalan: cf. Recasens 2008; Navarretta 2008; Navarretta & Olsen 2008).

Assuming equivalence between the original text and the translation, we would expect to find only pronoun–to–pronoun mappings (and adverb–to–adverb, if adverbs had been included in the markable set). Our data does not confirm this equivalence. In the corpus DE_o–to–EN_t, only 65% (132) of the pronominal markables are translated as pronouns, see Table 6, first row.

Table 6: Pronouns: Categorial transposition types

	Pronoun to pronoun		Pronoun to NP		Pronoun to other		Sum	
DE_o–to–EN_t	65.0%	(132)	9.4%	(19)	25.6%	(52)	100%	(203)
EN_o–to–DE_t	70.3%	(173)	7.3%	(18)	22.4%	(55)	100%	(246)

Other target categories of translated pronouns included NPs, cf. (5), and adverbials such as *so, likewise* — which were then added to the English markable set.[18]

(5) EN_o: I do not necessarily support this.
      DE_t: Diesem Standpunkt schließe ich mich nicht notwendigerweise an.
      DE_{lit}: This position I do not necessarily support.   (ep-00-10-03/15)

In examining the EN_o–to–DE_t corpus, we found similar results (Table 6, second row). The proportional distributions between DE_o–to–EN_t and EN_o–to–DE_t do not differ significantly.[19]

The bar plots in Figure 3 provide a more general overview by summarizing the relative frequencies of grammatical categories in the Anaphora Corpus. The

---

[18] DE_{lit} provides a literal translation of the German sentence.
[19] Chi-squared test: $\chi^2 = 1.5185$, $df = 2$, $p = .468$

top chart displays the data for pronominal anaphors in the source languages. For example, EN_O starts out with a larger set of markables than DE_O due to its inclusion of non-pronominal, adverbial types.

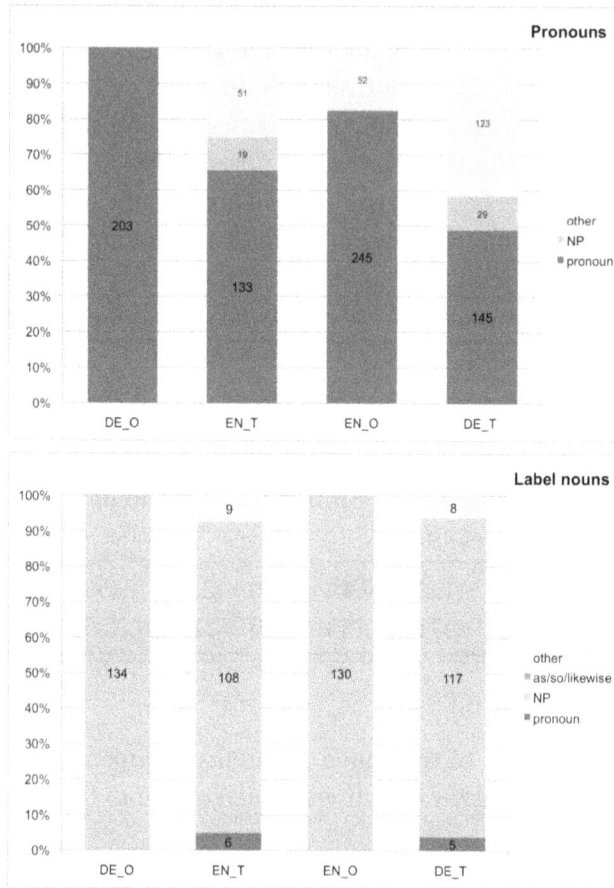

Figure 3: Relative frequencies of grammatical categories. Top chart: figures of pronominal anaphors; bottom chart: figures of the label nouns. Class 'as/so/likewise' is the markable type introduced in EN_t. Class 'other' (the white parts) consists of other cases with structural mismatches in the translations (such as translations by clauses), or cases in which anaphors could not be aligned to corresponding material in the translation.

It is clear that German and English show the same preferences with respect to the categorial realization of abstract anaphors. Similarly, translations of pronominal anaphors to more elaborate NP anaphors can be observed in both translation directions (see the column 'Pronoun to NP' in Table 6, and the bars 'EN_t' and 'DE_t' in the top chart in Figure 3). This effect might be attributable to the translation process (and could be an example of explicitation).

However, to fully exclude language-specific tendencies, we would also need to compare relative frequencies in the comparable$_{trans}$ corpora (between DE_o and DE_t, and EN_o and EN_t, respectively), which is not possible at the current stage of the project because of the different sets of markables used in the rounds of annotation.

Table 7: Label nouns: Categorial transposition types

	NP to NP		NP to pron		NP to other		Sum	
DE_o–to–EN_t	87.2%	(102)	5.1%	(6)	7.7%	(9)	100%	(117)
EN_o–to–DE_t	90.0%	(117)	3.8%	(5)	6.2%	(8)	100%	(130)

Abstract anaphors with demonstrative label nouns   Another kind of counter-check can be performed by investigating original NP anaphors and their translations. If many NPs were unexpectedly translated by pronouns, categorial transpositions from pronouns to NPs or vice versa would seem to be done at random.

In the Anaphora Corpus, the vast majority of label noun anaphors is translated by NPs, independent of the translation direction, see Table 7.[20] Only 4.5% of the label nouns are translated as pronouns (or as pronominal adverbs).

We conclude that there is a language-independent tendency that pronominal anaphors will be translated into full NPs, and that full NP anaphors till tend to remain full NPs in translation. This would conform with the explicitation hypothesis. §5.4 discusses individual translation examples in more detail.

4.3 Grammatical function

Pronominal abstract anaphors   In the annotation of pronominal anaphors, only coarse-grained functions were annotated: *subject, object,* and *other.* Table 8 shows the translation equivalences for subjects and objects in both translation directions, DE_o–to–EN_t and EN_o–to–DE_t. As can be seen in the figure, German

---

[20]There are no significant differences between the two translation directions.

subject anaphors usually remain subjects in the English translation, whereas German object anaphors tend to become subjects in English as well. The non-literal translation in (6) results in such a transposition.

(6) DE_o: Das kann man nicht einfach so geschehen lassen.
     EN_t: It is not such a simple matter.
     DE_{lit}: That you cannot simply let happen.   (ep-04-03-09/31)

Table 8: Pronouns: Transpositions of the functions *subject* and *object*

German original		English translation		English original		German translation	
Function	Freq	Function	Freq	Function	Freq	Function	Freq
subject	147	subject	107	subject	177	subject	114
		object	5			object	10
		other	35			other	53
object	55	object	27	object	37	object	18
		subject	12			subject	5
		other	16			other	14

As in §4.2, the bar plots in Figure 4 present a more general overview by summarizing the relative frequencies of grammatical functions in the Anaphora Corpus. The top chart in Figure 4 summarizes the distribution of grammatical functions with respect to pronominal anaphors and their translation equivalents. The cross-linguistic comparison of subjects and objects indicates significant differences: English uses more anaphoric subjects than German does.[21] In the comparable$_{trans}$ sets, we observe an overuse of anaphoric subjects in DE_t, which could be interpreted as a *shining-through* of English preferences.

Abstract anaphors with demonstrative label nouns   In the annotation of the label nouns, we extended the set of functions, including a class *argument-after-preposition* ('arg-after-prep') to capture both prepositional objects and prepositional adverbials, and a class *attribute* to be used for all (prepositional and nominal) attributes of noun phrases.

In the majority of the translations, the original function is also used in the translated unit (DE_o–to–EN_t: 71.55% (83), EN_o–to–DE_t: 73.38% (91)).[22]

---

[21]Chi-squared test: $\chi^2 = 5.3953$, $df = 1$, $p < .05$

[22]The proportions do not differ significantly, according to a Chi-squared test: $\chi^2 = 0.0301$, $df = 1$, $p = .8622$.

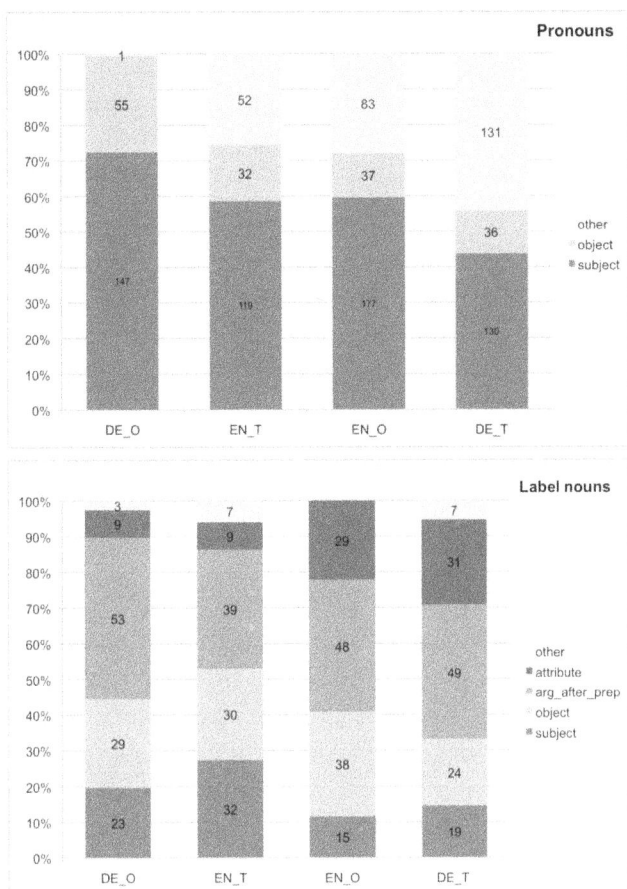

Figure 4: Relative frequencies of grammatical functions. The top chart refers to pronominal anaphors in the source languages and their translated equivalents, the bottom chart to label nouns.

However, there are some divergences: see Table 9, which lists interesting cases of transpositions of label noun functions. 17% of the 'arguments-after-prepositions' in DE_o are translated into subjects in EN_t. This is not mirrored in the opposite translation direction: only two out of 48 arg-after-preps in EN_o are translated as a subject in DE_t. We interpret this as a tendency for German prepositional phrases to be translated as subjects in English. An example is provided in (7).

(7) DE_o: Sie haben die Chance, <u>in diesem Wettbewerb</u> wirklich sehr vieles zusammenzuführen; regionale Kulturen können grenzüberschreitend zusammenarbeiten.

Table 9: Label nouns: Transpositions of functions. Only pairs discussed in the text are listed.

	Arg-after-prep to subject	Attribute to attribute	Object to attribute
DE_o–to–EN_t	17.0% (9/53)	66.7% (6/9)	3.5% (1/29)
EN_o–to–DE_t	4.1% (2/48)	72.4% (21/31)	18.4% (7/24)

EN_t: This competition gives them the opportunity to bring a very great deal of elements together; there can be cross-border cooperation between regional cultures.
DE_{lit}: They have the opportunity to bring a very great deal of elements together in this competition ...   (ep-06-04-04/317)

English shows a characteristic tendency to realize abstract anaphors as NP attributes, in contrast to German, cf. Figure 4: 22.3% (29) of the abstract nouns in EN_o are realized as attributes, versus 7.8% (9) in DE_o.[23] If we examine the language pairs from the parallel corpora, the number of attributes do not significantly differ, because attributes are usually translated as attributes in both translational directions (cf. Table 9). The conservative mappings result in a *shining-through* effect in both directions.

As just noted, German generally avoids anaphoric attributes. Surprisingly, there are some cases in which English objects are translated by German attributes (7 cases, see the third column in Table 9), but there is only one case in the opposite direction. This is the effect of a strong tendency for nominalization in German. In (8), the English object of a subordinate clause is translated as an NP attribute in German.

(8) EN_o: Not all the decisions will be taken when we vote this report through.
      DE_t: Mit unserer Zustimmung zu diesem Bericht werden nicht automatisch alle Entscheidungen getroffen.
      DE_{lit}: With our agreement to this report not all points are decided automatically.   (ep-00-05-16/19)

---

[23]The observed difference is significant, according to a Chi-squared test: $\chi^2 = 7.368, df = 1, p < .01$.

Finally, the bottom chart in Figure 4 shows the distributions of the functions observed with label nouns. The results are similar to those regarding pronominal functions.

Since the set of markables differ among the corpora, these are only preliminary conclusions. Further investigation is needed to verify the observed biases.

4.4 Clausal position

Grammatical categories (pronouns, full NPs, etc.) and grammatical functions (subject, object, etc.) are very similar in German and English, and the two languages can be directly compared to each other rather easily in these respects. In contrast, word order regularities are very different in the two languages. English has a fixed word order (S–V–O), whereas main clauses in German are *verb-second* (i.e., they allow any grammatical function to appear in the preverbal position, also called the *prefield* position).

Both languages have extra ways to mark or highlight constituents, such as cleft or topicalized constructions, which serve to place a constituent intended to be emphasized at the beginning of a sentence. Such special constructions are more often used in English than in German, probably because the prefield position in German already serves this purpose to some extent.

Sentence-initial positions play an important role in information structure: Old information tends to occur early in the sentence, new information towards the end. As abstract anaphors refer to previously mentioned referents, they represent old information. We therefore hypothesize that anaphors will tend to occur in topicalized or prefield positions.

(9) shows a relevant case: A German prefield instance is translated by a topic construction (*that is something*) in English.

(9) DE_o: Wenn es leichter ist, an die Subventionen zu gelangen, dann steigt auch die Nachfrage dafür. Dies halten wir gerade bei kleinen Programmen für notwendig.
   EN_t: If subsidies are more readily obtainable, the demand for them will rise, and that is something we regard as needed, particularly by small programmes.
   DE_{lit}: ...This we regard as needed, particularly by small programmes. (ep-05-10-24/68)

Our annotation distinguishes between three different positions for anaphors: in the *matrix* clause, in a *subordinate* clause, or in a sentence-initial position, which includes topic-like constructions in English (annotated as *topic*) and the *prefield* position in German.[24]

However, as explained above, we cannot directly compare these positions to each other, due to language-inherent differences in syntax. Therefore, we must restrict our comparisons to the comparable$_{trans}$ corpora in this case.

Pronominal abstract anaphors The top charts in Figure 5 show the relative proportions of pronominal anaphors across the clausal positions.

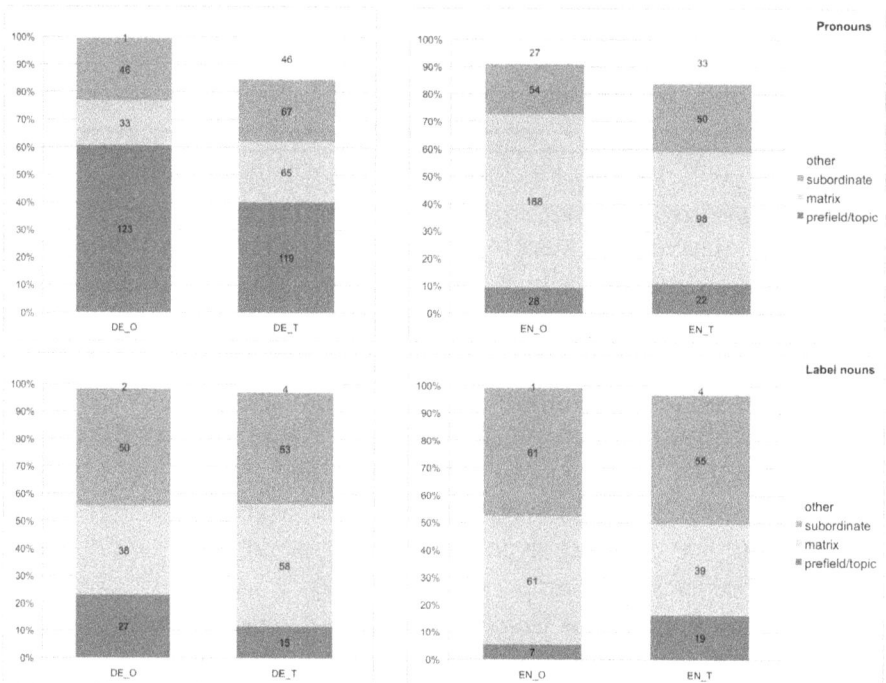

Figure 5: Relative frequencies of clausal positions. The top charts refers to pronominal anaphors, the bottom charts to label nouns. Only the pairings DE_o–DE_t and EN_o–EN_t can be compared to each other.

In comparing the two German corpora, we observe a significant underuse of prefield anaphors in DE_t: that is, pronominal anaphors in DE_o occur considerably more often in the prefield and less frequently in the (rest of the) matrix

---

[24]Note that our label *matrix* is assigned to constituents in the matrix clause, *except for* constituents in the topic or prefield position.

clause.[25]This indicates that translated texts do not follow our hypothesis to the same extent as original texts do.

A different effect is observed in the English corpora: EN_t shows a significant underuse of anaphors in the matrix position; this is counterbalanced by an overuse of anaphors in subordinate clauses.[26]Anaphors in topic positions are very rare, contradicting our (simplistic) hypothesis.

Abstract anaphors with demonstrative label nouns   The distribution of label nouns clearly differs from the distribution of pronominal anaphors, as can be seen in Figure 5. Whereas pronouns in German are preferably realized in the prefield position (cf. top charts), there is no such preference for label noun anaphors in our data (cf. bottom charts). Instead, label nouns are preferably realized in matrix and subordinate positions.[27] For English, we observe a significant overuse of anaphors in topic constructions in EN_t.[28]

It would be interesting to relate these observations to *shining-through* effects; however, we cannot draw this conclusion on the basis of our annotations. The annotated concepts (topic, prefield) would first have to be calibrated to each other.

5 Edit operations and lexical specificity: Case studies

The previous section presented quantitative results from the comparison of our parallel and comparable$_{trans}$ corpora, focusing on various properties of pronominal and label noun anaphors, such as grammatical category and grammatical function. In this section, we investigate a range of case studies in hopes of shedding light on selected details of our data.

We focus on examples in which the translated anaphor differs from the pattern of its source, i.e., cases in which material has been added, omitted, or substituted.

---

[25]Proportion of matrix in DE_o: 60.9% (123/202) versus DE_t: 96.7% (119/123); Chi-squared test: $\chi^2 = 7.6415, df = 1, p < 0.01$.

[26]Proportion of matrix in EN_o: 69.6% (188/270) vs. EN_t: 57.6% (98/170); Chi-squared test: $\chi^2 = 6.0677, df = 1, p < 0.05$. Proportion of subordinate in EN_o: 20.0% (54/270) vs. EN_t: 29.4% (50/170); Chi-squared test: $\chi^2 = 4.6114, df = 1, p < 0.05$.

[27]The observed asymmetry between pronouns and label nouns is probably a reflection of the universal tendency of pronouns to occur very early in the sentence, whereas no such general tendency exists for full NPs.

[28]Proportion of topic in EN_o: 5.4% (7/129) vs. EN_t: 16.8% (19/113); Chi-squared test: $\chi^2 = 7.0016, df = 1, p < .01$.

We call these processes *edit operations*, following the common terminology in computational linguistics (Levenshtein 1965). An obvious (and highly simplistic) hypothesis would be that an increase in the length of translated anaphors could be an effect of explicitation.[29]

There are numerous ways to add, omit, or substitute material in a label noun NP, and we examine some of these in detail. We investigate the addition or omission of adjectives in label noun NPs (§5.1), the substitution of nouns by more general or more specific nouns (§5.2 and §5.3), the substitution of full NPs by pronouns and vice versa (§5.4), and the substitution of the demonstrative determiner by various types of expressions (§5.5).

Edit operations often have an effect on the *specificity* of anaphors. We refer to an expression as being *more specific* than another expression if it has fewer possible interpretations. Very often, the addition of material (such as the addition of adjectives, or the expansion of a pronoun to a full NP) results in higher specificity. As the discussions in the next sections show, translations both increase and decrease the specificity of anaphors (contrary to the assumptions made by the explicitation hypothesis).

5.1 Adjectival modifications

In this section, we consider NPs with adjectives in either the original or the translated sentences. The examples illustrate that some of these adjectives contribute to the specificity of the NP, while others do not. We observed both situations: adjectives being added in the translation, and adjectives omitted. In the Anaphora Corpus, relevant cases were found only in the translation direction EN_o–to–DE_t (but not in DE_o–to–EN_t).

In several cases, the German translated NP contains the adjective *vorliegend* 'present', but there is no correspondent in the original English sentence, cf. (10). This adjective clearly serves only a deictic function, i.e., it assumes the meaning of *this* in the English NP. Consequently, in all these cases, the demonstrative article *this* is translated by the definite article in German (which is fused with the preposition: *in dem* 'in the' becomes *im*). Thus, the German version of the abstract NP is in fact a very close translation of the original NP in English.

---

[29] Of course, there are clear cases of length differences that must be removed from such considerations, such as multi-word expressions and compounds, which are usually spelled in one word in German and in several words in English. Further counter-examples to this hypothesis are presented in the following subsections.

(10)   *EN$_o$*: This exercise has been made possible in <u>this case</u> because of the
        work of national and international bikers' rights organisations
        coordinated by the Federation of European Motorcyclists, or FEM.
        DE$_t$: Ein solcher Dialog wurde <u>im vorliegenden Fall</u> durch die vom
        Verband Europäischer Motorradfahrer, VEM, koordinierte Arbeit
        nationaler und internationaler Organisationen für die Rechte von
        Motorradfahrern ermöglicht.
        DE$_{lit}$: This exercise has been made possible in <u>the present case</u> ...
        (ep-96-06-18/252)

In other examples, adjectives are omitted. In several cases, this concerns the
adjective *whole* not being translated in the corresponding German sentences.[30]
In these examples, the information provided by the original English *whole*-NP is
more elaborate than the translated German NP. For instance, in the German part
of (11), it is not specified that the *whole* area is involved. It would therefore be
possible to continue the clause by actually limiting the area in the following way:
*(much progress has been made in this area) — not in all parts/aspects, but in most
of them.* This reading is not possible for the English original NP. In this sense, we
can state that the original NP in English is indeed more specific than its German
counterpart in these examples.

(11)   *EN$_o$*: We have to note that much progress has been made in <u>this whole</u>
        <u>area</u>.
        DE$_t$: Wir müssen feststellen, dass in <u>diesem Bereich</u> große Fortschritte
        erzielt wurden.
        DE$_{lit}$: We have to note that in <u>this area</u> much progress has been made.
        (ep-97-04-08/304)

Finally, in one example, the adjective *particular* has been omitted, see (12). The
contribution by this adjective is different from the contribution of *whole* above.
Here, the adjective serves as a marker of focus. In contrast to the above example, omitting the marker in German does not allow a different interpretation of
the respective NP. Hence, we would not classify the German translation as less
specific. (Of course, the German translation lacks the contribution of the focus
marker, but this seems unrelated to specificity.)

(12)   *EN$_o$*: As a British Member, I am optimistic that the British Presidency can
        maintain the momentum that was picked up originally by the

---

[30]In one case, the adjective *ganz* 'whole' was added in the translation.

Luxembourg Presidency and that will be carried on through the Austrian and German presidencies because there is much to do in <u>this particular area</u>.

DE$_t$: Als britischer Abgeordneter bin ich zuversichtlich, dass die britische Präsidentschaft den Prozess, der ursprünglich von der luxemburgischen Präsidentschaft begonnen wurde, in Gang halten wird und dass er auch unter dem österreichischen und deutschen Vorsitz weitergeführt werden wird, denn in <u>diesem Bereich</u> gibt es noch viel zu tun.

DE$_{lit}$: ...because in <u>this area</u> there is still much to do.　　(ep-98-02-19/225)

Comparing these three examples ((10)–(12)), we see that only one type of adjective actually has an impact on the specificity of the abstract NP.

5.2 Lexical semantics of nouns

In this section, we consider examples in which the lexical semantics of the nouns has an effect on the specificity of the abstract NP. Either the original or the translated noun can be more specific.

Most of the examples are found in *EN$_o$*–to–*DE$_t$* translations. In most of these cases, the German translations are more specific than the English originals. A clear example is provided in (13). The original English noun, *issue*, is highly generic: if one did not know the context, a large set of interpretations would be possible. In contrast, the German translation, *Erweiterung* 'expansion' is much more specific.

(13)　*EN$_o$*: I would ask the President-in-Office to continue to champion <u>this issue</u> and emphasise it consistently in Göteborg, especially with a view to enabling the Irish to say "yes" to enlargement there.

　　DE$_t$: Ich bitte die Ratspräsidentin, ihr Engagement für <u>die Erweiterung</u> fortzusetzen und dieses Thema auch in Göteborg konsequent in den Vordergrund zu rücken, damit die Iren sich auf diesem Gipfel klar und deutlich für die Erweiterung aussprechen können.

　　DE$_{lit}$: I would ask the President-in-Office to continue to champion <u>the expansion</u> ...　　　　　　　　　　　　　　　(ep-01-06-13/8)

Similar, if somewhat more ambiguous examples, can be seen in (14) and (15). In (14), the English original noun *message* is less specific than the German translation *Zusage* 'assurance'. Out of context, the English noun *message* could refer to an assurance or a denial. The *denial* reading is obviously not possible in the

German translation, which makes it more specific than the English original in this respect.

(14) EN_o: If we reverse that message now we run the risk of undermining all the reforms which have taken place at great pain in Central and Eastern Europe.
        DE_t: Wenn wir jetzt von dieser Zusage abweichen, gefährden wir alle Reformen, die in Mittel- und Osteuropa mit großer Mühe unternommen wurden.
        DE_{lit}: If we depart from this assurance now we run the risk of undermining all the reforms ...   (ep-96-04-17/58)

Similarly, in (15), the German translation *Zwecke* 'purposes' is more specific than the original English noun *way*. For example, *spending money in that way* could refer to spending money for a specific purpose, or to spending money over a certain amount of time. In contrast, the German noun *Zwecke* only permits the first interpretation.

(15) EN_o: The continued spending of money in that way is unacceptable.
        DE_t: Die fortgesetzte Verwendung von Mitteln für diese Zwecke ist unvertretbar.
        DE_{lit}: The continued spending of money for these purposes is unacceptable.   (ep-01-04-03/46)

It should be noted that although most of the translated nouns are more specific than the original nouns, rare examples in the other direction also exist. For example, (16) involves *request* as the original English noun. The German translation is *Fall* 'case', which is clearly less specific than the English original (but connects back to a previous use of the word 'case' in the same sentence).

(16) EN_o: But the third came with the thumbprint of Government on it, unlike this request, so it is an inadequate precedent, even if it is a modest step in that direction.
        DE_t: Beim dritten Fall war die Regierung involviert, anders als in diesem Fall, weshalb er als Präzedenzfall ungeeignet ist, selbst wenn er ein bescheidener Schritt in diese Richtung ist.
        DE_{lit}: In the third case, the Government was involved, unlike as in this case, so it is an inadequate test case ...   (ep-01-05-02/31)

5.3 Impact of context

Consideration of the lexical semantics of nouns can help to locate translation examples in which specificity differs between the original and translated texts. However, it is not enough to simply consider pairs of nouns or NPs. If there is a mismatch between the NPs, the missing information can also be expressed in other parts of the sentence.

In (17), the English translation *thing* seems to be much less specific than the German original noun *Forderung* 'request'. However, the meaning corresponding to *Forderung* is instead expressed in the English verb *calling for*.

(17) DE_o: Ich sehe diejenigen, die jetzt in Briefen an uns eine Maximalharmonisierung fordern – gerade im Bereich des Verbraucherschutzes –, schon wieder sagen: Das ist zu viel Harmonisierung! Stichwort: Verbraucherkreditrichtlinie; daher sollten die Marktteilnehmer sehr vorsichtig mit dieser Forderung umgehen.
EN_t: I can imagine those who currently write to us demanding maximum harmonisation in consumer protection matters saying – yet again – that we are taking harmonisation too far with the Consumer Credit Directive; that is why they should be very careful when calling for such a thing.
DE_{lit}: ...therefore the market players should be very careful with this request.   (ep-05-04-27/120)

Further apparent specificity mismatches can arise when the sentence structure is changed considerably during translation. In (18), the German original NP, *diese Strategie* 'this strategy', is less specific than the translated NP *the Lisbon strategy*. However, the English translation does not actually provide any more information than the original German sentence: The German NP *diese Strategie* refers back to the antecedent *Lissabon-Strategie* (printed in bold in the example). In the English translation, the sentence structure has been changed so that the NP in question is the first mention of the abstract object, and therefore refers to *Lisbon* (the second mention being *it*).

(18) DE_o: Ich danke dem Kok-Bericht; das, was wir jetzt dringend brauchen, ist eine Ausrichtung **der Lissabon-Strategie**, denn diese Strategie ist richtig.
EN_t: I am grateful for the Kok report; what we now urgently need – as the Lisbon strategy is the right one – is an orientation for it.
DE_{lit}: ...what we now urgently need is an orientation for **the Lisbon strategy**, as this strategy is right.   (ep-04-11-17/38)

This discussion demonstrates that we must be careful in drawing conclusions from purely statistical data. Even detailed information about word-to-word correspondences (such as the noun pairs discussed in this section) can be misleading. It is therefore important to also consider the noun pairs in context. However, analysis of statistical counts and noun pairs as a first step can help to detect noteworthy examples.

5.4 Pronouns vs. NPs

As discussed in §4.2, pronouns are often translated into full NPs, both in DE_o–to–EN_t and EN_o–to–DE_t. In this section, we examine some of these cases in greater detail.

For example, in (19) (= 5), the English pronoun *this* corresponds to the full NP *diesem Standpunkt* 'this position' in the German translation. The pronominal anaphor *this* in the English original sentence can in principle refer to different kinds of objects, such as a process, a rejection, an undertaking, etc. This flexibility is eliminated in the German translation, in which it is explicitly specified that the speaker does not support the *position*.

(19) EN_o: I do not necessarily support this.
      DE_t: Diesem Standpunkt schließe ich mich nicht notwendigerweise an.
      DE_{lit}: This position I do not necessarily support.   (ep-00-10-03/15)

In a similar way, the German original pronominal anaphor *das* 'that' is less specific than its English translation *this threat* in (20). The pronominal anaphor could also refer to a development, for example, an interpretation that is unlikely for the corresponding English expression *this threat*. In the German sentence, however, the verb *abwenden* 'avert' provides important clues and restricts the set of possible referents to those with negative connotations.

(20) DE_o: Das konnte durch die glänzende Vorsitzführung von Frau
      Cederschiöld, aber auch durch die sehr substanzielle Hilfe der
      Kommission abgewendet werden, und deswegen können wir diesem
      Kompromissergebnis zustimmen.
      EN_t: Thanks to Mrs Cederschiöld's inspired leadership, but also due to
      the very substantial support from the Commission, this threat has been
      averted, so we can now vote in favour of this compromise result.
      DE_{lit}: That could be averted by Mrs Cederschiöld's inspired leadership,
      but also due to the very substantial support from the Commission ...
      (ep-04-01-28/109)

These examples were taken from a wide range of sentences in which an original pronominal anaphor was translated with a more specific full NP. In the other direction (i.e., from original abstract demonstrative NPs to translated pronouns), only rare examples can be found. (21) is such an example: German *diese Ansicht* 'this view' is translated with the pronominal *that* in English. The verb *agree*, however, is only compatible with a small range of readings for the pronoun: *that* could refer to, e.g., a judgment, assessment, opinion, or the like—quite similar concepts. Due to the use of the verb *agree*, the pronominal translation is only marginally less specific than the original full NP.

(21) DE_o: Sie schreiben, dass es nicht sinnvoll ist, Beihilfen für Investitionen an Unternehmen zu geben, die profitträchtig sind. Diese Ansicht teile ich.
       EN_t: He writes that it makes no sense to give aid to businesses that are already profitable, and in that I agree with him.
       DE_{lit}: He writes that it makes no sense to give aid to businesses that are already profitable. This view I share. (ep-06-02-13/115)

There are some very unusual examples in which the translated sentence is indeed less specific than its original counterpart. In (22), *dieser Effekt* 'this effect' in German corresponds to the English pronoun *this*. English *this* could refer to a development or a threat that has been exacerbated, but the German full NP does not allow these readings.

(22) DE_o: Dieser Effekt wird noch dadurch verstärkt, dass junge Mädchen nicht mehr zur Schule gehen können, weil sie ihre an Aids erkrankten Eltern pflegen müssen.
       EN_t: This is exacerbated by the fact that young girls are no longer able to attend school because they have to care for their parents who are sick with AIDS.
       DE_{lit}: This effect is exacerbated by the fact that ... (ep-04-01-13/306)

Taking prior context into account, the discourse model that speakers and hearers have built up thus far might provide very clear constraints for the reference of *this*, so that no further specifications (such as using the noun *effect*) would be necessary. The issue of interest to us is that in most cases in which the original contribution uses a full NP, the translator also uses a full NP. In other words, if the author of the original contribution finds it necessary to spell out the referring expression in detail, this detail is probably required in order to avoid misinterpretation, and the translator will face the very same situation in the target language (especially for languages as similar as German and English).

Thus, whenever the translator deviates from the original version in this way, it could indicate an interesting example for detailed examination, both in the original and in the translated texts.

5.5 Transposition of the demonstrative determiner

In this subsection, we investigate cases that involve translations without (canonical) demonstrative articles. Remember that in the annotations with label nouns, only those noun chunks that contained a demonstrative determiner were pre-marked. We therefore expect close translations to contain a demonstrative determiner as well.

In total, we found 20 instances in EN_t that did not contain such a determiner, and 34 instances in DE_t. In many cases (14 in EN_t and 13 in DE_t), the abstract NP is translated either by a pronoun or by a diverging syntactic construction.

Some instances in DE_t employ a strategy that we addressed above (see Section 5.1): Adjectives, such as *vorliegend* 'present, at hand' and *last-mentioned* are used to convey the deictic meaning.

In some cases, the demonstrative pronoun is replaced by a possessive in the translated sentence. In our corpus, this occurs in English original sentences and their German translations. Some examples also involve minor changes in the overall structure of the sentence. In (23) (=4), the English speaker thanks the rapporteur for producing the report. In the German translation, *producing* is not translated but is instead replaced by the possessive pronoun.

(23) EN_o: Madam President, I would like to thank the rapporteur for producing <u>this report</u> because it is a very important one.
  DE_t: Frau Präsidentin, ich möchte dem Berichterstatter für <u>seinen Bericht</u> danken, denn es handelt sich um einen wirklich wichtigen Bericht.
  DE_{lit}: Madam President, I would like to thank the rapporteur for <u>his report</u> because it is a very important report.   (ep-98-11-17/284)

In the remaining cases, we observe a variety of situations. In some sentences, the specificity of the anaphoric noun seems considerably reduced in the translation. In most of these examples, *such (a)* serves as a substitute determiner, see (24). Like canonical demonstratives, *such* has a deictic component but points to a type or set of entities that share certain properties rather than to a specific entity. In another example, the demonstrative NP is translated by an unspecific negated NP, see (25).

(24) EN_o: The Commission, however, intends [to] bring forward a Council regulation on the control of unloading and transfers: <u>this proposal</u> is already being prepared and the Commission believes it should provide a more appropriate framework.
DE_t: Die Kommission beabsichtigt vielmehr, eine Verordnung des Rates betreffend die Kontrolle von Aus- und Umladungen vorzuschlagen: <u>Ein solcher Vorschlag</u> wird bereits vorbereitet und dürfte nach Ansicht der Kommission einen angemesseneren Rahmen bilden.
DE_{lit}: ...<u>such a proposal</u> is already being prepared ...   (ep-98-03-13/71)

(25) EN_o: It is regrettable that we cannot yet achieve <u>that full agreement</u>.
DE_t: Es ist bedauerlich, daß wir noch <u>keine vollständige Einigung</u> erzielen können.
DE_{lit}: It is regrettable that we can yet achieve <u>no full agreement</u>.
(ep-97-04-08/304)

Finally, in (26) (= 13), the abstract label noun is translated by a lexically more specific noun. As a result, the space of possible references is narrowed and therefore use of the demonstrative determiner seems superfluous (see the discussion in §5.2).

(26) EN_o: I would ask the President-in-Office to continue to champion <u>this issue</u> and emphasise it consistently in Göteborg, especially with a view to enabling the Irish to say "yes" to enlargement there.
DE_t: Ich bitte die Ratspräsidentin, ihr Engagement für <u>die Erweiterung</u> fortzusetzen und dieses Thema auch in Göteborg konsequent in den Vordergrund zu rücken, damit die Iren sich auf diesem Gipfel klar und deutlich für die Erweiterung aussprechen können.
DE_{lit}: I would ask the President-in-Office to continue to champion <u>the expansion</u> ...   (ep-01-06-13/8)

6 Conclusion

In this paper, we have presented a bootstrapping approach to the annotation of pronominal and label noun anaphors. Based on our annotated data, we investigated selected properties of the anaphors in greater detail. Before summarizing our findings, we would like to emphasize that all our results should be understood as valid only for the particular type of language represented in the Europarl corpus — namely, spoken and translated parliamentary debates. This holds for both the differences between original and translated texts as well as for the language-specific properties that we have identified. It remains to be seen to what extent our findings will generalize to other domains and text types.

Lexical choice   Original and translated texts showed identical preferences with regard to pronominal anaphors: *das* 'that' in German, and *this, that* in English. Translated German texts showed an interesting significant overuse of *dies* 'this', which might be an effect of *shining-through*, reflecting the high frequency of its English counterpart *this*.

Certain label nouns occurred very often in our data. This is related to the domain of our data: parliamentary debates. Nevertheless, when we compared the frequencies of selected label nouns in original and translated turns thoughout the entire Europarl Corpus, interesting (and statistically significant) discrepancies stood out.

Based on our annotated data, the German noun *Angelegenheit* 'issue' seemed to serve as a kind of "dummy" translation. With the noun *Bereich* 'area', we observed an interesting asymmetry: When translated into English, a variety of English expressions were used (e.g., *area, issue, subject, sphere*), whereas German translators employed *Bereich* quasi-exclusively as the translation for *area*.

Category, function, position   Translations in general tended to preserve the anaphor's categories, functions, and positions; however, some interesting differences were observed.

With regard to category, we observed a clear asymmetry: A considerable number of pronouns were translated as full NPs, while the reverse was not true. Since the asymmetry appeared in both languages, this might have been an effect of the translation process, perhaps due to translational conventions (in the form of "do not use pronouns"). Very rarely could the opposite mapping be observed. As in the case of lexical semantics (see below), the context sometimes compensated for the loss of specificity.

At the functional level, we observed a preference for anaphoric attributes in original English texts, in contrast to German. This resulted in an overuse of these attributes in DE_t and an underuse in EN_t, i.e., a *shining-through* effect in both directions.

Finally, with respect to the positional properties of the anaphors, both languages exhibited language-typical patterns in both original and translated texts. *Shining-through* effects were found here as well: DE_t underused anaphors in the prefield position, while EN_t underused matrix anaphors in comparison to subordinate anaphors.

Adjectival modifications Adjectives such as *whole* were sometimes omitted, even when this could result in under-specification and various possible interpretations. Such omissions mainly occurred in the translation direction EN_o–to–DE_t. That is, in these cases, the German translations were less specific than their sources.

Lexical semantics Most of the cases in which the original and translated nouns differed with respect to their specificity were found with EN_o–to–DE_t translations. The German translations were generally more specific than their English counterparts. (This might outweigh the tendencies described in the previous paragraph to some extent.)

In certain cases, the immediate context (e.g., the main verb) compensated for the loss of specificity in the nouns.

Transposition of demonstratives Two cases were of interest here: First, specific demonstrative NPs were sometimes translated by *such* (or its German equivalent). The speaker no longer referred to the specific entity in question but to all entities of the same kind. Second, the demonstrative article was sometimes translated by a definite article. In these cases, the deictic function of the demonstrative often seemed to be taken over by adjectives such as *vorliegend* 'present'.

The amount of data that we examined was rather small, so we consider the research reported here to be a pilot study that can serve as a starting point for further in-depth analyses. In order to derive more reliable conclusions, we need more data. This can be achieved in several ways.

In the next annotation round, the translated nouns that have not yet been included in our label noun list will be added and annotated.

We also plan to provide the annotators with translation candidates that have been automatically selected from all noun chunks in the aligned translated turn. To this end, we intend to use heuristics derived from our present findings, e.g., using the most common translation equivalents for nouns and marking NPs containing modifiers such as 'present' or 'at hand' as promising candidates (in addition to demonstrative NPs). Pre-selecting such candidates in the aligned translated turns will make the annotation procedure simpler and more efficient.

Thus far, we have only annotated and aligned pairs of turns that contain the pronouns *it, this,* and *that* (and their German equivalents) and demonstrative

NPs with label nouns in the original turns. No such restrictions applied to the translated turns; here the annotators were free to mark arbitrary strings as the expression that represented the translation of the anaphor in the original text. As we have seen, however, translators very often stay close to the original. Therefore, we cannot expect to discover exceptional ways of referring to abstract entities in translated texts very often. To complement our 'restricted' approach, it would be useful to annotate a sample of running text, marking all types of abstract anaphors that appear.

Finally, we would like to take advantage of the fact that Europarl provides debate protocols in many other languages, and expand our studies to include additional languages.

References

Asher, Nicholas. 1993. *Reference to abstract objects in discourse.* Boston: Kluwer.

Becher, Viktor. 2011. *Explicitation and implicitation in translation: A corpus-based study of English–German and German–English translations of business texts.* Universität Hamburg dissertation.

Blum-Kulka, Shoshana. 1986. Shifts of cohesion and coherence in translation. In Juliane House & Shoshana Blum-Kulka (eds.), *Interlingual and intercultural communication*, 17–35. Tübingen: Gunter Narr.

Byron, Donna K. 2003. *Annotation of Pronouns and their Antecedents: A comparison of two domains.* Technical Report, University of Rochester.

Cartoni, Bruno, Sandrine Zufferey, Thomas Meyer & Andrei Popescu-Belis. 2011. How comparable are parallel corpora? Measuring the distribution of general vocabulary and connectives. In *Proceedings of 4th workshop on building and using comparable corpora, at ACL-HLT 2011*, 78–86.

Čulo, Oliver, Silvia Hansen-Schirra, Stella Neumann & Mihaela Vela. 2008. Empirical studies on language contrast using the English-German comparable and parallel CroCo corpus. In *Proceedings of the LREC workshop on comparable corpora*, 47–51. Marrakesh.

Dipper, Stefanie, Christine Rieger, Melanie Seiss & Heike Zinsmeister. 2011. Abstract anaphors in German and English. In Iris Hendrickx, Sobha Lalitha Devi, António Branco & Ruslan Mitkov (eds.), *Anaphora processing and applications: 8th discourse anaphora and anaphor resolution colloquium, DAARC 2011. revised selected papers*, 96–107. Berlin: Springer.

Dipper, Stefanie, Melanie Seiss & Heike Zinsmeister. 2012. The use of parallel and comparable data for analysis of abstract anaphora in German and English. In *Proceedings of the LREC-12.* Istanbul.

Dipper, Stefanie & Heike Zinsmeister. 2009. Annotating discourse anaphora. In *Proceedings of LAW iii,* 166–169.

Dipper, Stefanie & Heike Zinsmeister. 2010. Towards a standard for annotating abstract anaphora. In *Proceedings of the LREC 2010 workshop on language resource and language technology standards,* 54–59. Valletta.

Dorr, Bonnie J. 1994. Machine translation divergences: A formal description and proposed solution. *Computational Linguistics* 20(4). 597–633.

Francis, Gill. 1994. Labelling discourse: An aspect of nominal group lexical cohesion. In Malcolm Coulthard (ed.), *Advances in written text analysis,* 83–101. London: Routledge.

Gries, Stefan T. 2005. Null-hypothesis significance testing of word frequencies: A follow-up on Kilgarriff. *Corpus Linguistics and Linguistic Theory* 1. 277–294.

Halteren, Hans van. 2008. Source language markers in EUROPARL translations. In *Proceedings of the 22nd international conference on computational linguistics COLING 08,* 937–944.

Hedberg, Nancy, Jeanette K. Gundel & Ron Zacharski. 2007. Directly and indirectly anaphoric demonstrative and personal pronouns in newspaper articles. In *Proceedings of daarc-2007: 6th discourse anaphora and anaphora resolution colloquium,* 31–36.

K. Byron, Donna. 2002. Resolving pronominal reference to abstract entities. In *Proceedings of the acl-02 conference,* 80–87.

Klaudy, Kinga. 2008. Explicitation. In Mona Baker & Gabriela Saldanha (eds.), *Routledge encyclopedia of translation studies. 2nd edn.* 104–108. London: Routledge.

Koehn, Philipp. 2005. Europarl: A parallel corpus for statistical machine translation. In *Proceedings of MT summit.*

Levenshtein, Vladimir I. 1965. Binary codes capable of correcting deletions, insertions, and reversals. *Doklady Akademii Nauk SSSR* 163(4). 845–848.

Müller, Christoph. 2007. Resolving *it, this,* and *that* in unrestricted multi-party dialog. In *Proceedings of acl-07 conference,* 816–823.

Müller, Christoph & Michael Strube. 2006. Multi-level annotation of linguistic data with MMAX2. In Sabine Braun, Kurt Kohn & Joybrato Mukherjee (eds.), *Corpus technology and language pedagogy: New resources, new tools, new methods,* 197–214. Frankfurt a.M.: Peter Lang.

Navarretta, Costanza. 2008. Pronominal types and abstract reference in the Danish and Italian DAD corpora. In *Proceedings of the second workshop on anaphora resolution*, 63–71.

Navarretta, Costanza & Sussi Olsen. 2008. Annotating abstract pronominal anaphora in the DAD project. In *Proceedings of LREC-08*.

Poesio, Massimo & Ron Artstein. 2008. Anaphoric annotation in the ARRAU corpus. In *Proceedings of LREC-08*.

Pradhan, Sameer, Lance Ramshaw, Ralph Weischedel, Jessica MacBride & Linnea Micciulla. 2007. Unrestricted coreference: identifying entities and events in OntoNotes. In *Proceedings of the ieee-icsc*.

Recasens, Marta. 2008. Discourse deixis and coreference: evidence from AnCora. In *Proceedings of the second workshop on anaphora resolution*, 73–82.

Schmid, Helmut. 1994. Probabilistic part-of-speech tagging using decision tree. In *Proceedings of international conference on new methods in language processing*.

Teich, Elke. 2003. *Cross-linguistic variation in system and text: A methodology for the investigation of translations and comparable texts*. Berlin: De Gruyter.

Vieira, Renata, Susanne Salmon-Alt & Caroline Gasperin. 2002. Coreference and anaphoric relations of demonstrative noun phrases in a multilingual corpus. In *Proceedings of daarc-2002: 4th discourse anaphora and anaphora resolution colloquium*.

Vinay, Jean-Paul & Jean Darbelnet. 1958/1995. *Comparative stylistics of french and english: A methodology for translation*. Amsterdam: Benjamins.

Weischedel, Ralph, Sameer Pradhan, Lance Ramshaw, Jeff Kaufman, Michelle Franchini, Mohammed El-Bachouti, Nianwen Xue, Martha Palmer, Mitchell Marcus, Ann Taylor, Craig Greenberg, Eduard Hovy, Robert Belvin & Ann Houston. 2010. *OntoNotes Release 4.0, with OntoNotes DB Tool v. 0.999 beta*. Tech. rep. http://www.bbn.com/NLP/OntoNotes.

Name index

Name index

of machine translation and post-editing on translations and translators. These topics are much discussed - and rightly so! - in the field of post-editing. However, little work has been done so far on how to model machine translation in terms of translation-theoretic models. Exceptions are, for instance, Rozmyslowicz (2014) who discusses whether translated texts produced by a machine can be counted as translations even though functional translation theory requires agency for the production of a translation, or Lapshinova-Koltunski (2013) who treats machine-translated texts as a text type in its own right and analyses them for their linguistic variation. While the latter is not actually a contribution in terms of theoretical modelling of machine translation, it does represent an interesting shift in perspective on how machine-translated texts are treated. Čulo (2014) makes an attempt at classifying machine translation from the viewpoint of functional theories, albeit on a rather abstract level.

This re-issue contains two new paradigms besides the corpus paradigm which have gained ground in all of the fields addressed here: the cognitive and process-based research paradigm, which interact heavily. With techniques such as eye tracking and key logging, we gain insight into micro and macro processes in various types of text processing, including post-editing, which also brings Machine Translation into focus Carl et al. (see e.g. Carl & Dragsted, this volume; 2016). We hope that this re-edition will give another impulse for connecting Translation Studies with its neighbouring fields, potentially discovering new (common?) grounds.

Leipzig, Germersheim and Aachen, September 2017
Oliver Czulo, Silvia Hansen-Schirra, Stella Neumann

References

Carl, Michael, Srinivas Bangalore & Moritz Schaeffer. 2016. *New directions in empirical translation process research: Exploring the CRITT TPR-DB*. Cham: Springer International Publishing.

Čulo, Oliver. 2014. Approaching Machine Translation from Translation Studies: a perspective on commonalities, potentials, differences. In *Proceedings of the Seventeenth Annual Conference of the European Association for Machine Translation (EAMT)*, 199–208. Dubrovnik, Croatia.

Gast, Volker. 2015. On the use of translation corpora in contrastive linguistics: A case study of impersonalization in english and german. *Languages in Contrast* 15(1). 4–33.

Preface to the new edition

This volume is a re-issue of the second of three volumes made up of previous issues of the open access journal "Translation: Computation, Corpora, Cognition" (TC3) which was transformed into the book series "Translation and Multilingual Natural Language Processing" (TMNLP) at LangSci Press. The underlying TC3 issue focused on the potential of exchange between the three fields Contrastive Linguistics, Translation Studies and Machine Translation. Today, we can look back and ask what has changed in the last five years.

The corpus paradigm proved a way to establish an intensified exchange between Translation Studies and Contrastive Linguistics, both in terms of methodology and theory. It seems, however, that the flow of information is stronger in one direction: translation scholars have adapted and evolved approaches from Contrastive Linguistics, yet our observation is that this has happened to a lesser extent in the opposite direction.

In Contrastive Linguistics, there has been a growing interest in the analysis of translations from various viewpoints, though apparently not so much in translation theory itself. Among those who integrate translations in their analysis of language contrasts is Gast (2015) who makes use of the Europarl corpus to study impersonalisation strategies in English and to contrast those to strategies found in the German data. Levshina (2017) investigates the use of *t/v* forms (formal vs. informal forms of addressing) in various languages by means of a parallel corpus of subtitles. While the design of these studies may be carefully crafted around the specificities of translated language, one should not forget the methodological drawbacks of using parallel data for contrastive studies: Translated language is influenced by the translation process and potentially by the source language. If not analysed with this in mind, translation data can be misleading, as Neumann & Hansen-Schirra (2013) show in their discussion of the differences between the translational and the contrastive perspective.

For Machine Translation and Translation Studies, the topic of post-editing was and is a point of convergence. After all, this is the point at which humans and machines meet. Typically, the topic of machine translation is addressed from angles such as quality issues, evaluation of machine translation or the impact

Contents

Oliver Czulo & Silvia Hansen-Schirra (eds.). 2017. *Crossroads between Contrastive Linguistics, Translation Studies and Machine Translation: TC3 II* (Translation and Multilingual Natural Language Processing 4). Berlin: Language Science Press.

This title can be downloaded at:
http://langsci-press.org/catalog/book/102
© 2017, the authors

ISBN: 978-3-946234-26-5 (Digital)
       978-3-946234-98-2 (Hardcover)
ISSN: 2364-8899
DOI:10.5281/zenodo.1019701
Source code available from www.github.com/langsci/102
Collaborative reading: paperhive.org/documents/remote?type=langsci&id=102

Cover and concept of design: Ulrike Harbort
Typesetting: Sebastian Nordhoff, Iana Stefanova, Florian Stuhlmann
Proofreading: Felix Kopecky, Jean Nitzke, Valeria Quochi
Fonts: Linux Libertine, Arimo, DejaVu Sans Mono
Typesetting software: X∃LATEX

Language Science Press
Unter den Linden 6
10099 Berlin, Germany
langsci-press.org

Storage and cataloguing done by FU Berlin

Freie Universität Berlin

Crossroads between Contrastive Linguistics, Translation Studies and Machine Translation

TC3 II

Edited by

Oliver Czulo

Silvia Hansen-Schirra

language science press

Translation and Multilingual Natural Language Processing

Editors: Oliver Čulo (Universität Leipzig), Silvia Hansen-Schirra (Johannes Gutenberg-Universität Mainz), Stella Neumann (RWTH Aachen), Reinhard Rapp (Johannes Gutenberg-Universität Mainz)

In this series:

1. Fantinuoli, Claudio & Federico Zanettin (eds.). New directions in corpus-based translation studies.

2. Hansen-Schirra, Silvia & Sambor Grucza (eds.). Eyetracking and Applied Linguistics.

3. Neumann, Stella, Oliver Čulo & Silvia Hansen-Schirra (eds.). Annotation, exploitation and evaluation of parallel corpora: TC3 I.

4. Čulo, Oliver & Silvia Hansen-Schirra (eds.). Crossroads between Contrastive Linguistics, Translation Studies and Machine Translation: TC3 II.

5. Rehm, Georg, Felix Sasaki, Daniel Stein & Andreas Witt (eds.). Language technologies for a multilingual Europe: TC3 III.

6. Menzel, Katrin, Ekaterina Lapshinova-Koltunski & Kerstin Anna Kunz (eds.). New perspectives on cohesion and coherence: Implications for translation.

7. Hansen-Schirra, Silvia, Oliver Čulo, Sascha Hofmann & Bernd Meyer (eds). Empirical modelling of translation and interpreting.

8. Svoboda, Tomáš, Łucja Biel & Krzysztof Łoboda (eds.). Quality aspects in institutional translation.

ISSN: 2364-8899